# University Campus Barnsley

Telephone: 01226 216 885

Catalogue: https://webopac.barnsley.ac.uk

Class No: ............070.4....MAI...........

**This book is to be returned on or before the last date stamped below. Thank you!**

| | | |
|---|---|---|
| | | |
| | | |
| | | |
| | | |
| | | |
| | | |
| | | |
| | | |
| | | |
| | | |
| | | |
| | | |

Published 2011 by Abramis academic publishing

www.abramis.co.uk

ISBN 978 1 84549 483 4

Printed and bound in the United Kingdom

Typeset in Garamond 12pt

Abramis is an imprint of arima publishing.

arima publishing
ASK House, Northgate Avenue
Bury St Edmunds, Suffolk IP32 6BB
t: (+44) 01284 700321

www.arimapublishing.com

# Contents

# Acknowledgements

The Editors would like to thank the following for their invaluable help in mounting the Face the Future Conference in November 2010 at Coventry University and in pulling together this volume: most importantly the speakers and writers – all 45 of them. In addition, thanks go to:

- the BBC College of Journalism (Kevin Marsh, David Hayward, Angelique Halliburton and Jon Jacob)
- Coventry University's Vice-Chancellor Madeleine Atkins for unstinting support
- Coventry University Pro Vice-Chancellor David Pilsbury for financial support
- Coventry School of Art and Design Associate Dean Martin Woolley for financial support
- Lincoln University School of Journalism
- Richard Franklin at Abramis academic publishing
- The Frontline Club, in London, for hosting the book launch
- Finally, our loved ones for being patient as we lived with the project.

*John Mair and Richard Lance Keeble*
*Oxford and Lincoln, March 2011*

# The Editors

John Mair is Senior Lecturer in Broadcasting at Coventry University. He has won the Cecil Angel Cup for enhancing the prestige of Coventry University in 2009 and 2010. He invented and produces the weekly Coventry Conversations. He is a former BBC, ITV and Channel 4 producer/director on a wide range of programmes from daily news to investigative documentaries on *World in Action* to more considered pieces on *Bookmark*. A Royal Television Society Journalism Award winner, he publishes widely in the media and journalism press including the *Guardian*, bbc.co.uk/journalism and journalism.co.uk. This is his fifth co-written or edited book. For the BBC, he co-wrote *Marx in London*, with Asa Briggs, in 1981. With Richard Lance Keeble, he edited *Beyond trust* (2008) *Playing footsie with the FTSE? The great crash of 2008 and the crisis in journalism (2009)* and *Afghanistan, war and the media: Deadlines and frontlines* (2010), all published by Abramis academic, of Bury St. Edmunds. He is on the editorial board of *Ethical Space* and chairs the Institute of Communication Ethics. He is also a judge for the RTS Journalism Awards and the Society of Editors Press Awards.

Richard Lance Keeble has been Professor of Journalism at the University of Lincoln since 2003. Before that he was the executive editor of *The Teacher*, the weekly newspaper of the National Union of Teachers and he lectured at City University, London, for 19 years. He has written and edited 19 publications including *Secret state, silent press: New militarism, the Gulf and the modern image of warfare* (John Libbey, Luton, 1997); *The newspapers handbook* (Routledge, 2005, fourth edition); *Ethics for journalists* (Routledge, 2008, second edition); *The journalistic imagination: Literary journalists from Defoe to Capote and Carter* (Routledge, 2007, with Sharon Wheeler) and *Communicating war: Memory, media and military* (Abramis academic, Bury St Edmunds, 2007, with Sarah Maltby). He is also the joint editor of *Ethical Space: The International Journal of Communication Ethics.*

# Foreword

# In place of paper

**Jeremy Vine**

We gathered, a small group of us, on the other side of the traffic lights. I wished I had worn warmer clothing – the bright sunshine that morning had misled me. This was a bracing Coventry day, and there was not much of a welcome on other fronts either.

Across the road was the office where I had started my career. More than an office: the words *COVENTRY EVENING TELEGRAPH* were bolted to the front and side of a four-storey building which, my dusty memories told me, dominated the entire city centre.

I squinted at the place. The memories must have played me wrong. Sure, the building was still four storeys. But a reconditioned theatre and modernised shopping mall took the eye away, and the pedestrians passing did not shoot the newspaper office even a glance.

*We* looked, of course. The building was the reason we were back for our reunion. Organised by BBC environment correspondent Roger Harrabin, who normally covers the destruction of the planet, these former journalists with the *CET* had returned to reflect on the distress of a somewhat smaller world: newspaper journalism.

I have much to be grateful to the *Telegraph* for. It took me on as a trainee in 1986 and taught me that the first sackable offence in regional reporting is to spell someone's name wrong. Even worse was for the first name of the principal character in a news story to change mysteriously during the copy (yep, I did that once). The paper impressed on me law for journalists, shorthand and the importance of detail.

I once came back from reporting on a compulsory purchase order to make way for a new road and, despite having spoken to all the people who were losing their homes, I was bawled out for not asking what the new road would be called. The *Evening Telegraph* gave its trainees the fundamental journalistic insight: what is a story and what is not. "A man comes up to a woman and shouts 'I want sex' is not a story," the deputy news editor lectured me sternly, "because everyone wants sex. The story is that she fought him off with a shoe."

## When the *Telegraph* was a powerhouse in Coventry

The editor, Geoffrey Elliott, was a stickler who sent us a weekly briefing containing gems I have never forgotten: "Do not use the words *incident* or *situation* in the paper," he once wrote imperiously, "for they have no meaning." In those days the *Telegraph* had 85 editorial staff, numerous sub-offices in places such as Nuneaton, and was a powerhouse in the city. What you typed in the morning could fly off the presses and be sold on street corners that same afternoon. I had never felt so excited in my life as I did when I saw my first front page lead hit the desk beside my typewriter. And it really was a typewriter, with a ribbon: there were no computers back then. We used carbon paper to create second and third copies of what we typed.

Which is why the sight of the paper now was a sobering one for our group. More than 20 years on, the editorial staff was down from 85 to less than twenty (the ghost of the news editor appeared before me as I wrote that: "'Less than twenty?' How many exactly? Haven't you checked? Why not *fewer*?") The paper no longer occupied all four storeys

– in fact, it apparently had trouble filling one. When I worked there, aged 21, I would walk out past the deafening presses to collect my bicycle. Now the printing was done in Birmingham to save money, and "paper" was almost the wrong word. The *Coventry Evening Telegraph* had become a website.

So if ever there was a day that demonstrated the pulverising power of technological change, that visit to Coventry was it. I think we all felt sad, standing across the road in the chill wind and looking at the bedraggled giant we had abandoned two decades before. But a sense of the inevitable takes the edge off any sadness: it had to happen, didn't it?

All around us we see the effects of technological change. Born in 1965, I had my childhood in black and white. Not just the small TV in the corner of the living room that took two minutes to warm up, but all the holiday photographs too. We now live in a world in technicolour. I do the BBC election graphics – VR, they call them, virtual reality: because they are that close. Augmented reality, 3D, 3G, use whatever term you like. The change has sucked the air out of our lungs.

The great irony is that newspapers were supposed to use all this innovation to coast into a new and greater age. During my brief time in Coventry I had seen the city squad win the FA Cup and the first delivery of enormous desktop computers (in fact, I tripped over the boxes in reception: just like the newspaper, I was not looking where I was going). Soon after I left, the *CET* printed the odd picture in colour. But somehow the technology started as slave and ended as master. In America, many towns are without any printed newspaper now, and there have been predictions that before 2050, on an unspecified street corner in the USA, the very last newspaper will be folded and thrown into a bin.

**What the case of Phil Laing tells us about the power of Google**
I was struck by the case of Phil Laing, a first-year sports technology student at Sheffield Hallam University who urinated on a war memorial while drunk. Someone took his picture. Twenty years ago it would have gone into his local newspaper, and, if he was especially unlucky, a national tabloid might have printed it and lived off the reaction for a couple of days. Now the image went global. People abused him on YouTube from places as far afield as Sydney. If you Google Phil Laing you see pages and

pages of photographs and rabid commentary. He was tried and convicted by Google before he ever saw the inside of a courtroom. The image is permanent – it will outlive Phil – and will be instantly searchable forever. Phil has become the image. That is the change.

Power has shifted to the hands – and keyboards – of a new army of internet warriors, variously described as bloggers, citizen journalists, trolls, tweeters and many other things. They do not have a boss and their name appears on no one's payroll. Their activities can suddenly coalesce like a swarm of hornets and then just as quickly they are gone in their different directions. It makes the solid four walls of the *Coventry Evening Telegraph* look like a positive disadvantage, and the same goes for many other old media outposts, even though some have bent over backwards to embrace the change. I regret not seeing how big this was going to become in the early nineties; or, come to think of it, the early eighties, when my dad bought one of the first retail computers and I used the entire memory by typing in song titles from my record collection.

So if you are reading this because you are about to "go into journalism", good luck. You have chosen the worst time and the best. They used to say you needed an eye for detail and a nose for a story. Now it would be best to have an ear for what is coming around the corner. The only reassurance I can offer is this: the values I was taught on that newsroom floor in Coventry have not died. A journalist must fight to gain attention and trust. That has become harder to do, but more important than ever.

- After his stint reporting on the *Coventry Evening Telegraph*, Jeremy Vine joined the BBC in 1987. He currently hosts the BBC Radio 2 programme, *Jeremy Vine*, which presents news, views and interviews with live guests.

# Section 1. We have faced the future, and it works for us

**John Mair**

This collection of essays by practitioners, academics and media students is unashamedly about the future of journalism – if it has one! The internet is just twenty years old but has been the Great Disruptor of our age. No more so than in journalism worldwide. Those who "got" the digital revolution from the start have survived and some thrived; those who did not are struggling to play catch up. The status quo is on shifting sands; sticking to print or linear broadcasting is not an alternative in 2011. Like it or not, you have to face the future as a publisher, journalist, journalism educator or student.

First the big guns and the grey beards of our trade: Alan Rusbridger, Editor in Chief of the *Guardian* and *Observer*, "got" the revolution early as did John Birt at the BBC. They are reaping the digital dividends if not always being able to pay for it. Rusbridger's contribution – an edited extract of his Andrew Olle Memorial Lecture – is a digital manifesto *tout*

1

*court.* Mike Smartt invented BBC News Online – the most trusted journalism website in the world – in 1997. In the commercial world he would be a billionaire on that intellectual property alone. He looks back at the early days and his home computer in the corner of the newsroom with some nostalgia. So, too, the doyen of the British media press corps, Raymond Snoddy, who is a very old dog in the journalism trade but has taught himself (or been taught by his tyro son, Oliver, as he explains) some new digital tricks. He is a convert.

Peter Barron was an early adopter of social media when editor of *Newsnight* at the BBC. His on and off screen innovations led to a running commentary, not always in positive terms, by the presenter, Jeremy Paxman. It was digital Punch and Judy. Barron defected three years ago to join the new behemoth, Google, where he now heads up external relations for half the world. He is very upbeat about the possibilities presented to journalism by the tools of the modern media; perhaps he has to be.

Jon Snow, of *Channel 4 News*, is another old dog who has gone big time on the new tricks. Snow is an inveterate blogger and now tweeter from wherever he is reporting in the world. Teo Beleaga traces the journey of a national news treasure from news on film to news on Twitter. Finally, Kevin Anderson, who has been at most of the digital cutting edges on the *Guardian* and the BBC, traces his own journey from cub reporter in the US to digital guru worldwide.

All of these big hitters leave one in no doubt: face the future – it is the only direction to take.

- *Face the future* comes out of the Third Coventry Conversations/BBC College of Journalism International Conference held in Coventry in November 2010. The second led to *Afghanistan, war and media: Deadlines and frontlines* (Abramis, Bury St. Edmunds, 2010), also edited by John Mair and Richard Lance Keeble. The third book, *Investigative journalism: Dead or alive?* will be published in the autumn of 2011 after another Coventry Conversations Conference in March 2011.

# If you want to find out where (most) things happen first – go to Twitter

**Alan Rusbridger**

The digital space is – without going into complex arguments about net neutrality – owned and regulated by no-one. So it raises very unique kinds of problems. It's developing so fast, we forget how new it all is. It's totally understandable that those of us with at least one leg in traditional media should be impatient to understand the business model that will enable us magically to transform ourselves into digital businesses and continue to earn the revenues we enjoyed before the invention of the web, never mind the bewildering disruption of Web 2.0. But first we have to understand what we're up against.

It is constantly surprising to me how people in positions of influence in the media find it difficult to look outside the frame of their own medium and look at what this animal called social, or open media does, how it currently behaves, what it is capable of doing in the future. On one level there is no great mystery about Web 2.0. It's about the fact that other people like doing what we journalists do. We like creating things – words, pictures, films, graphics – and publishing them. So, it turns out, does everyone else!

For 500 years since Gutenberg they couldn't, now they can. In fact, they can do much more than we ever could. All this has happened in the blink of an eye. That's one problem – the rapidity of the revolution, the bends – and the other is that we find it difficult to look at what's happening around us and relate it to what we, as journalists, have historically done. Most of these digital upstarts don't look like media companies. EBay? It buys and sells stuff. Amazon? The same. Tripadvisor? It's flogging holidays. Facebook? It's where teenagers post all the stuff which will make them unemployable later in life. If that's all we see when we look at those websites then we're missing the picture.

Very early on I forced all senior *Guardian* editors onto Facebook to understand for themselves how these new ways of creativity and connection worked. EBay can teach us how to handle the kind of reputational and identity issues we're all coming to terms with our readers. Amazon or Trip Advisor can reveal the power of peer review. We should understand what Tumblr or Flipboard or Twitter are all about.

## Misguided views about Twitter as "inane stuff"

I've lost count of the times people – including a surprising number of colleagues in media companies – roll their eyes at the mention of Twitter. "No time for it," they say. "Inane stuff about what twits are having for breakfast. Nothing to do with the news business." Well, yes and no. Inanity – yes, sure, plenty of it. But saying that Twitter has got nothing to do with the news business is about as misguided as you could be. Here, off the top of my head, are 15 things which Twitter does rather effectively and which should be of the deepest interest to anyone involved in the media at any level.

1.  It's an amazing form of distribution: it's a highly effective way of spreading ideas, information and content. Don't be distracted by the 140-character limit. A lot of the best tweets are links. It's instantaneous. Its reach can be immensely far and wide. Why does this matter? Because we do distribution too. We're now competing with a medium that can do many things incomparably faster than we can. It's back to the battle between scribes and movable type. That matters in journalistic terms. And, if you're

trying to charge for content, it matters in business terms. The life expectancy of much exclusive information can now be measured in minutes, if not in seconds. That has profound implications for our economic model, never mind the journalism.

2. It's where things happen first. Not all things. News organisations still break lots of news. But, increasingly, news happens first on Twitter. If you're a regular Twitter user, even if you're in the news business and have access to wires, the chances are that you'll check out many rumours of breaking news on Twitter first. There are millions of human monitors out there who will pick up on the smallest things and who have the same instincts as the agencies – to be the first with the news. As more people join, the better it will get.

3. As a search engine, it rivals Google. Many people still don't quite understand that Twitter is, in some respects, better than Google in finding stuff out. Google is limited to using algorithms to ferret out information in the unlikeliest hidden corners of the web. Twitter goes one stage further – harnessing the mass capabilities of human intelligence to the power of millions in order to find information that is new, valuable, relevant or entertaining.

4. It's a formidable aggregation tool. You set Twitter to search out information on any subject you want and it will often bring you the best information there is. It becomes your personalised news feed. If you are following the most interesting people they will in all likelihood bring you the most interesting information. In other words, it's not simply you searching. You can sit back and let other people you admire or respect go out searching and gathering for you. Again, no news organisation could possibly aim to match, or beat, the combined power of all those worker bees collecting information and disseminating it.

## Twitter as a great reporting tool

5. It's a great reporting tool. Many of the best reporters are now habitually using Twitter as an aid to find information. This can be simple requests for knowledge which other people already know, have to hand, or can easily find. The so-called wisdom of crowds comes into play: the "they know more than we do" theory. Or you're simply in a hurry and know that someone out there will know the answer quickly. Or it can be reporters using Twitter to

find witnesses to specific events – people who were in the right place at the right time, but would otherwise be hard to find.

6. It's a fantastic form of marketing. You've written your piece or blog. You may well have involved others in the researching of it. Now you can let them all know it's there, so that they come to your site. You alert your community of followers. In marketing speak, it drives traffic and it drives engagement. If they like what they read they'll tell others about it. If they really like it, it will, as they say, "go viral". I only have 18,500 followers. But if I get re-tweeted by one of our columnists, Charlie Brooker, I instantly reach a further 200,000. If Guardian Technology pick it up it goes to an audience of 1.6m. If Stephen Fry notices it, it's global.

7. It's a series of common conversations. Or it can be. As well as reading what you've written and spreading the word, people can respond. They can agree or disagree or denounce it. They can blog elsewhere and link to it. There's nothing worse than writing or broadcasting something to no reaction at all. With Twitter you get an instant reaction. It's not transmission, it's communication. It's the ability to share and discuss with scores, or hundreds, or thousands of people in real time. Twitter can be fragmented. It can be the opposite of fragmentation. It's a parallel universe of common conversations.

8. It's more diverse. Traditional media allowed a few voices in. Twitter allows anyone.

9. It changes the tone of writing. A good conversation involves listening as well as talking. You will want to listen as well as talk. You will want to engage and be entertaining. There is, obviously, more brevity on Twitter. There's more humour. More mixing of comment with fact. It's more personal. The elevated platform on which journalists sometimes liked to think they were sitting is kicked away on Twitter. Journalists are fast learners. They start writing differently. Talking of which...

## Twitter's level playing field

10. It's a level playing field. A recognised "name" may initially attract followers in reasonable numbers. But if they have nothing interesting to say they will talk into an empty room. The energy in Twitter gathers around people who can say things crisply and entertainingly, even though they may be "unknown". They may

speak to a small audience, but if they say interesting things they may well be republished numerous times and the exponential pace of those re-transmissions can, in time, dwarf the audience of the so-called big names. Shock news: sometimes the people formerly known as readers can write snappier headlines and copy than journalists can.

11. It has different news values. People on Twitter quite often have an entirely different sense of what is and what isn't news. What seems obvious to journalists in terms of the choices we make is quite often markedly different from how others see it both in terms of the things we choose to cover and the things we ignore. The power of tens of thousands of people articulating those different choices can wash back into newsrooms and effect what editors choose to cover. We can ignore that, of course. But should we?

12. It has a long attention span. The opposite is usually argued – that Twitter is simply a, instant, highly condensed stream of consciousness. The perfect medium for goldfish. But set your Tweetdeck to follow a particular keyword or issue or subject and you may well find that the attention span of Twitterers puts newspapers to shame. They will be ferreting out and aggregating information on the issues that concern them long after the caravan of professional journalists has moved on.

13. It creates communities. Or, rather communities form themselves around particular issues people, events, artefacts, cultures, ideas, subjects or geographies. They may be temporary communities, or long terms ones, strong ones or weak ones. But I think they are recognisably communities.

14. It changes notions of authority. Instead of waiting to receive the "expert" opinions of others – mostly us, journalists – Twitter shifts the balance to so-called "peer to peer" authority. It's not that Twitterers ignore what we say – on the contrary (see distribution and marketing, above) they are becoming our most effective transmitters and responders. But, equally, we kid ourselves if we think there isn't another force in play here – that a 21-year-old student is quite likely to be more drawn to the opinions and preferences of people who look and talk like her. Or a 31-year-old mother of young toddlers. Or a 41-year-old bloke passionate about politics and the rock music of his youth.

15. It is an agent of change. As this ability of people to combine around issues and to articulate them grows, so it will have increasing effect on people in authority. Companies are already learning to respect, even fear, the power of collaborative media. Increasingly, social media will challenge conventional politics and, for instance, the laws relating to expression and speech.

## And now – some irritating aspects of Twitter

You could write a further list of things that are irritating about the way people use Twitter – it's not good at complexity though it can link to complexity; it can be frustratingly reductive; it doesn't do what investigative reporters or war correspondents do; it doesn't, of itself, verify facts; it can be distracting, indiscriminate and overwhelming.

Moreover, I'm simply using Twitter as one example of the power of open or social media. Twitter may go the way of other, now forgotten, flashes in the digital pan. The downside of Twitter also means that the full weight of the world's attention can fall on a single unstable piece of information. But we can be sure that the motivating idea behind these forms of open media isn't going away and that, if we are blind to their capabilities, we will be making a very serious mistake, both in terms of our journalism and the economics of our business.

We can now glimpse better what Raymond Williams was anticipating when he wrote about what he thought of as true communication 60-odd years ago. For him it meant what he called "active reception and living response". For that to exist, he thought, you needed "an effective community of experience" and a "recognition of practical equality". Indeed, Williams thought we could not survive as a common culture without such a mechanism.

## Let's not elevate social media above traditional media

Of course, social media is not enough on its own. I'm not in any way trying to elevate it above traditional media. We should be pleased, not resentful, that Twitter is in some measure parasitical – that many of the referrals and links take people to so-called legacy media companies, who still invest in original reporting, who still confront authority, find things out, give context and explain. But I do believe we should be relentless in learning all we can about how people are using this post-Gutenberg ability to create and share...and import those lessons back into our own journalism and businesses.

It's not about all rushing to be on Twitter. We can make our own media collaborative and open, too. Distribution, breaking news and aggregation? At the *Guardian* and *Observer* we have more than 450 people on Twitter, together with 70 different single subject sites or section feeds. Our journalists are out there, reaching a different audience from the core *Guardian* readership, seeking help, ideas, feedback, joining in the common conversations. Reporters use open media as a way of finding sources, communities and audiences. The notion of a story – with a finite starting and finishing point – is changing. Live-blogging can bring audiences of millions around specific events. Linking allows you to place your journalism at the heart of issues, news and information.

Instead of trying to write everything ourselves we're increasingly a platform as well as publisher. It started with Comment is Free in 2006. Soon our cultural coverage will be just as open and collaborative. We've done it with our network of environmental and science blogs: traffic on the former has risen by 800 per cent since the start of the year. We benefit from expert content and increased audiences. They share the revenue. We can trace the beginnings of a virtuous circle.

We harness readers in our shoe-leather investigations, whether it's hunting down tax avoidance, or tracing people who might have digital records of police assaults or enlisting 27,000 readers to sift through 400,000 records of MPs' expenses or alerting readers to super injunctions that stop us telling them things. Guess what? The readers love to be involved. They, too, like being critics, commentators and photographers. They love helping to defeat injunctions and being asked to share their particular knowledge or pool their expertise.

**Let's learn from EBay about reputations, rankings and identity**
You harbour a feeling that some of the stuff they create is poor? I agree. Let's learn from EBay about reputations, ranking and identity. We're experimenting with open data and open APIs. We want to experiment distributing our content to where the audiences are – preferably with advertising attached. Some of the more radical ideas will work, some won't. But a failure to experiment is more dangerous than trying new things.

This open and collaborative future for journalism – I have tried the word "mutualised" to describe something of the flavour of the relationship this new journalism has with our readers and sources and advertisers – is already looking different from the journalism which went before. The more we can involve others the more they will be engaged participants in the future, rather than observers or, worse, former readers. That's not theory. It's working now.

And, yes, we'll charge for some of this – as we have in the past – while keeping the majority of it open. My commercial colleagues at the *Guardian* firmly believe that our mutualised approach is opening up options for making money, not closing them down. I won't criticise people who want to try a different path...you can't preach plurality and argue for a single model of journalism or against attempts to find alternative ways of financing what we do.

I've always argued it's a good thing that different organisations are trying different routes to the future. And the models that are currently emerging are very different. Our web traffic last month averaged just over 2m unique browsers a day. One independent company which measured *The Times*'s UK web audience during September 2010 found that their web traffic – not including ipad apps – had fallen by 98 per cent per cent as people progressed past the paywall.

**Jury still out on the different financial models**
More sophisticated analysts than me calculate that the content behind the paywall is therefore generating a total global audience of about 54,000 a month, of whom about 28,000 are paying for the digital content (the remainder being print subscribers). That's not a criticism of *The Times*, that path may well make sense for how they see the future. The jury on the relative financial models for different approaches will remain out for a while yet. But these comparative figures point to completely different ideas of scale, reach, audience, engagement, ambition...and of journalism itself.

So that is a very brief tour around this splintered Fourth Estate. I suspect we would never invent the BBC or ABC today – the spirit of the age is against it. The issues about plurality are complex. When things are threatening to disintegrate it needs the greatest wisdom to know how and when to intervene both to enable change while preserving what's precious

– or, more than that, necessary. As for digital, I am with the utopians – fully aware that some see that as a term of abuse. To quote one blogger, the social web is not really about the end of what came before, but the starting point for what comes next: richer and more complex societies.

As with the early 16th century, it's our privilege, as a generation, not only to imagine the future of information, but to take the first steps on the road to re-crafting the ways in which it is created and spread. As the great editor, C. P. Scott wrote about the technological changes in the air when the *Guardian* celebrated its first 100 years in 1921: "What a change for the world! What a chance for the newspaper!"

# How the BBC puts its news online

**Mike Smartt**

It is difficult to overstate the influence the digital revolution now has on all our lives. Just take a look at any main street in the developed world. People striding along in their own little universe, "consuming content" – as the phrase now goes – from cavernous solid-state memories in tiny mobile devices. Or ambling forward, eyes fixed on a screen as they text furiously and expect fellow citizens to step aside.

It is not just the interesting, acquisitive and trivial things we do with the new and fast-developing technology: shopping online, arranging travel, keeping in touch and building huge virtual warehouses of music and movies. The serious stuff – how our countries are organised and defended – also relies, entirely in many cases, on bits and bytes and the ability and motives of those administering and maintaining them.

Many of us take all this modern technology for granted. Young people cannot imagine life without it. Connection to the world wide web is now considered a real priority. Some argue it is a human right. And there are few places where change has been more profound than in news. And yet, only thirty years ago all this was the stuff of science fiction and children's comics. At that time just a few outside academia, where it was used for swapping documents, had ever heard of the internet. When it did begin to catch on, Bill Gates felt it was so vulnerable that Microsoft might be able to replace it with a proprietary system. There was little general concept of what digital media meant.

At the BBC in the early 1980s, radio was still using tape which was edited using razor blades and stuck back together again with other bits of tape. Television news was beginning to cast aside the shackles of film, which took an age to process so that pictures of events when they were eventually shown were not so much instant as historical by today's standards. In both cases, digital technology was soon to revolutionise the recording, editing, manipulation and constant re-use of broadcast material.

But even fifteen years ago, the internet was still not used widely, except for email. CNN had just launched its news website and early adopters, especially in the United States, were logging on regularly. But elsewhere it was all still a bit of a mystery. A few at the top of the BBC saw early on that that there was a place for news online: principally the Director General, John – now Lord – Birt, the Chief Executive of News, Tony Hall – also now ennobled – and the man soon to succeed him, Richard Sambrook, who initially asked me in 1995 to examine what BBC News could do on the net.

There were a few others running news who were curious and some enthusiastic about new technology but most had their hands full running programmes on radio and TV that millions of people actually cared about. One, who was later to be one of its most passionate supporters, stormed out of a couple of early presentations of how BBC News Online would work declaring it all a waste of time.

A handful remained hostile, even after the service was launched in 1997. Putting web links on television would merely bamboozle viewers, they argued. Announcing them on radio news would be worse and take up precious time. These were, in fact, reasonable points as most of the general public had no idea what the world wide web was and suggesting visits to "www dot bbc dot co dot uk forward slash radio four forward slash the world tonight" would merely have prompted a million scratched heads.

### Special funding for digital

Some programme makers saw the internet as a rival service – why would producers be urging people to abandon their broadcast and log-on to a competing platform? Worse still, money was being diverted from budgets in traditional media to pay for digital development, although eventually some extra cash for digital was added to the licence fee.

But then the eagerness from above filtered down, even to the last-remaining doubters who realised that at least some investigation of what was happening online might be a good career move. And the web began to be seen as a valuable partner to traditional broadcast where further information could sit and add considerable value. Then, of course, everyone began to want a website for their own particular programme. Tomorrow please and "here are a few suggestions for how it might look".

Editors naturally wanted control over content on their sites and many over design and production tools too. It was explained that if all BBC News material were to be accessible forever – an early policy decision – sites would very soon contain thousands and then millions of archived pages.

Effective cross linking between all these news pages and programme sites was vital if traffic was to be driven to all corners of BBC News Online. Each page must contain hyperlinks to and from other relevant ones but to put these in manually and keep up with the constant changes demanded by an up-to-date news service was never going to be remotely possible. The best way to avoid chaos was for all BBC content within News to have a common look and feel and be produced on a single production system by a properly-trained central team of journalists.

### *Today* goes it alone

Every programme eventually agreed on this strategy with the single exception of Radio Four's flagship *Today*, who decided to set up and produce their own site with a decidedly modernist design in stern red and black. Producers on the programme were soon complaining that their efforts were not recording the number of "hits" they had expected, partly because of an absence of links to and from main news.

The strength of BBC News Online was always going to be the Corporation's journalism. It was – and remains – the best in the world of broadcasting. So it was decided early on to reject the policy of some early rivals who were posting unedited text from big news agencies, such as the Press Association and Reuters. Good as this material undoubtedly is, what would make the BBC's site stand out was a mixture of this agency copy – vital if comprehensive and up-to-the-minute coverage was to be achieved – with reportage from the BBC's own men and women on the spot, all part of the world's biggest broadcast news team. So no agency copy was to be published without being rewritten or added to, to some degree.

Achieving this was helped greatly by a vital relationship forged long before launch with the BBC World Service, who offered all their valuable material so that foreign coverage was the best on the web from the start. In return, their most important non-English language services were to be launched within their own pages with the help of the News Online technical team.

But the BBC and other broadcasters were at a distinct disadvantage in the early days. Newspapers, their trade being text and still pictures (which was all that was possible online then) could repurpose their publications for online relatively easily and cheaply. Some automated the process completely. But with the exception of Ceefax, the one thing the BBC News did not do was produce text for publication. And what online news sites needed then – as now – was text, in large quantities. This provided a once-in-a-life time opportunity.

When people take over managerial jobs, they normally inherit a team – the good, the bad and the ugly. But in this case we could recruit one from scratch, choosing everyone we wanted personally. Bob Eggington, an experienced and highly regarded senior executive, had been appointed Project Director to get News Online up and running. His long career in BBC Radio News meant he already knew everyone in that department. I knew pretty well everyone in BBC TV News, after more than 20 years there. So, we were ready for all those who would no doubt be queuing round the block to join the digital revolution. But we waited in vain.

## When News Online lacked glamour

Journalists generally join the BBC to work in the glamorous worlds of radio and television. But one thing News Online certainly lacked was glamour, at that time anyway. So, apart from a few prescient individuals who were keen to be in at the beginning of this new adventure, few in the Corporation, it seemed, were interested in a career online. Ceefax, of course, had some of the most highly skilled text journalists in the business but even though we were already in the same department – Continuous News – we could not poach them as they were needed to maintain one of the BBC's most popular services. However, the experience of those running Ceefax, most notably its editor Peter Clifton, was invaluable early on and he eventually became the editor of News Online too.

So, the editorial team which put BBC News on the web in 1997 contained some BBC News bodies keen to explore the new journalism but many more from newspapers outside, big and small, a few of whom already had experience of early news sites elsewhere. Their challenge was to implement a very simple editorial policy – to report the world to the world online to the same high standard as all other BBC News outlets. From day one.

## Dedication, enthusiasm and sheer hard work

That they managed to achieve this with a measure of dedication, enthusiasm and sheer hard work that was well beyond the call of duty suggested that during Managing Editor Dave Brewer's exhaustive series of selection boards we had picked the right people.

This team in the London newsroom handled the writing, rewriting and repurposing of the daily flow of news around the clock. Soon, the BBC English Regional and other National newsrooms – in Wales, Scotland and Northern Ireland – set up their own teams to provide a constant stream of stories from every corner of the UK.

Everyone learned on the job because no-one in the Corporation, or pretty well anywhere else for that matter, had done internet journalism before. People who were to become departmental heads and editors had to work ordinary shifts on the news desk to start with, no matter how senior they had been elsewhere (and this requirement did put off one or two from joining). A news web site soon becomes a vast collection of interrelated stories and how to build and maintain this ever-growing monster was all part of learning the new craft. How long stories should be and in what style they would appear gradually evolved in the early days. The novelty of the medium meant that inevitably, and for a short time, we were making it up as we went along. And, together with journalists in the new 24-hour radio and TV operations, the old concept of deadlines was forgotten. Stories went live whenever you pressed the publish button, which put extra pressure on checking every one thoroughly.

The icing on the cake was to be material from BBC Correspondents, both specialists at home and those based abroad. But many initially avoided the extra chore of producing reports especially for online. Bi-medialism was being introduced under which reporters were, for the first time, expected to file for both radio and TV on some stories – often simultaneously – and their already taxing workloads were further growing as a result.

We resisted asking the Head of News to make filing for online compulsory, hoping persuasion would be more effective. To start with, a few reporters did respond enthusiastically to calls from the online team for special coverage. Then, gradually, almost all discovered there was space online to write at length again, as many had in earlier careers on newspapers. They could use much of the extra material collected on stories for radio and television but which is inevitably squeezed out in a short, one-and-a-half minute broadcast. And they could forge a relationship with the audience through the interactive nature of the medium, blogging and email.

There was an extra attraction for television correspondents posted abroad. When video became technically feasible online, they could watch their output in the context of a bulletin for the first time. Up until then they had had to rely on news desks to pass on whether reports had been broadcast, reduced in length or cut altogether at the last minute – something I knew from experience kind-hearted foreign duty editors had been known to fib about when events forced lovingly-crafted journalism off the air.

### Facing the biggest challenge
The other big challenge, of course, was technical. Everything about the internet was new and most was largely untried and perplexing. So, when shortly before launch our Technical Director left, we looked scuppered. But then Bob Eggington heard that the technical boss at News International's ISP Lineone, Matthew Karas, wanted to leave. At

interview, he told us he could bring most of his team too (geniuses all, as it turned out). Things looked up again.

A tour of other teams in the United States preparing to put news online revealed that they, too, were flummoxed. Journalists untrained in web production were being instructed to include code to format their stories. This was madness, as any rookie who has tried raw HTML knows: a single wayward backslash can often result in a page of gibberish.

A further requirement was that the Director General, John Birt, was insisting the BBC's news site should be updated constantly from launch without waiting for radio and TV bulletin times. Many other organisations were proposing to refresh their sites only at regular intervals, following the newspaper principle of editions.

In double-quick time, our new team of programmers and designers developed what was almost certainly the world's first production system of its scope and type, the basics of which still remain today. It enabled whole teams of journalists to write, publish and revise multiple versions of stories continuously and for linking between pages to update automatically. No coding was necessary – in fact, the use of HTML by writers became a sackable offence.

With three weeks to go, we took our designs to the BBC's authority on such matters for what we assumed would be a formal nod of approval. Luck intervened, though, when someone in the guru's office noticed that what we intended to serve up – though brilliant – would take several hours to render on people's screens down ponderous dial-up internet connections.

Our Design Director Matt Jones, to his eternal credit, worked feverishly to produce a set of much less ambitious page structures and it was to be sometime before technology was able to handle the great ideas he had originally proposed.

### Problems come – as a result of success
But our real problems began after launch and were due, ironically, to the almost immediate success of the site. We had assumed that because the traditional BBC News audience tended to be middle-aged, they were less likely to be engaged with the world wide web and so traffic to the site could be slow to grow.

This was despite one justification for the service being the need to re-engage the young in news. Research showed that they were less likely to read newspapers than they were (if they ever really did) and were no longer watching as much news on television. But it was known that they were using the internet and it soon became clear that in the absence of much of the vast amount of content online today, they were visiting BBC News Online.

Computers could even then accurately measure within 24 hours what stories people were actually reading online (today, the process is almost instantaneous) and by far the most popular tended to be about celebrity and technology. Day after day, it seemed those pesky youngsters were choosing to read about what they were actually interested in.

No matter how deeply within the site a story about the current stars of the time – Britney Spears or the Spice Girls – resided, the number of page views it attracted would often far outweigh those for more serious news, of which there was no shortage.

One result was that traffic to BBC News Online grew quickly – much faster than expected – and the ability to deliver material to the growing number of users at all times soon began to falter. At one point, the server technology wobbled and for several hours, as an emergency measure, the BBC News website was pushed out to the world from a laptop in the corner of the newsroom.

The trouble was that the economics of the web differed hugely from those of established broadcast. When the *10 O'clock News* is broadcast on radio or television, it is received by its audience at the same time. To all intents and purposes, it costs the same to deliver whether ten people or ten million are watching or listening.

Online it was the opposite. When a site visitor chooses to view a certain page, the whole page – text and images – has to be sent individually to that person's computer to be displayed by a browser. Bandwidth is used to deliver that material and as a site grows in popularity, demand for bandwidth increases. In the early days of BBC News Online, bandwidth was rare and expensive. Add to that big audio and video files, as they were eventually introduced, and costs rocket. With BBC income fixed by the licence fee, this became a real problem.

## Providing more and more of that pricey bandwidth

Worse still, when bandwidth ran out, access to the site was not cut off from the most recent user connected as one might assume. The service gradually slowed for everyone and, as demand continued to grow, all screens eventually went blank. This happened very rarely but always at important times, just when visitors were most hungry for information. The answer was to provide more and more of that pricey bandwidth. But the profile of the average visitor was changing. Millions of older people were catching the internet bug and usage was exploding. Demand for more mainstream news, rather than just the latest in entertainment and technology, grew.

The problem was most acute during big news stories. No-one running a website could afford to pay every day for enough bandwidth to deal with all possibilities. Fixed events – such as the Budget or elections – were a little easier to plan for and have extra bandwidth ready. But even then demand, particularly from the increasing number of people using computers at work where there were no alternative sources of news, stretched resources to breaking point.

News Online's technical team kept things running by using every trick in the book – but due to lack of precedent, there were very few of those. When things started to get really busy, they would monitor how many people were successfully connecting. But when the site went down due to bandwidth shortage, it became impossible to measure how many more people were attempting unsuccessfully to access the site – it could have been thousands (or millions). So there was no way to estimate how much more bandwidth to provide next time round.

Breaking news was the most difficult. Because it was unexpected and in many cases dramatic – an earthquake perhaps or a plane crash – demand was big and immediate. Because all news sites wanted extra bandwidth, it ran out quickly. Eventually, what became known as 9/11 led to every big news site on the web disappearing from view. Millions of people opened their browsers at once and were greeted by empty screens. It took the biggest US sites many hours to recover.

Today bandwidth is more plentiful and cheaper. There are now companies who will sell it only when it is needed. Compression techniques have improved so that delivery of large files is much more efficient. Connections are better and download speeds faster. The next time records were broken – on the day of the world's fifth strongest earthquake on record in Japan in March 2011 – sixteen million unique users visited News Online and the site remained accessible as usual throughout.

When asked before launch what BBC News Online would become, we would say "the top national and international news service on the web with the best of audio and video available". As politicians are fond of saying, this was an aspiration rather than a commitment because it took some years before video, in particular, became a realistic proposition. Eventually, though, newspapers' early advantage online waned as broadcasters were able to use their huge resources of sound and vision to compliment text and still images. And although the papers are now streaming audio and video, too, in many cases, it is not their core activity and they still have much catching up to do.

## Interactive nature of the web

The real game changer, though, was the interactive nature of the web. Whereas in the past broadcasting meant just that – editors deciding what the audience would see and hear and pushing it at them – the new online platform meant the public could have their say. And have it they did.

On one level, it was easier for visitors to the service to talk to the people behind News Online. Email made it simple and a new two-way conversation evolved. Time dealing with the sheer volume of the new electronic correspondence created its own problems, of course. But we literally asked for it – inviting our users, soon numbering millions worldwide, what they wanted from their news service. How could it be improved? What ideas did they have for better coverage?

On another level, we already knew what they were reading most from our own electronic statistics and could improve how the content was presented and prioritised based on this new knowledge. Then there was opinion. Oodles of it. Asking people for their views on the news soon resulted in a massive stream of comment.

Within the team there was much debate about how this material should be handled. Some argued that the culture of the internet had already established that all comment should be free and unfettered. And undoubtedly there is much excellent material on forums and online opinion sites – sometimes better than professional journalism. But it is all too often hidden in a sea of dross where the same points are made badly and repeatedly amidst abuse and aggression. The prevailing view was that there were already plenty of sites which allowed instant and uncontrolled postings and that people would expect the BBC to use some discretion and editorial control.

So an area called "Talking Point" was established where incoming comment was read by a team of journalists and the best edited to reflect arguments fairly. The aim was to provide the best experience for visitors – such as the "Letters to the editor" columns in newspapers for hundreds of years. Live online interviews, with visitors putting questions in real time to world leaders in some cases, also became a popular feature.

It worked well editorially but the small team of journalists was soon overwhelmed and it became clear that only a tiny proportion of contributions could ever be read and considered for publication. However, a fear that users would stop sending comments when only a few would ever appear was unfounded. Opinion just continued to increase.

## Moving away from the open forum principle
Recognising that these days discussion about BBC News stories often takes place elsewhere – on social networks such as Twitter, Facebook and the like – the site is moving away from the open forum principle to one in which comment is invited, moderated and published alongside specific stories, and the sharing of links is encouraged. This should further improve the reader experience and reduce the unrealistic cost of moderating huge quantities of material.

The development that was, arguably, of most value was interactivity's capacity for users' participation in the journalistic process. In August 1999, a huge earthquake in Turkey killed a thousand people. As soon as agency material arrived, we included for the first time a request on the webpage for any information from the scene, more in hope that expectation. Early reports from quakes are notoriously difficult as they often occur in isolated areas where the damage wrought wipes out power and communication for some time. But within minutes, emails started to arrive. Many were from outside Turkey – friends and relatives of people in the area asking for news. But a few appeared to be from the quake-stricken region with details of the terrible situation there.

There were some doubts about these reports. How could computers and connections still be operating? Could they be from pranksters, or worse, pretending to be in Turkey when they were actually sitting at home in Perth or Pimlico? We emailed back, asking for a telephone number so we could call and check. In some cases, we had no reply because either the emails were hoaxes or genuine authors could no longer communicate or were otherwise busy. But we did manage to contact one or two whose material we could use within news stories and we passed on contact details to radio and television news so they could record interviews. The rule, thereafter, was that no matter how good on-the-spot material appeared to be, its veracity had to be established before it appeared as part of a BBC News Online report.

This now, of course, happens all the time on all types of stories but the first inkling of the power of this new type of reporting – at News Online anyway – was that day in 1999. Just over two years later, after the attacks in America on 9/11, much of the most moving material from the scenes was emailed in by ordinary people in the midst of the drama.

**The challenge continues**
In the decade since, of course, the media landscape has continued to change at breathtaking speed. The term New Media no longer applies as digital activity in its various forms is now the norm. At the BBC, the pioneering separate online team at news is no more. Journalists have for sometime operated alongside colleagues from radio and television in an integrated unit. And online skills are now amongst the most valued across the board.

The future offers many challenges. As newspaper and magazine publishers fight falling circulations by migrating to the web, hoping to persuade people used to free online news to start paying for it, fingers are crossed that it could eventually be the salvation for professional journalism.

The explosion in social networking provides fresh newsgathering opportunities. As the man running multi-media at Reuters, ex-BBC Head of Newsgathering Chris Cramer, put it: "These days journalists rarely break the story, most compelling pictures come from eyewitnesses, and not from journalists…citizen journalism is not a fad or an intriguing addition to traditional journalism, but here to stay."

So, would those people emailing the BBC from the Turkish earthquake or from Ground Zero now be texting Twitter and Facebook instead? And the generation of youngsters who research suggests now spend whole chunks of their lives swapping news, as they see it, with friends via social networking. They are the potential online news consumers of tomorrow. But when the time comes, will they get the habit? As always, interesting times ahead.

**Note on the author**
After 20 years as a BBC television reporter, correspondent and presenter, Mike Smartt was tasked with investigating how BBC News could put itself on the world wide web. It was, he says, because his bosses noticed he had being using a very early laptop to write scripts on location "without seriously injuring himself or anyone else". He was appointed launch editor of BBC News Online in 1997 and subsequently became Editor-in-Chief of BBC News Interactive, which also included interactive television and Ceefax.

# Staring into the crystal ball – and seeing a bright future for journalism

Peter Barron

I have spent most of my working life as a journalist. When I started in BBC News, scripts were written on manual typewriters on five-ply carbon paper, wire copy was delivered in baskets by messengers, and if you needed to look up an old story you would walk down the corridor to a place called News Information where a researcher would pull out a folder of hand-clipped newspaper articles, which may – or may not – contain the story you had in mind. That was only 20 years ago!

Yet news in those days was a growth industry, hiring was buoyant and the budgets generous. Today, the impact of the internet on the news industry has led some to worry about the very survival of high-quality journalism. In this chapter I will argue that, rather than seeing the looming extinction of journalism, we are seeing its reinvention. It will no doubt be a painful reinvention, but you need only look back to the advent of radio, television and cable news to see that disruption caused by technological innovation is nothing new. So, what might this future for journalism look like? No-one knows for certain of course, but here's my bet on some of the key developments we will see.

## Journalism will be more open-form

The internet has changed the way people consume news. In newspapers, articles are presented in a context. They come with a rating of importance (page 1 versus page 23, size of headline, position on page), they are clearly categorised by section, they may have related coverage alongside or be part of an ongoing series of articles on a given topic.

Online, that's not the case. More often than not, online articles are read in isolation. People follow a link – from a search engine, a blog, or a tweet – and navigate straight to the article. Once they have read it they often disappear, unless you are lucky and they come across something else on the site that grabs their attention. It's a far cry from the days when readers sat back and thumbed through their newspaper from beginning to end.

This way of consuming news is a bit like grabbing a snack rather than sitting down to a full meal. Nowadays the opportunity is always there for people to look at an article on impulse, while at work or on their mobile phone. Some have called this breaking down news to its "atomic level of consumption". It's an interesting way to put it, not least because when you see something broken down to its most basic components, it's only natural to think about how the parts might be re-assembled.

I'm not suggesting we will stop snacking on news, but I do believe news organisations will find ways of serving up our news diet in ways that will appeal to individual desires and needs. News is about to become more personalised. Just as my ideal meal is going to be different to yours, the same is true for news. Whereas I might be happy with just a two paragraph summary, you might want a six-page feature. Or, rather than stories in written form, you might prefer to see them in the form of photographs with captions that you could click on for more information.

Even for the same person the ideal news package can change over time. For instance, I have a holiday to Seville planned in a couple of months, so until then, I'm interested in hearing about upcoming cultural events there. After that, it should stop as I'll just find it irritating to see what I missed. Similarly, when I'm scanning the news on the bus in the morning rush hour on my mobile, I want just the top stories that get straight to the point. When I'm relaxing on the sofa at home with my iPad, I want to read features and trust in serendipity that an article on a seemingly random topic might prove fascinating.

We're still at the beginning of experimenting with how this kind of tailoring could change the way news is presented. But the early signs are promising. For instance, consider Flipboard. It's an iPad app that combines links shared by your friends on Facebook and Twitter with your choice of a selection of curated news topics. The whole thing is displayed in an engaging magazine-like fashion complete with photographs and virtual pages. It's a long way from being perfect, but it gives a glimpse at the potential for drawing on social connections to craft a personal news package.

## The emergence of the "read later" tool

Or how about Instapaper? It's a free "read later" tool designed for when you stumble across an article you'd like to read but can't spare the time that instant. You can add articles to your reading pile via a button in your web browser. You can then return to the articles at any time, even when you are offline. One of my colleagues uses Instapaper to get a bundle of full length stories sent to her Kindle every day.

It's already possible to train algorithms to do a good job at predicting things you might like. In a news context, an algorithm could learn from the articles you spend time reading as opposed to the ones you skipped. It could learn from the ratings you gave to its suggestions, or the recommendations of your friends. It could learn through your answers to carefully crafted (and fun to do) quizzes to see what your interests are. All with your permission, of course.

No-one has come close to applying this kind of technology in news yet – and when they do you would want to balance personalisation with the kind of serendipitous story selection that newspapers do so well – but there are already some incredibly good tools for predicting taste more generally. I've been buying from Amazon for years and it's stunning how good its recommendations for books and music have become – these days it often knows what I'm looking for before I know. By combining more than five years of my browsing and buying history with that of millions of others, it is able to get its recommendations uncannily spot-on.

Taking the notion of predicting tastes even further is Hunch. Hunch describes itself as a tool to "personalise the internet" and aims to provide recommendations on thousands of topics. It begins with some entertaining and addictive quizzes, then starts predicting things. You have the fun of seeing what it guesses about your tastes – and correcting its mistakes – and before you know it you have answered hundreds of questions and it is predicting even quite obscure things with astonishing accuracy.

## Doing clever things with technology
Opening up the form in which news is packaged – making it more varied and flexible – will mean doing clever things with technology. But on its own technology will not be enough. In the future, the true journalistic stars will be not just those adept in one medium – writing words or ad-libbing on air – but those who open themselves to innovation and who develop the skills-spanning genres that let them match the style of storytelling to the setting.

Consider the case of local Russian newspaper *Kurer-Sreda*. They were inspired by *The New York Times*'s "One in 8 million" series featuring New York residents so decided to try something similar featuring the people in their own small town of Berdsk. Their tiny newsroom did not have the resources to emulate *The Times*'s fancy Flash-based styling, so they went low-tech. Reporters used Microsoft's free Movie Maker tools to craft their own multimedia shows from the photographs and videos they had taken, then uploaded them to YouTube and to the newspaper's website. The resulting "One in 97,000" series may not be as glossy as that in *The New York Times*, but it's still a great watch (see http://goo.gl/zEBr1).

Or take the story that the investigative reporter Bill Dedman put together for MSNBC about a wealthy elderly heiress. Rather than writing it in the usual prose form, he submitted it in the form of a lengthy slideshow with captions. Within a month the story had been viewed 78 million times online and elicited 500 emails from readers – more than any other story he had written (see http://goo.gl/ZozNp).

## Changes in the conventions and structure of story-telling
So far I have focused on the way stories are packaged and presented. A related and equally profound change will be in the conventions and structure of story-telling. Traditional journalistic processes have been

honed to suit a world of periodical (as opposed to continuous) publication, and a format of tightly constrained (as opposed to infinite) space.

In the digital world, coverage can be much faster and much more iterative. Online articles can be published as soon as the news becomes available, then corrected and extended on the fly. Just as CNN invented a new style of live rolling news, in marked contrast to that of traditional nightly bulletins, online journalism is having a radical effect on the way newsrooms operate.

On the web there is no need to worry about column inches or airtime. The only scarcity is people's attention. So far, news organisations have found it difficult to hold readers' attention online. On an average day, US newspaper subscribers spend about 25 minutes reading their print copies, but the average web user spends only about 70 seconds per day at newspaper websites (see http://goo.gl/sLqBq). Talk about a light snack.

In the future, news organisations – and the journalists they employ – will become ever more adept at structuring their offerings in ways that draw online readers in, whether exploring a story angle in more depth, or being hooked by a totally different subject. It's still early days but we are already seeing some promising experiments. For instance, adding a social layer is a great spark to exploratory reading. Who hasn't been intrigued by the "most shared" links on the BBC News site? Now imagine what it would be like if you could tailor it to see the most shared articles among circles of people relevant to you – say those with the same profession (for business news), or who live within a five-mile radius (for local news), or who share a similar lifestyle ethos (for fashion, travel, and so on).

Joris Luyendijk, a much-lauded Dutch newspaper reporter, has an interesting viewpoint on this, as it relates to the story format itself. In a recent *Guardian* interview, he told how he moved out of conventional journalism as he wanted to tell more open-ended and less linear stories – difficult in the confines of a traditional newspaper model but perfectly suited to online. Luyendijk's thesis is that every situation has the potential for many stories, most of which are currently left languishing because there is not enough space or they lack clear conclusions. But once newspapers cease to be printed on paper (as he believes will ultimately happen), the constraint on the kind of stories that can be told will lift (http://goo.gl/J01rP). In parallel with this more open-ended style of content we will also see a greater diversity in the stories being pursued – enabled by the opportunity to involve a much wider range of people.

## Journalism will be more open-minded

Since I have been working at Google a couple of things strike, and rather disturb, me about how news works. First, whenever almost any story about Google breaks – large or small, positive or negative – it will generate several hundred cuttings of the story in Germany. Most are almost identical, taken from an original agency source, but they nevertheless require precious resources – re-writing, editing, printing, paper – to produce. Similarly, in the UK, when one newspaper breaks an exclusive about Google, reporters from the other newspapers will follow up within the hour to write an almost identical version.

Of course this is understandable, but it is also terribly inefficient. Does the world really need multiple versions of the same article? Wouldn't the reader – and society – be better served by presenting a wider range of perspectives? It was frustration with the narrowness of news coverage in the US around 9/11 that led to the invention of Google News. Krishna Bharat, an Indian-born engineer then working in California, found he had to visit news sites in Europe and Asia in order to get a broader understanding of the world's reaction. It was a hassle, so to make it easier for himself and others, he came up with the idea of aggregating links to the world's news – and the idea for Google News was born.

Of course, providing more diverse perspectives is easier said than done in a time of scarce resources and ever shorter deadlines. It isn't that journalists don't wish to do it, it just takes time to analyse a story and explore multiple viewpoints – time they don't have. So a key way to encourage more diversity in coverage will be to free up more time.

For example, newspapers often used to send junior reporters out to do "vox pops", the view of the man or woman in the street. What they were after were a few punchy one-liners rather than an expert or representative opinion. As newsroom resources became stretched, this became less common, and one albeit trivial source of diversity in coverage declined. Then along came Twitter. Now there's an abundance of "vox pop" comments that take minutes rather than hours to unearth. In terms of news value, the tweets have the same flaws and the same advantages as quotes from the street – they just take much less work. It's a source that news organisations all over the world are beginning to embrace.

## Pooling resources and sharing content
Another approach to free up journalists' time is to pool resources and share content. Of course, this is not a new tactic. The Associated Press traces its origins back to 1846, when daily newspapers in New York set up a cooperative venture for staying abreast of news about the Mexican war (http://goo.gl/JD7Z1). In recent years, economic pressures have led to content-sharing arrangements popping up all over the place, even among once bitter rivals.

The danger, of course, is that this could lead to a greater homogenisation of coverage, but not if pooling frees up resources to concentrate on more distinctive or investigative journalism. A great example is the coverage of Wikileaks. Three leading international newspapers – *Der Spiegel*, *The New York Times* and the *Guardian* – worked closely to analyse the Wikileaks material. All the findings were pooled, then each team went off to write their own stories. What is particularly fascinating is that this collaboration was apparently initiated by Wikileaks' founder Julian Assange who made it a condition of sharing the materials in advance. He had learned that putting raw materials on a website, open to everyone to analyse, paradoxically, meant that few did. By joining forces, more material could be analysed, providing each paper with more to write about than if they had worked on their own. And because each paper served a different constituency there was variety in the stories and angles emphasised, even though there was apparently no formal agreement (http://goo.gl/tmiOI).

## Transformation in the way story ideas emerge
Aside from giving journalists more time, another way to boost the diversity of coverage is to inject more ideas. In the future, I think we will see a transformation in the way story ideas emerge and are prioritised. Think about a typical editorial meeting. It's a lively debate about the most newsworthy stories and the relevant angles to emphasise – taking into account the public interest as well as the interest of the public. But it is limited to the views of those people in the room, however talented they may be. In the future, there will be processes that help bring a wider variety of suggestions and diverse views to the table.

We are already seeing examples of this. Look at Wikipedia. Although it isn't a news organisation, it does act surprisingly like one in terms of the intensity of discussion around articles involving breaking news. For instance, within a day of the 2008 terrorist attack in Mumbai, the Wikipedia article about it had been edited more than 360 times by 70 different people referring to 28 separate news sources (http://goo.gl/VO5YF).

Another illustration is the way the *Guardian* crowdsourced its investigation of the MPs' expenses scandal. Readers were asked to review the raw data and flag things they found that they thought merited looking into further. More than 20,000 people helped and over 170,000 documents were reviewed in the first 80 hours alone. Their efforts turned up many leads for the professional journalists to pursue – helping ensure better coverage than would otherwise have been possible (http://goo.gl/CTTFr). These examples are illustrations of a kind of "citizen journalism", which lead me to my final prediction.

## Journalism will be increasingly open-sourced

Let's be clear – I'm not suggesting for a moment that citizen reporters will or should replace professional journalists. Healthy democracies stay strong in part due to journalistic oversight. The financial models to support journalism in future may still be fuzzy (more on that shortly), but professional journalists carry out a vital public service and, like other such services, they must be funded.

That is not to say that the army of amateurs can't make an important contribution – although I know this is an uncomfortable notion for some. Often, when I talk at an event and mention citizen reporting, someone will ask if I would be happy to fly in a plane flown by a citizen pilot. It's a good quip, but is it a good analogy? When flying a plane the cost of failure is very high; that isn't the case with journalism. Anyone can write an article or blog and post it on the web – if it is very poor it does not matter much, but the good stuff will be recognised and rise to the top. When established news organisations adopt citizen journalists they do not tend to use them to do specialised jobs such as political analysis or editing the front page: they use them to reach parts that their own resources can't reach. And they should and do check that what the citizen journalist has written is accurate.

There are numerous examples of citizen reporters playing a valuable role at filling gaps in coverage for key stories. For instance, in October 2009, the *Guardian* was banned from reporting the contents of a parliamentary question relating to allegations of toxic dumping by Trafigura. They knew it was an important story but their hands were tied. So the *Guardian*'s editor, Alan Rusbridger, alerted readers to his frustration with a tweet. This sparked a flurry of online sleuths who tracked down and circulated the details, resulting in Trafigura being unmasked in less than 24 hours (http://goo.gl/hmJjA).

## Citizen reporters handling stories professional journalists are unable to cover

Through Twitter and blogs, citizen reporters are also stepping up to report on stories that, for safety or logistical reasons, professional journalists are unable to cover. In Mexico, they are covering the country's drug wars after violent retaliations by the cartels forced newspapers to cut back (http://goo.gl/WCLsx). During the recent battles in Rio slums, a 17-year-old student sent real-time updates using the Twitter handle "@vozdacomunidade" (voice of the community) (http://goo.gl/bOi94). And, of course, in Iran and Egypt citizens gathered imagery from the streets that the professionals were blocked from collecting.

Looking forward I think we will see news organisations making more and more use of citizen contributions, even for events they would once routinely have flown out a team to cover. For any newsworthy event – floods, toxic sludge, earthquakes, you name it – local people will always be at the scene faster than journalists, and thanks to the rise of web-enabled smartphones, they are well-equipped. It may not always be necessary to send a crew to film what's happening on the streets if the people living there are already filming and uploading it to YouTube.

Such collaboration does not have to be ad hoc. We are also starting to see citizen journalists playing a more organised role in supporting their professional counterparts. I have already talked about the *Guardian* enlisting readers to help with research. Other news organisations have taken this further. Korea's OhmyNews employs just 55 editorial staff, but they are backed by 65,000 volunteer contributors. All contributions are fact-checked, and 70 per cent of submissions are published (http://goo.gl/9bV4V).

We are even seeing experiments in crowd-funding, in which readers are given the chance to contribute towards the reporting costs for individual stories. For example, Spot.Us, backed by the Knight Foundation, offers a channel for the public to commission reporting on important and perhaps overlooked topics. One such report, successfully funded and placed in *The New York Times* via Spot.Us, highlighted the "Pacific garbage patch" (http://goo.gl/FSYNk). So...open-form, open-ended, open-minded and open-sourced. That's all very well, but how exactly is it going to be paid for?

## The future of funding journalism

There are undeniably immense financial pressures on news organisations, particularly newspapers. Subscription revenues continue to decline as younger generations fail to embrace the print habit. Print display advertising fell through the floor in the economic downturn, and faces tough competition as digital marketing grows. Classified advertising, for so long a cash cow, has all but disappeared from most newspapers, moving to new online platforms. Any one of these changes would have been enough to disrupt a newspaper's business model: to have all three combined is a challenge indeed.

So far, no one pretends to have the magic solution. It's easier to see where we are heading than how we will get there. I echo James Fallows' view that "ten years from now, a robust and better-funded news business will be thriving. What next year means is harder to say" (http://goo.gl/uBZ4t). I also share Clay Shirky's sentiment: "Nothing will work, but everything might" (http://goo.gl/I7Npk). It's hard to see how any single action could solve a problem of this scale; instead, what is more likely is a kind of death by a thousand cuts in reverse – how about life by thousand band-aids?

In the past, newspapers supported the high cost of doing the serious news by packaging it with lighter features and pull-outs full of advertising. The problem now is that that package has fallen apart, and few advertisers want their ads to appear alongside hard-hitting news. Serious news, standing alone, has never had a business model and is unlikely suddenly to find one.

And from an editorial perspective, the notion of making serious news directly pay its way presents dangers. The risk is it leads news organisations to gloss over awkward details or favour topics that you know will be pleasing – to readers and advertisers – while more socially important but less popular stories fall through the cracks. It's the age-old argument for the "church/state" separation between editorial and advertising, and it's a fundamental tenet of journalism.

Of course, that is not to say journalists should pretend their readers are fascinated by every worthy story. It's helpful to know readership by article, if only because the ultimate goal of writing is for people to read it. That's why many newsrooms now monitor the readership of their articles online, but it is important for popularity not to become the only yardstick for success.

## Getting the personalisation right

In the longer term a mutually reinforcing model is likely to emerge. If news organisations get their personalisation right they will have something that is incredibly powerful for advertisers. If you know someone well enough to deliver them personalised news, then you are likely to be able to take a pretty good guess as to the kind of advertising that will appeal.

Of course, there are all sorts of challenges to overcome in doing this. It is vital that privacy be respected, in terms of both deed and spirit. It will require new processes and new tools. The ads themselves will need to evolve in form. It will mean a new kind of relationship between news organisations and their readers. But it should be possible.

Can readers be persuaded to pay for news content behind paywalls? I don't think there is a one-size-fits-all solution; it depends on the nature of the service. If you offer a unique perspective on business topics that affect people's livelihoods – as do the *Financial Times* and *Wall Street Journal* – it is clear readers are prepared to pay. If you offer a community – an exclusive place to discuss and debate the news with like-minded contributors – that might work too for certain brands.

Ultimately I expect there will be many different charging formats. Some will support micropayments for access on an article-by-article or day-by-day basis; others will lock out everyone except subscribers. Some will offer a certain amount of content free upfront – a model already used successfully in iPad Apps – others will not. Perhaps, for some, payment will be in the form of time rather than money – for instance, giving readers the option to fill in a survey in exchange for time-limited access.

Maybe we'll even see voluntary contributions. Already a model for this exists via Readability, in which people can donate a set amount each month to be divvied up between publications – newspapers, magazines, blogs alike – in accordance with the number of articles read. Or there's Flattr, offering a tip jar version, in which people can choose to contribute after they have read and enjoyed an article. Overall, it's too soon to tell what will work and what won't, but charging models are likely to make up one part of the solution.

## The role of Google

Finally, 1 would be remiss if I did not also address the debate that swirls around Google's role in all of this. Particularly since I have had the benefit of having a foot in both camps. Some have singled out Google as being to blame for journalism's woes. Unsurprisingly, I disagree. If Google didn't exist, the same problems – the loss of classified ad revenue, the economic crisis, the decline in subscriptions – would all still exist.

There have been accusations that Google is making big profits on the back of newspaper content, with Google News siphoning away readers. That's simply not true. First, Google does not sell advertisements on the Google News homepage, and the revenue from advertisements shown alongside news-related queries is tiny. Just as brands do not tend to advertise against serious news stories in papers, the same is true online. The vast majority of Google's revenue is generated from people searching for products – try searching for "digital camera" and then "David Cameron" and compare the number of advertisements on each results page.

 Second, people do not read the news at Google News, they use it as a signpost towards the websites of news providers. We show a headline and couple of lines from each story – enough for people to tell if they want to read on. And they do. Google News sends more than a billion clicks a month from interested readers to news websites. And if publishers don't want to use that model it is easy for them to opt out.

The truth is, Google wants to support news organisations in finding their way through the current challenges. We work with publishers who have chosen the ad-supported model to help find ways to engage readers for longer, making the advertisements more valuable. We have built the One Pass payment tool to make it easier for publishers who want to charge for their content online, giving them flexibility to choose what content they charge for, at what price, and how – daypass, one time access, subscription and so on. And we are investing in not-for-profit organisations to encourage the kind of innovation in digital journalism discussed in this article (http://goo.gl/Zai6D).

## Will journalism get better?

Let's go back to the newsroom I described at the beginning of this chapter, before email, mobile phones and the internet. Is the state of journalism better or worse than it was in 1990, back at the beginning of the technology revolution?

There were many great journalists operating then, of course, and there will be exceptions to any rule, but I think most would agree that overall the quality and breadth of journalism on television, radio, in the newspapers and online has risen, fuelled by a transformation in our ability to communicate, to gather information and to publish it.

Will journalism be better still, or worse, in another 20 years? I believe it will be better. In an era in which – through the supercomputers they carry in their pockets – almost everyone will be able to access the world's information, everyone can be news gatherers and publishers, the possibilities for journalism are surely immense.

It will be a big challenge for existing news organisations to adapt to this world, to harness the technologies and find better ways of researching and presenting stories and, crucially, and sustainable business models. Can it be done? As a former journalist, and a lover and avid consumer of journalism, I'm optimistic.

## Note on the author

Peter Barron has been Google's Director of External Relations for Europe, Middle East and Africa since January 2011. He joined Google in

2008 and was previously Director of Communications and Public Affairs for North and Central Europe. Before joining Google he was editor of BBC2's *Newsnight* programme from 2004-2008 and worked in TV News and Current Affairs for almost twenty years. He has also been deputy editor at *Channel 4 News* and *Tonight with Trevor McDonald* and devised and edited the future-gazing BBC Current Affairs drama-documentary series *If...*

# How after Mosaic, the Brave New World of the web opened up for me – and I never looked back

**Kevin Charman-Anderson**

I first glimpsed the future of journalism in a student computer lab at the University of Illinois in August 1993. I was returning from summer break and my friends were all buzzing about some software, developed on campus, called Mosaic.

When I started at university, you could only use the internet if you knew its arcane text commands. Mosaic was one of the first graphical web browsers, and it made the internet point-and-click. It was a revelation. As a journalism student, I knew that this would radically change my career. Suddenly, a world full of information and instantaneous communication was available with a click of the mouse.

I graduated in 1994, and leaving university for the workplace felt like going back to the present. Few newspapers had websites, and internet access was still rare. I became a regional reporter for a small newspaper in western Kansas, covering agriculture, school board meetings, tornadoes and Bob Dole's presidential campaign.

Local journalism was immensely satisfying. Despite being an outsider, I was able to provide coverage no one else was, and my readers told me they appreciated it. The newspaper was progressive and was already building an online presence. They realised that the web could deliver news faster and more cheaply than trucks could deliver newspapers to the edges of our coverage area, hundreds of miles away.

But by 1996, I was restive. I was getting job offers based on my internet skills, but they were not in journalism. In Illinois, I had seen the beginning of an information and communication revolution as historic as the creation of movable type, and I desperately wanted to be a part of it. It is a passion that still propels me.

I shared that passion with members of an early online journalism email discussion list and caught the attention of a Knight-Ridder technology writer who tried to recruit me to the news group. Newspapers were still struggling after the recession of the early 1990s and, like many other groups and papers at the time, Knight had a hiring freeze in place.

## The power of virtual connections

But just as economic uncertainty has been a constant during my career, so has the power of virtual connections. A television station in Michigan was launching a new website in partnerships with fast-rising internet company, Yahoo. They contacted the tech writer at Knight-Ridder, headhunting for their first internet news editor. Before I knew it, I was on a flight to Kalamazoo.

As with most digital journalism jobs I have had, I had to learn new skills, teaching myself HTML from a fat computer book so that I could code web pages by hand. Although much of my job was to build and maintain the news website, I also got my start in broadcasting when the television news team needed background for internet stories.

A year later, I got a new job: special projects producer for a regional news website, part of Advance Internet, the internet division of Newhouse Newspapers and Condé Nast. I started doing multimedia packages, mostly images with stills, and some early data journalism, such as a project to see how responsive state lawmakers were to email. However, I also did a lot of "repurposing" content from newspapers.

But I missed reporting. I applied for a few newspaper jobs only to find that newspaper editors did not consider my last two years of online work as journalism. Luckily, demand for online journalists was increasing and soon I found an advertsiement for a six-month experimental posting with the newly-created BBC News website in its Washington bureau. I leapt at the chance and, at 26, I became the BBC's first online journalist outside of the UK.

In a little more than four years, I had gone from being a regional reporter at a small local newspaper to the Washington bureau of the BBC. That's a rare trajectory, and I credit my early embrace of the internet as the catalyst for the quick progression of my career. Two years of internet journalism experience was not common at the time, and as the opportunities for online journalists increased, I was placed to take advantage of them.

Working for the BBC News website in Washington was a great opportunity. I was fortunate to have experienced colleagues and bureau chiefs such as Andrew Roy and Martin Turner to mentor me as I carved out what was an entirely new position. With my online colleagues in London, we worked to create public service journalism for the internet. Although I produced a lot of stories by the radio and television correspondents, I also did my own reporting. As time went on, I expanded from simply writing reports for the web to covering major technology stories, such as the Microsoft anti-trust trial, for web, radio and TV. I was the BBC journalist in the courtroom when Bill Gates gave testimony.

## Golden age for online journalism at the BBC

It was a golden age for online journalism at the BBC. During the 2000 presidential election, Tom Carver and I took a trip across the US using broadcasting technology that would become commonplace to provide coverage in Afghanistan for webcasts. My editors in London, Nic Newman and John Angeli, had the idea of asking our audiences to help set the agenda of our coverage. It was some of the first user-directed coverage the BBC would do.

That trip was one of the most demanding in my career and is a classic of example of how flexible and improvisational you will need to be for a career in digital journalism. In six days, we travelled coast-to-coast across the United States. The first day we flew from Washington to Miami to interview university students about voter apathy amongst young people in an open-air bar with the portable satellite dish perched precariously off the balcony. The next day we were off to Texas to interview state politicos who could explain George W Bush to our audience.

There was one small hitch. The webcasting gear looked robust enough, but when I opened it up in Austin Texas, only one sad amber light came on. When I called London, a technician on the other end asked: "Do you have any tools?" No: carrying nearly 70 pounds of satellite, broadcasting and computer gear, I had neglected to bring my set of hex wrenches.

We recorded the interview and then rushed to the edge of town to the nearest DIY store for the required tools. After two aborted attempts to bring the video gear back to life, I gave it a gentle whack, and it blinked back to life just as it looked as if we might miss our satellite window to file the video. One of the store staff ambled up and asked what we were doing with my small satellite transmitter on the boot of the car connected to a box full of wires and lights. Fortunately, this was before the 11 September attacks so the question was friendly. I replied: "We're feeding video to London, sir."

In a Texas drawl he said: "No shit!" He offered to help, and I said that it would be great if he would keep people from walking in front of the satellite. Like a folksy traffic warden, he waved his arms and told anyone within earshot: "Stand back! Stand back! They're feeding video to London." Satellite equipment field repair was not in any of my courses at university – I just had to improvise.

Fortunately, the BBC is good about training staff. Not only did I learn the art of improvisation in the field, I also learned how to record and edit audio, shoot video and edit basic video packages. I learned how to interview and be interviewed on television, although it still could not prepare me to look calm and collected on air as a Fox producer elbowed me in the kidneys as we encroached on her live position on the red carpet at Elton John's after-Oscar party.

Then came the dot.com bust. While it is true that it wiped out a lot of charlatans, it sadly also wiped out a lot of good companies and even more good digital journalists. Most digital journalists I knew in Washington lost their jobs, and more than half left journalism entirely, dejected not only by the collapse of the boom but also how they had been treated by an industry which did not value their knowledge or experience.

I rode out the crash at the BBC, where we continued to innovate. After the 11 September 2001 attacks, we increased our live webcasts and multimedia coverage. Then in 2004, world editor Rachel Nixon asked me to blog the presidential election, a request which would change the course of my career again. Blogging was a revelation for me. When I left Kansas, I lost the direct connection with my audience that had been so satisfying. On this new blog I could take questions from BBC viewers around the world. Blogging restored and expanded that connection with my audience.

## How blogging and social media have transformed my career

Blogging and social media have transformed my career in other ways too. The next year, I came to London to write a strategic white paper on blogging for BBC News. I also helped launch two innovative and interactive programmes based, respectively, on global audience participation and sourcing stories from social media: *World have your say* on the BBC World Service, and *Pods and blogs* on BBC 5Live (now called *Outriders*).

In 2006, with my secondment in London drawing to a close, I was searching for a new job so that I could stay in the UK. Blogging had not just changed my career, it has also led me to the woman who would become my wife, Suw Charman. I contacted an editor I knew at the *Guardian* and, two days later, I had a meeting with Emily Bell, director of digital content. "I've read your blog, and we're on the same page," she said. A job offer came soon after, and I became the first blogs editor at the *Guardian*.

My time at the *Guardian* would draw on all of the digital and journalism skills that I had developed during my previous eight years with the BBC and make me dust off technical skills that I had not used since the mid-1990s. During the three-and-half years I was at the *Guardian*, the organisation went through dramatic changes. They redesigned and relaunched the website including the blogs which, as the editor, required me to develop technical project management skills. The newspaper moved into new offices at Kings Place with greatly expanded digital and multimedia facilities, and the newspaper and online newsrooms were brought together, something that the organisation is still trying to digest more than two years later.

In 2008, the *Guardian* sent me back to the US to reprise the election trips that I had done in 2000 and 2004 for the BBC. In the eight years since the first trip, the 70 lbs of gear I had carried to stream video, take digital stills and edit had shrunk to 15 lbs and fit easily into a small backpack. In the four years since the last trip, social media had exploded moving beyond blogs to include social networks such as Facebook and micro-blogging platforms such as Twitter.

Mobile technology had also made incredible advances since 2000. Back then, I had an adapter so that I could use my phone as a data modem, but it was incredibly slow. I could not use it reliably to file copy or pictures. By 2002, I was using a data modem that boasted ISDN speeds of 128 kbps. In covering the one-year anniversary of the 11 September attacks, we finished our coverage at the concert in Central Park. Using my wireless modem, we had pictures and copy filed before Billy Joel played the last chords of New York State of Mind. In 2004, wifi was widely available in the US, and by 2008, DSL-class wireless blanketed the US.

In 2008, my phone, a Nokia N82, had a 5-megapixel camera and could shoot standard-definition photos. Using the built-in GPS, I could record the location of every photograph I took. Using Twitter, I could post short updates along the trip, flag up interesting stories that I was reading and also post photos from interviews, campaign rallies and the celebrations outside the White House on the night of Barack Obama's historic victory.

I drove 4,000 miles, shot more than 2,000 photographs and uploaded them to photo sharing site Flickr, posted 1,600 updates to Twitter, wrote 50 blog posts and recorded the audio for two podcasts. Emily Bell had also asked me to connect with *Guardian* readers in the US, and I hosted four blogger meet-ups including one jointly with National Public Radio in their Washington headquarters. The blogger meet-ups were good outreach for the *Guardian,* and interviews with politically savvy bloggers across the country also provided insight and material for my journalism.

Twitter proved invaluable in covering the rapidly developing, rolling new story that is an election, as many journalists have found in subsequent years. I could update Twitter either using an app on my phone or by simply sending a text message. The trip in 2008 was the realisation of several dreams that I had as a digital journalist.

In 2004, we did the best we could with the technology that we had, and the blog was as interactive as we could make it. However, we did not have live comments. They were all screened and posted by colleagues in London. I wanted more immediate interaction, and Twitter provided that. People could send me questions, and they would arrive via a text message on my mobile phone. I also wanted a way to keep updating a story without having to find a place to crack my laptop.

We had an easy way for Twitter to automatically post to the *Guardian* site so that I could easily continue coverage without ever breaking away from the story, whether it was live updates during the presidential debates or live coverage, including pictures, of the celebrations in Washington. One of the most popular updates, measured by the number of retweets, was when I quoted crowds outside of the White House chanting: "Whose house? Whose house? Obama's House! Obama's House!" It still gives me chills.

More than the technology, I embraced social media because I saw it as a way to directly engage audiences in important stories. By developing a relationship with my audience, I felt I could more easily stimulate their curiosity about serious issues that would affect their lives. At the start of my trip, Ralph Torres contacted me about the housing crisis in California. His family had been in the real estate business for 40 years, and he said to tell the story I really needed to come to his neighbourhood in Riverside. Five houses had foreclosure signs just on his block alone, and our interview made the basis not only for a blog post but also for a podcast. Ralph started following me on Twitter, and the day after the election, he sent me this message publicly on Twitter: "Big thanks to @GuardianUS08 [the Twitter account I used for the election] for last month's visit and chat and for pulling me further into the conversation." Result.

## Taking responsibility for my own career

During eight years at the BBC and three and a half years at the *Guardian*, I witnessed deep cuts. Soon after I arrived in London in 2005, I realised that I had to take more responsibility for my own future. In 2006, I started writing on a blog that my wife Suw started two years earlier.

I'm not naturally self-promoting, but I'm passionate about digital journalism. Just as I shared that passion with that early email list, I now use blogs to connect with other digital journalists. I have used my blog and social media to build an audience for my journalism and to network with my peers and future clients. This allowed me to take the next step in my career after taking voluntary redundancy from the *Guardian*. I am now an independent journalist and digital media strategist working with news organisations around the globe, continuing to pursue my passion of creating a new medium for journalism.

## Note on the author

Kevin Anderson is a freelance journalist and digital strategist with more than a decade of experience with the BBC and the *Guardian*. He has been a digital journalist since 1996 with experience in radio, television, print and the web. As a journalist, he uses blogs, social networks, Web 2.0 tools and mobile technology to break news, to engage with audiences and tell the story behind the headlines in multiple media and on multiple platforms. From 2009-2010, he was the digital research editor at the *Guardian* where he focused on evaluating and adapting digital innovations to support the *Guardian*'s world-class journalism. He joined the *Guardian* in September 2006 as their first blogs editor after eight years with the BBC working across the web, television and radio. He joined the BBC in 1998 to become their first online journalist outside of the UK, working as the Washington correspondent for BBCNews.com.

# You *can* teach an Old Dog new tricks

**Raymond Snoddy**

Sometimes it seems as if the internet is wasted on the young. It is surely the army of superannuated hacks, their souls still haunting Fleet Street pubs, who have the most to gain from the deft application of the latest communications technology to maintain presence and visibility.

It goes without saying that any aspiring journalist of today must be a master of the web and all the latest iterations of social media. They must be able to take multi-tasking in their stride, and as for multi-media, the words, sound and pictures should be like the holy trinity – impossible to separate. To stand any chance of achieving that most elusive of contemporary states – decently paid media employment – you probably need to have launched your first blog by the age of 12 and have your tweets followed by Stephen Fry. Or that, at least, is the theory.

In reality, however natural a digital native you are, three significant barriers, almost biblical trials, stand in the way of becoming a professional

47

journalist nowadays. The first is the most bizarre and inexplicable of all: more and more young people want to become journalists at the very time that more and more jobs, money and, above all else fun, are being squeezed out of the trade. The majority of those taking media and journalism courses will not become journalists – at least, not in the traditional meaning of the term.

They should not despair. The development and encouragement of curiosity, the ability to impose order on apparently unrelated facts, the habit of working accurately to tight deadlines and the pursuit of literacy are desirable and saleable skills elsewhere. The minority who will make it are the ones most determined to do so.

Much has changed since the late Bob James, head of training at the then Westminster Press, summed things up with Geordie precision: "Journalism is the worst of jobs – unless you happen to think it is the best." Then again, perhaps not so much has changed after all.

The second obvious barrier is the fact that for some years now it has become less and less clear who is a journalist and who is not. Old craft and trade union restraints limiting and controlling access to the media now look medieval and have mercifully been swept away by the internet. Openness, freedom and democracy have been well served by the ability of any citizen anywhere in the world to seek, and sometimes find, an audience for their ideas and opinions.

## What is a journalist?

But what then is a journalist? There are two workable attributes or characteristics – one with an idealistic tinge and the other deeply practical. The gathering and checking of facts or images, as part of a journalistic tradition, clearly has something to do with it.

Alan Rusbridger, editor-in chief of the *Guardian*, put it well when he spoke of the importance to society of the provision of "independently verifiable" information. People who collect and verify information, as opposed to merely transmitting unchecked rumours, can call themselves journalists – though their exclusive right to such a title may be disputed. The other much cruder determinant is money. A journalist is someone who gets paid for the practice of journalism. It may look dangerously like a circular argument but it is a definition that works perfectly well for other occupations.

Because of the remorseless laws of supply and demand some would-be journalists may have to defer the pleasure of earning money to achieve that state at a later date. Working shifts for free is hardly desirable but is can serve a higher, longer-term purpose. My daughter, Julia, secured jobs at the *Guardian* and the BBC after doing work experience at Kelvin Mackenzie's late, lamented L!ve TV. She once climbed into the station's trademark News Bunny suit and waved her tennis racket in the background of L!ve's news bulletins from Wimbledon. It has graced her CV ever since.

In the end, however, no pay equals philanthropy, not journalism. The final trial is an ancient one – how to get noticed and stand out from the crowd when no-one knows who you are? Something interesting in your CV, preferably more substantial than pulling on the hot and sticky News Bunny outfit, always helps. So can an unusual degree. A young aspiring journalist once applied for the political editor's job at LBC radio without much noticeable experience of either radio or politics. She was asked what she had studied at university. "Egyptology" was the answer. "I like Egyptology," replied the interviewer and she got the job.

## Inside always better than outside

Here at least the internet comes to the aid of young would-be journalists. They can blog or post a radio or television piece on the web. They can demonstrate what they can do – if only they can get noticed. For those for whom journalism remains "the best of jobs" despite any evidence to the contrary, then the traditional advice remains – get inside a news organisation and appear enthusiastic in almost any capacity. Inside is always better than outside.

Aged hacks are, however, the ones who can, in relative terms, benefit most from engagement with the latest communication technologies. Until recently, when they were finally found out, or shown the door because £2 million had to be taken out of the budget and they were too highly paid, that was that. After the redundancy cheque had been gratefully received there was little for it but PR, reminiscing into their pints about long-forgotten stories or editing their local community newsletter.

Now for the first time journalists who haven't had enough, who still want more of the fun and more of the mischief, despite the passing years, can continue to do so. While money is still very acceptable, thank you very much, to pay for expensive bad habits such as Convent Garden or football season tickets, redundancy payments and pensions help to take the edge off the necessity.

Take the case of Revel Barker, former *Daily Mirror* reporter and newspaper adviser to Robert Maxwell. He lives in Gozo, the small island half an hour's ferry ride from Malta. It must be one of the more remote spots in Europe yet he has managed to create a much-admired web site for former journalists – gentlemenranters.com – and established an imaginative publishing house specialising in work by and about journalists. Ten years ago Barker would have had little option other than to enjoy the wine and the sun and contemplate writing his memoirs.

The site he created in three days is the equivalent of a virtual Fleet Street pub for those who still want to rant and set the world to rights. Though just occasionally the word apocryphal springs to mind, who would not warm to stories from a past era such as "I knew Eric Wainwright" by former *Mirror* journalist Colin Dunne. Wainwright was the legendary *Mirror* journalist who, it is said, survived in paid employment despite failing to file a story for six years.

But Barker went further and set up what he calls ironically a "macro" publisher specialising mainly in the out-of-print works of famous journalists, sometimes extended and brought up-to-date. His first was an updated version of the 25-year-old *Forgive us our press passes* by the freelance journalist, Ian Skidmore. Soon after publication it got into the top 10 of the Amazon best-seller's list.

**"The best book about journalism – ever"**
Other titles include *Slip-up: How Fleet Street found Ronnie Biggs and Scotland Yard lost him*, by Anthony Delano, and Murray Sayle's devastating portrait of Fleet Street, *A crooked sixpence*. The novel was first "published" in 1961 except that it had to be pulped when one of Sayle's former editors spotted too close a resemblance between himself and the fictional characters described and unleashed the libel lawyers. The book has been brought back from the dead by Barker and the distinguished investigative

reporter Phillip Knightley has described *A crooked sixpence* as "the best book about journalism – ever".

There is, of course, an inevitable air of nostalgia about the activities of Barker and his gentlemen ranters but a much more modern journalist, the former media editor of *The Times*, Dan Sabbagh, used the web to keep his career alive after resigning from the Murdoch daily. While waiting for opportunity to knock again, Sabbagh set up his beehivecity website and blog to continue to cover media stories and keep both his reputation and his contacts warm. Before long he was appointed head of media and technology at the *Guardian*. Moreover, he remains in control of beehivecity and can link it to MediaGuardian as part of the newspaper's general commercial philosophy – "links not walls".

But if you are about to start drawing your old-age pension and are neither resting between jobs nor yearning for a wallow in a virtual Fleet Street pub what, then, can the internet do for you? Quite a lot, actually, though admittedly it helps if you have offspring to open the door to the social media and do a bit of necessary cajoling and even bullying when required.

It is the modern equivalent of getting your child to programme the video-recorder. So let's take for granted that as a hack of a certain age you have been completely comfortable for years with email, lap-tops, Google, HD television and Personal Video Recorders and don't run around complaining there is nothing to watch on television when there is.

**When aged parent finally signs up for the social media…**
What about the social media? Here there is definite possibility that the natural response will be to Harrumph and say you can't for a moment see the point at all and have no intention of signing-up. Along comes Oliver Snoddy and, without consultation, signs the aged parent up for linkedin.com and continues the spoon-feeding by running up a quick profile and posting a photograph.

Suddenly the sceptical one is linking up with all and sundry and before you know it has reached the honoured ranks of the 500 + brigade and, yes, I really do know who most of them are. You bump into a lot of people in decades of journalisms. But that's it. Professional contacts are one thing. They might open up lucrative opportunities. You never know. But Twitter? What on earth is the point of that telling people which café you are in or revealing to the world that the sun is shining or that you have the biggest hangover ever.

Absolutely no way! Twitter is obviously a waste of time for those with nothing better to do. Then the son strikes again. The Twitter account is set up complete with profile without the slightest by-your-leave. Naturally the love affair with Twitter is instantaneous and before too long 3,000 followers will have been amassed, perhaps not in the Fry class but it's the quality that counts.

The attempt to say something meaningful in 140 characters represents a perpetual challenge. I know you are supposed to keep it shorter than 140 to make it easier for people to reply but this is outweighed by the sheer bliss of getting to exactly 140 characters – no more no less. Now the lad senses a pattern here and closes in for the kill and goes for the big one – Facebook.

Further Harrumph, no way etc to the accompaniment of assurances that it will be only a matter of time, it's the largest social network in the world, worth $50 billion blah, blah. Not on this occasion. "No" really does mean "No". Facebook is a step too far for the grumpy old man with no desire to post his holiday snaps or interact with a large proportion of the entire world's population. Not everyone, after all, wants to voluntarily give up all rights to privacy.

Even if you are not looking for a conventional job these days the very thought of those who have never reached their full potential because of Facebook boasts about their sexual predations or drunken escapades is enough to make the stoutest heart shudder. So under protest the unsought Facebook profile is removed. This is obviously a minority opinion. If Facebook works for you whatever your age – fair enough.

### Is engaging with the digital world activity for its own sake?
Engaging with the digital world and being connected to at least some social networks is fine and dandy but is it merely an illusion? Activity for its own sake? Does any of it cut the mustard? For hobbyists not seeking to make any money it's a wonderful outlet while for journalists of mature years, or freelancers of all ages, the issue is more problematical and the benefits often intangible.

Undoubtedly, the web gives a presence, a voice, albeit it one among many. The better known you are before you hit either linkedin or Twitter the more useful it can be. To those that have shall be given. What is obviously true is that for journalists of a certain age total invisibility can easily amount to professional death. By putting yourself about online there is at least the chance of a useful tie-up or unexpected commission – and the usual amount of unsought abuse. There are a lot of very rude people out there.

What you are saying is that you are still here, still sentient, interested in being a player and available for writing, interviewing, chairing and appearing on panels. All the usual stuff. If you are suddenly short on a Sunday of some nice quotes for an article that should have been written days ago emails to a number of relevant linkedin connections can produce the goods within hours.

## Using Twitter to promote articles, ideas, programmes
Some are perfectly happy to use Twitter for inconsequential chit-chat and, indeed, that was its initial purpose. It can also be used by journalists to promote articles, ideas, programmes and views about society and has become a news vehicle in its own right breaking and influencing stories. Twitter, for instance, has the power to undermine the misuse of "super-injunctions" where not even the subject matter of injunction can be revealed.

Admittedly it would be extremely difficult to produce a cash-flow analysis of the benefits of online activity. Perhaps it is a little too early to know for sure. The most problematical issue is whether it is wise for professional freelance journalists to start writing blogs – giving the work you might otherwise sell for nothing. Unless you are able to take a long-term view and hope that eventually you will have enough readers to attract advertising, sponsorship or the attentions of publishers then it is not a brilliant idea.

For the more mature journalist the social media represents a second chance – and probably the only chance. In an ideal world it should be possible to combine young and old, new and traditional media. That is why I have set up a new website Old Media New Media with my social media mentor and tormentor, Oliver Snoddy, digital services director of the New York advertising and marketing consultancy, Doremus.

There he will try to tell me that advertising is dead and that influential marketing is the thing and I will try to convince him that traditional advertising is far from dead and remains the most effective way to launch new products and market big corporate brands. Something might come of the inter-generational dialogue. You never know.

## Note on the author

After studying at Queen's University, in Belfast, Raymond Snoddy worked on local and regional newspapers, before joining *The Times* in 1971. Five years later he moved to the *Financial Times* and reported on media issues before returning to *The Times* as media editor in 1995. At present, Snoddy is a freelance journalist writing for a range of publications. He has presented *NewsWatch* since its inception in 2004. The programme was launched in response to the Hutton Inquiry, as part of an initiative to make BBC News more accountable. His other television work has included presenting Channel 4's award-winning series *Hard News*. In addition, Snoddy is the author of a biography of the media tycoon Michael Green, *The good, the bad and the ugly*, about ethics in the newspaper industry, and other books. Snoddy was awarded an OBE for his services to journalism in 2000.

# From "clunky Motorola radios" to Twitter: A brief account of Jon Snow's reporting journey

**Teodora Beleaga**

*"The social network is on fire.* Despite Egypt's best efforts, the revolution is under way. Whether it ends in Mubarak or no Mubarak, *the movement for change travels on the shoulders of the web,"* blogs Jon Snow, the Face of Channel 4 News, from Egypt's capital, Cairo. Snow published this comment (2011a) as soon as the telephone lines and internet connections were reinstated in the country, on 29 January 2011, after more than 48 hours of "blackout".

He also acknowledged the gravity of Egypt's authorities' decision to interrupt virtual communication in a tweet to a 24-year-old budding journalist from Glasgow: "@journodave you get the Tweets badly spelt or not at all! Very up and down web connection here in Cairo: *hence effective silence for some days."* But there was no silence in the news, as some Communication Satellites (COMSATs), which were in use long before social media and mobile phones, did their job rather well. Thus, despite the "blackout", Jon Snow still presented Channel 4's *7 O'Clock News.*

Since journalism "put simply, is a form of communication" (Niblock 2010: 1) one would not be too far from the truth in assuming that any developments in the means of communication would have a form of impact on journalism. Yet, what Snow has proven through his "get straight out there and see what's going on" approach (Snow 2005: 179) is that, regardless of the constant renewal of the technological means of transmission, journalism remains governed by the same old principles – some of which are yet to be agreed on by academics, but are nonetheless recognised by professionals (i.e. news values).

This is a brief incursion into Jon Snow's reporting journey with a focus on the way his packaging of news has changed over the years as a result of technological developments. Although Snow is currently still classed just as a "presenter" in his biography page on the Channel 4 News website (2010), his current responsibilities also include operating a SnowMail, SnowBlog and Twitter account. With modesty, he told the Institute for International and European Affairs' (IIEA) audience: "I'm not a great internet wiz, although I use it a great deal," adding what it meant for him to go from working for a television station to working for a multiplatform newsdesk in less than four years "I probably work three times harder than I've ever worked before" (2009a).

Consequently, Jon Snow writes a daily account of the evening bulletin's headlines, posts at least one blog entry a day sharing his opinion on current events and tweets as events unfold. On Friday, 4 February 2011, between 4 am and 5 am (UK time), he tweeted from Cairo as American tanks manipulated by the Egyptian army were attacking the peaceful, anti-Mubarak protesters; his last tweet, minutes before 5 am, reflects his passion for reporting: "I'm going to try to sleep, but if tank fire resumes I will tweet again; if internet sustains…it needs to because they can't reopen the banks without it" (2011b). And he woke up in less than three hours tweeting the night's aftermath: "As usual…the morning reveals slow movement in Freedom Sq despite horrific night... 4 dead, 800 injured...Handful Mubarakists, 3,000 protesters?" (ibid).

Originally from Haywards Heath, Sussex, Jon Snow has been presenting the Channel 4 News since 1989. His journalistic career started by chance in 1973 at LBC (London Broadcasting Company) and continued at ITN and ABC. In his almost 40 years of reporting, Snow has travelled in more than 85 countries and has interviewed the likes of Ronald Regan, Nelson

Mandela, Margaret Thatcher, Alistair Campbell, Monica Lewinsky, Bill Gates and many, many more. His many notable honours include the Richard Dimbleby Bafta award for Best Factual Contribution to Television (2005) and Royal Television Society awards for Journalist of the Year (2006) and Presenter of the Year (2009). On his reporting genius, Andy Kershaw, the BBC One DJ, says that Snow "whipped the floor" with the other journalists in his reporting of the 2010 Haiti earthquake " (2011).

When Jon Snow was starting his reporting career with the LBC, he recalls: "There were no mobile phones in those days, but we had clunky Motorola radios, which within five miles of the office could transmit a just-about viable signal" (2005: 74). Snow successfully used one of these radios to report live on the IRA bombing of the confines of the Houses of Parliament in 1974. Of his early time in television, to which he moved in 1976, he reminisces: "In the 1970s there was no lightweight video, you could not carry a video camera into the field; it was too heavy. One person could not carry a video camera and the recording mechanism was so large, you'd need a wheelbarrow" (2009a).

But in 1977, when he found himself alone with just the soundman, having to do a package from Somalia's front line, Snow attempted to film his own piece-to-camera. After having received a brief tutorial from a French cameraman, he recounts the experience:

> I tried to establish myself with the camera, keeping the lens wide as instructed, but every time someone opened fire I gave an involuntary jerk in response. My pictures would be all over the place. Somehow I had to grab a piece-to-camera to prove I had ever been there. I found a ledge near the top of my trench, perched the camera, turned it on, ran back and gave a breathless account, trying to connect this chaotic scene with the unsuspecting viewer at home (2009: 120-121).

This relationship with the viewer is most important to Snow as he asserts it to be at the centre of reporting. Aside from the ease of collecting news today – his above-mentioned package would have resulted in much better quality image with current video cameras – Snow is most grateful to networked journalism because content producers, such as himself, are now answerable to content consumers. "For a boring several decades we were able to travel a one-way street and push material out with no consequences at all, as long as we kept within the bounds of the regulator...Suddenly you've got to be accountable not to the regulator, but to the viewer...What a delicious situation! What a vast improvement from the previous set up," says Snow (2009a).

Still, in the late 1970s, the technical problems for the television journalist were still substantial. In 1979, for instance, having taken the first interview in English with the Pope (John Paul II), Snow and his crew could not synchronise the Pope's lip movement with his words. This ended in ITN using a mere two minutes of the interview and with Snow throwing the whole recording from the transmission tower in Santo Domingo into the Caribbean Sea. "I was, of course, a complete idiot," admits Snow. "Very soon, new video and digital technology would come along that could synchronise the whole thing at the flick of a button" (2005: 133).

The 1980s would see the introduction of electronic lightweight cameras which produced instant video. Snow describes these as "magically fast and seductive" regardless of their being "twice as heavy as their film forebears" (ibid: 135). He was soon to get very familiar with these. When reporting from the Afghanistan front in 1980, he replied to the cameraman's account of the camera being dead by saying: "It's probably only frozen" (ibid: 173). They soon cooked the batteries on fire for approximately ten minutes and when replaced back in the camera it worked immediately. Thus his passion for the job prevailed once more.

From cooking batteries to revive a frozen film camera to being banned from tweeting the latest Egypt revolution, it's fair to assume that, at least as far as reporting technology is concerned, Snow has witnessed it all. In a lecture he delivered as a Visiting Professor at Coventry University, Snow spoke of a "massive speed of change", explaining with a sense of regret how "no one 'carries' the news anymore; they make it themselves or shove it off the internet and sell it to news corporations" (2009b). Internet-based media, he argues, are in desperate need of regulation.

But what he misses most today is the luxury to do personal research since instant processing has largely removed "the capacity to reflect, to consider, to write beautifully, to research properly, to talk to people, to ring people up, to spend time making sure that really what you were doing reflected what was actually going on" (Snow 2009a).

Snow's account of being a Washington correspondent presents the American President's residency as an open space to journalists: "I could wander in and out of the White House any time I chose, buttonhole an official, or wander into Speakes's [Press Secretary at the time] outer office to make a request for information or an interview." Yet today he looks back and sees the dangers of open access: "In reality, of course, it meant that journalists were so close to the centres of power that we were seduced by them: we rarely challenged them for fear of damaging our status, and we were frequently taken in by them. It took me some months to realise quite how quiescent the US press actually was" (2005: 213).

Despite his vast experience, Snow still describes his career as "short" (Snow 2005: P.S.8). And while he claims that "becoming a good journalist takes your entire life" he still stresses that "this is the best time to be a journalist" (Snow 2009b).

## References

Kershaw, A. (2011) No "off" switch. Lecture delivered at Coventry University on 27 January 2011

Niblock, S. (2010) *Journalism*, Oxford, One World Publications

Snow, J. (2005) *Shooting history*, London, Harper Perennial

Snow, J. (2009a) The impact of new media. Keynote speech delivered for the Institute of International and European Affairs, 4 September. Available online at http://iiea.com/events/jon-snow, accessed on 6 February 2011

Snow, J. (2009b) The best and worst of times – Who would be a journalist in the 21st century? Lecture delivered at Coventry University on 15 October 2009 at Coventry Cathedral. Available online at http://www.youtube.com/watch?v=bsUEba-4ZTI, accessed on 6 February 2011

Snow, J. (2010) Jon Snow, Channel 4 News. Available online at http://www.channel4.com/news/jon-snow, accessed on 6 February 2011

Snow, J. (2011a) *When revolution hits transmission problems*, 29 January, Channel 4 News. Available online at http://blogs.channel4.com/snowblog/revolution-hits-transmission-problems/14536, accessed on 6 February 2011

Snow, J. (2011b) @JonSnowC4, Twitter. Available online at http://twitter.com/#!/jonsnowC4, last accessed on 6 February 2011 at 10:52 pm

## Note on the author

Teodora Beleaga is a journalism student at Coventry University.

# Section 2. 140 characters that are changing the world

**John Mair**

Could Twitter, the microblogging site, be 140 characters that change the world? It is certainly the current tool of choice for many working (and not working) journalists. Some tweet so much you wonder if they have time to eat or sleep! It is possible using Twitter to follow most or all the gurus and thinkers of the journalism and hackacademic trade and share their thoughts and their recommended reading and viewing. It is a worldwide community of not necessarily like-minded individuals.

Judith Townend, a very early adopter of this technology and one of the movers behind the innovative "News Rewired" conferences hosted by journalism.co.uk in London. She offers some cautionary tales for tweeting journalists but maintains that Twitter has found an important place in the modern hack's toolbox alongside notebooks and cameras. Grander claims have been made for Twitter. The recent and ongoing uprisings in the Arab world – in Tunisia, Egypt, Bahrain and Libya – have been labelled by some as Twitter or Facebook "revolutions" because of the use of social media by the insurgents in fomenting change and communication with like-minded others worldwide.

Daniel Bennett, whose research at King's College, London, covers new media and war, examines critically the claims that Twitter is the engine of the new revolutions and the reporting of them.

So, can 140 characters micro-blogged change the world or is social change more deep-seated? You decide (120 characters).

# A Twitter revolution in breaking news

**Daniel Bennett**

"If you are in Cairo and you were waiting for something to happen to go to the protest. It's real. Time now to go," tweeted an Egyptian on 25 January 2011. In the days that followed thousands would go, pouring on to the streets with the intention of ending President Hosni Mubarak's thirty-year rule. Inspired by the toppling of President Zine El Abidine Ben Ali in Tunisia, an internet campaign had called for a "day of revolt"; protesters used Facebook, Twitter and other social networking sites to spread the message. The 25 January demonstration in Tahrir Square, Cairo, demanding reform from Egypt's repressive regime, was the start of a protracted political crisis which included protests in Alexandria, Suez and Ismailia.

The Egyptian regime responded by deploying the army to Tahrir Square, suspending public transport services to Cairo and blocking mobile phone and internet access on 27 January. Twitter had already been blocked on 26 January, forcing protesters to use proxy servers. Google and Twitter also set up a voicemail-to-tweet service in an attempt to keep the 140-character messages flowing. The events in Egypt reignited the debate over Twitter's role in the political process and whether the world has seen its first Twitter revolution.

Nearly two years earlier, the "Twitter revolution" headline for post-election protests in both Moldova and Iran spread widely. The idea that pro-Western digital revolutionaries could bring down Communist and theocratic governments using a trendy internet tool was an alluring news story readily seized upon by the media. There was much excitement about the Moldovan protesters' apparent use of Twitter to organise the demonstrations in the capital, Chisinau. But Twitter's role was exaggerated. One of the leaders of the Moldova protests, Natalia Morari, noted that there was almost no organisation at the site of the protest in Piata Marii Adunari Nationale Square whatsoever, let alone anybody conducting proceedings using Twitter (Morari 2009). Twitter had been used to publicise the protests but Morari said a much broader digital media campaign was pursued including email, blogs, text messages, Facebook and other social networks such as Odnoklassniki.

Similarly, in Iran, Clay Shirky argued that Twitter had caused the greatest impact as part of "the first revolution" that was "catapulted on to a global stage and transformed by social media" (Shirky 2009). But a "YouTube revolution" might have been an equally appropriate headline to describe the uprising against Mahmoud Ahmadinejad's re-election as President. The media relied heavily on video posted on the site to understand what was happening in Tehran and provide pictures for news reports. It was also the platform that supplied the harrowingly iconic image of demonstrator, Neda Soltan, dying on a street in the capital.

The contention that there has, as yet, been "a revolution" in either Moldova or Iran is also debatable. After the April protests in Moldova against the conduct of the election and the Communist Party's return to power, subsequent elections in July 2009 and November 2010 could not break the political deadlock. The pro-Western Alliance for European Integration was unable to win enough seats from the Communists to elect a President. In Iran, political gains were even more limited as members of the opposition Green Movement, who were demanding a re-run of the Iranian presidential election, were subjected to a brutal crackdown. There was a spike in the use of the death penalty and the regime arrested participants in subsequent demonstrations throughout 2009 and 2010 (UN 2010). Backed by the Revolutionary Guard, President Ahmadinejad remains in power.

President Ben Ali's decision to flee from Tunisia and the subsequent removal of most of the remnants of his regime from the cabinet represents a more compelling case for a revolution, (Zuckerman 2011). In Egypt, President Mubarak has also resigned – and protests have spread to Libya and elsewhere in the Arab world. But neither Twitter, nor social media more generally, cause revolutions *ex nihilo* – Moldovans, Iranians, Tunisians, and Egyptians rose against their respective governments as a consequence of varying and long-standing political, social and economic grievances (Noman 2011).

Twitter does facilitate the spread of news and information, enabling individuals to combat censorship and undermine the stranglehold of state-controlled media. It is undoubtedly playing a significant role in a rapidly evolving digital media landscape and 21$^{st}$ century politics. But journalists' dubbing of the events in Moldova, Iran, Tunisia and Egypt as "Twitter revolutions" is perhaps more reflective of the experience of their own changing working practices than the politics on the ground. It points to a Twitter revolution occurring in the newsrooms of media organisations, evident in the increasing importance of Twitter for journalists covering breaking news stories.

Created as little more than a simple way for a few people in the United States to tell each other what they were doing, Twitter has been adopted by a variety of individuals and organisations. It has developed into a powerful "real-time information network" (Twitter 2011) and an essential tool for journalists and media organisations. Initially sceptical, and faced with a number of challenges, journalists have learned how to harness its potential for news stories ranging from earthquakes to terror attacks. It enables reporters to monitor hundreds of sources of information simultaneously, to quickly contact eyewitnesses, to receive news faster than through traditional methods and to report news updates from their mobile phones. Twitter's ability to act as a customisable, searchable, global news wire and information network is transforming journalists' approach to breaking news.

## Twitter and journalists' early experiences

Twitter began in March 2006 and was the product of a brainstorming session at podcasting company Odeo (Malik 2009). Jack Dorsey, who would become the first CEO of Twitter, wanted a way of sending a text message that could be accessed by a small group of "followers" on their mobile phones but which would also be collated on a webpage. His idea was to harness the potential of the status update – a short, simple way of sharing information with anybody who was interested in where you were and what you were doing. Twitter gained a viral following in Silicon Valley and began to attract more widespread attention when the company won a web award at the South By Southwest festival in 2007. Dorsey believed that if a sufficient number of people contributed, Twitter would become an essential communication system.

Critics wondered whether Twitter's subsequent rapid growth would be sustainable and some journalists dismissed the 140 character updates as frivolous (Levy 2007). Twitter was not the first web-trend to be initially regarded as irrelevant to the practice of journalism. Previously "amateur" blogs had been regarded as an interesting media development but some journalists claimed they were not to be confused with the practice of "professional" journalism. Journalists' perceptions of blogs changed significantly when they began covering major news stories – the South Asian tsunami in 2004, the London bombings in 2005, the ongoing war in Iraq and a host of political stories. It was a pattern that was replicated with Twitter.

By 2008, Twitter was emerging as an important newsgathering tool for journalists in breaking news situations. As the microblogging site spread far outside the United States and began to be used for news and information, journalists could receive potentially newsworthy status updates from people all over the world. The 140-character limit encouraged brevity and immediacy while the ability to organise tweets using hashtags enabled a journalist to monitor hundreds of Twitter accounts that were providing information on the same topic. Twitter could be used as an adaptable and searchable breaking news wire that alerted journalists to stories exceptionally quickly.

The Chinese earthquake in May 2008 was one of the first global news stories where significant attention was paid to this phenomenon and the event convinced some of the sceptics that it might be more than worthwhile. The BBC's technology correspondent, Rory Cellan-Jones, for example, had been of the opinion that the microblogging service was "just another fad for people who want to share too much of their rather dull lives", but when he logged on to Twitter on the morning of 12 May, he was struck by the way that Twitter was "alive with tweets about the earthquake". He wondered whether this was the moment when "Twitter comes of age as a platform" (Cellan-Jones 2008a).

## The Mumbai attacks: Learning from challenges

A number of journalists and editors were becoming aware that Twitter was a useful place to search for breaking news. But harnessing its potential to cover a fast-moving breaking story such as the Mumbai terror attacks in November 2008 was far from straightforward. The 60-hour crisis in the Indian city, which left 174 dead and hundreds wounded, was discussed by thousands of people using Twitter. Some Twitterers were in the city, including individuals who were appealing for blood donors to go to the hospital in Mumbai; others were relaying information they had watched on television or were simply commenting from far flung places around the globe. The Mumbai hashtag (#Mumbai), which collated tweets about the incident, quickly became inundated and CNN estimated that 80 tweets were being sent every second (Busari 2008). Sifting through the stream of tweets, identifying useful Twitter accounts, and verifying the claims of Twitter users challenged journalists to apply existing editorial practices in a new environment.

The task of extracting useful information from these tweets was hindered by the fact that many journalists were also having to familiarise themselves with Twitter while attempting to report a complex breaking news story. BBC journalists covering the Mumbai crisis on the news website's live updates page, for example, had very little personal experience of Twitter but were urged by editors to incorporate tweets in their coverage. Fortunately, they could call on the expertise of journalists working on the BBC's User Generated Content (UGC) Hub – the Corporation's dedicated department for sourcing and verifying audience material. Nevertheless, the BBC still incorporated a tweet on their website which said that the Indian government had asked people to stop using Twitter – a claim which was subsequently demonstrated to have little, if any, basis in fact (Cellan-Jones 2008b). Steve Herrmann, the editor of the BBC News website, admitted that the Corporation was "still finding out how best to process and relay such information in a fast-moving account" (Herrmann 2008).

## Reporting the Iran election crisis: Changing mindsets and working practices

During the Iran election crisis in June 2009, there were also significant difficulties for journalists to overcome including: a large volume of noise and false information, inaccurate tweets, and a lack of balance given the almost exclusive use of Twitter by the Green Movement in Iran (Newman 2009). Information overload was even more acute. Former Director of BBC Global News, Richard Sambrook, estimated that at one stage up to 2,500 updates were being tweeted per minute (Sambrook 2009).

By 2009, however, journalists had more experience of using Twitter which helped them to access eyewitnesses and contacts, identify leads, and track links to images and video. In the context of a widespread media crackdown by the Iranian regime which included the jamming of satellites, the detention and expulsion of journalists and the blocking of internet websites, journalists were reliant on social networks for information. Twitter was particularly useful because it allowed "multiple paths in and out for data", meaning it was difficult for the Iranian regime to completely censor without cutting off Internet access altogether (Zittrain 2009).

Trushar Barot, who was working on the BBC's UGC hub during the Iran election crisis, said the BBC used Twitter to monitor rumours and "chatter" on the web, contact sources, and glean information on the time and location of future demonstrations. Information was circulated around the BBC via internal emails so that possible news lines could be followed up and BBC journalists were aware of potential developments. Barot noted that "after a week or so, there were certain bloggers and Twitter accounts that we could trust" because what they were saying was consistently confirmed by wire reports (Barot 2009). After this vetting process, several key Twitter accounts were identified as being reliable sources of information. The BBC's experience of covering Iran helped change mindsets among BBC journalists who were previously sceptical of the value of Twitter as a newsgathering tool.

Similarly, CNN's Deborah Rayner, the Managing Editor for Europe, Africa and Middle East, said the broadcaster's journalists covering Iran had "never experienced newsgathering like it". Journalists were "utterly overwhelmed" by the volume of information that was coming in from the streets of Tehran. Twitter and Facebook were used to source potential news stories and YouTube provided "an endless stream of video". CNN established a special Iran desk to cope with the influx of material and Rayner said journalists were constantly developing strategies to sift, verify and authenticate information. She claimed it "had been a revolution" in newsgathering; "the world had changed" (Rayner 2009).

## Twitter: An everyday tool for journalists working in breaking news

By 2010, Twitter had become "a more effective system than any single news organisation at servicing breaking news", according to Jay Rosen (see Boyle 2010). Twitter accounts had been started by charities, NGOs, corporations, politicians, governments, militaries, PR companies, sports stars and celebrities (Sambrook 2010: 33-36). The uptake of Twitter by a range of individuals and organisations as well as the widespread adoption of Twitter accounts by journalists and media organisations (Messner and Eford 2009; Hermida 2010) firmly established its role in the daily breaking news cycle. Twitter was not merely a tool a journalist would access in the context of an unusually significant breaking news crisis such as the Mumbai attacks and the Iran election crisis. For some journalists working in breaking news, such as the BBC's Defence and Security Producer, Stuart Hughes, and Sky News' Field Producer, Neal Mann, it has become an essential tool in their everyday journalism.

Stuart Hughes says previously he had a few main sources of information to track breaking news, but Twitter allows him to monitor those sources and several hundred others at the same time. He describes this development as "quite a significant shift" (Hughes 2010). Twitter has made contacting sources much faster which in turn speeds up the news cycle. Hughes says he is now rarely surprised by stories in newspapers because Twitter has already made him aware of the news and he is able to quickly monitor broadcast media competitors. Significant stories, such as the Domodedovo airport bombing in Moscow on 24 January 2011, continue to be broken first on Twitter which is having "a massive effect in the newsroom" (Hughes 2011).

Sky News journalist Neal Mann has discovered that regular tweeting, a systematic approach to following Twitter users who are "really interested in news", and the development of a significant number of Twitter followers (more than 4,000 at the beginning of 2011) means that people often contact him through Twitter with news and information (Mann 2011). For some stories, such as the ongoing activities of the whistle-blowing organisation, Wikileaks, Mann claims Twitter is the only way to fully follow developments as a journalist. He notes that Wikileaks often uses Twitter to break news about their organisation, while the decision by the judge to allow tweeting from the bail hearing of Wikileaks founder, Julian Assange, meant journalists would have missed significant news lines if they were not on Twitter.

The decision by Hughes and Mann to actively and regularly participate rather than merely turn to the Twittersphere in a crisis undoubtedly benefits their ability to extract relevant material from the network. Embedded in Twitter's online community they are able to build relationships and contacts, enabling them to establish an understanding of which sources on Twitter to trust before news breaks. This approach is far more effective than that used by many journalists during the Mumbai attacks, and to a lesser extent the Iran election crisis, whereby journalists delved into Twitter with little prior experience. Hughes and Mann are becoming known in the Twitter network as suppliers of breaking news and information, encouraging others to follow their Twitter accounts. In turn, these individuals and organisations offer Hughes and Mann news stories and alert them to breaking news.

## A Twitter revolution in breaking news

Twitter celebrates its fifth birthday in 2011 and media commentators are still debating whether the world has experienced a Twitter revolution (Zuckerman 2011; Frei 2011). Twitter's impact on the political process is part of a complex range of issues, but the increasingly important role it plays in the daily news cycle points to a burgeoning and rapidly advancing Twitter revolution in the practices of journalists covering breaking news.

A Twitter revolution in the practices of journalists covering breaking news has significant implications for journalism. It places pressure on the traditional news agency wires which are now regularly slower with the news than Twitter's easily-updated network. It thus increases the speed of the news cycle, enabling journalists to access sources very quickly in a breaking news crisis and it is part of a broader trend whereby journalists are operating in a "live" online news medium. The Twitter revolution in breaking news is far from complete: many journalists still rely on more traditional methods and it is merely one tool in an evolving digital media landscape. Journalists should be prepared, however, for a future where Twitter, or a similar web-based communication system that acts as a customisable and searchable global news wire, will become an indispensable tool for monitoring breaking news.

## References

Boyle, A. (2010) Msnbc.com acquires breakingnews.com, Msnbc.com. Available online at http://www.msnbc.msn.com/id/34694904/ns/technology_and_science-tech_and_gadgets/, accessed on 13 January 2011

Busari, S. (2008) Tweeting the terror: how social media reacted to Mumbai, CNN.com. Available online at http://edition.cnn.com/2008/WORLD/asiapcf/11/27/mumbai.twitter/ accessed on 28 November 2008

Cellan-Jones, R. (2008a) Twitter and the China earthquake, dot.life: A blog about technology from BBC News. Available online at http://www.bbc.co.uk/blogs/technology/2008/05/twitter_and_the_chi na_earthqua.htmla, accessed on 12 May 2008

Cellan-Jones, R. (2008b) Twitter – the Mumbai myths, dot.life: A blog about technology from BBC News. Available online at http://www.bbc.co.uk/blogs/technology/2008/12/twitter_the_mumbai _myths.html, accessed on 1 December 2008

Frei, M. (2011) Is this the Twitter Revolution? Available online at http://www.bbc.co.uk/blogs/thereporters/mattfrei/2011/01/where_is_ wikileaks_when_you_ne.html, accessed on 31 January 2011

Hermida, A. (2010) Twittering the news: The emergence of Ambient Journalism, *Journalism Practice*, Vol. 4, No. 3 pp 297-308

Herrmann, S. (2008) Mumbai, Twitter and live updates, BBC, The Editors. Available online at http://www.bbc.co.uk/blogs/theeditors/2008/12/theres_been_discussi on_see_eg.html, accessed on 4 December 2008

Levy, S. (2007) Twitter: Is brevity the next big thing, *Newsweek*. Available online at http://www.newsweek.com/2007/04/29/twitter-is-brevity-the-next-big-thing.html, accessed on 13 January 2011

Malik, O. (2009) A brief history of Twitter, GigaOm. Available online at http://gigaom.com/2009/02/01/a-brief-history-of-twitter/, accessed on 14 January 2011

Messner, M., and Eford, A. (2009) Twittering the news: How US traditional media adopt microblogging for their news dissemination. Paper presented at The Future of Journalism Conference in Cardiff, UK

Morari, N. (2009) Moldovan journalist and civil rights activist in panel discussion on Moldova's "Twitter revolution", Alliance for Youth Movements Summit, Mexico City, 16 October. See video at http://www.movements.org/case-study/entry/were-protests-in-moldova-a-twitter-revolution/, viewed on 12 February 2011

Newman, N. (2009) The rise of social media and its impact on mainstream journalism. Paper for the Reuters Institute for the Study of Journalism. Available online at http://reutersinstitute.politics.ox.ac.uk/fileadmin/documents/Publicatio ns/The_rise_of_social_media_and_its_impact_on_mainstream_journalis m.pdf, accessed on 12 February 2011

Rayner, D. (2009) Strategic communications and new media. Talk by Managing Editor for Europe, Africa and Middle East, Albany Associates Strategic Communications Conference, 25 June

Sambrook, R. (2009) Twittering the uprising, SacredFacts. Available online at http://sambrook.typepad.com/sacredfacts/2009/06/twittering-the-uprising.html, accessed on 14 June 2009

Sambrook, R. (2010) Are foreign correspondents correspondent? Paper for the Reuters Institute for Journalism. Available online at http://reutersinstitute.politics.ox.ac.uk/publications/risj-challenges/are-foreign-correspondents-redundant.html, accessed on 12 February 2011

Shirky, C. (2009) Q and A with Clay Shirky on Twitter and Iran, TED blog. Available online at http://blog.ted.com/2009/06/16/qa_with_clay_sh/, accessed on 16 June 2009

*Telegraph* (2009) Students use Twitter to storm Presidency in Moldova. Available online at http://www.telegraph.co.uk/news/worldnews/europe/moldova/511944 9/Students-use-Twitter-to-storm-presidency-in-Moldova.html, accessed 7 April 2009

Twitter (2011) http://twitter.com/about, accessed on 31 January 2011

UN (2010) *The situation of human rights in the Islamic Republic of Iran: Report of the Secretary General,* 15 September. Available online at http://www.un.org/ga/search/view_doc.asp?symbol=a/65/370&referer =/english/&Lang=E, accessed on 12 February 2011

Zittrain, J. (2009) Could Iran shut down Twitter, Future of the Internet. Available online at http://futureoftheinternet.org/could-iran-shut-down-twitter, accessed on 15 June 2009

Zuckerman, E. (2011) The first Twitter revolution? *Foreign Policy.* Available online at: http://www.foreignpolicy.com/articles/2011/01/14/the_first_twitter_re volution, accessed on 31 January 2011

## Author interviews and correspondence

Barot, T. (2009) BBC Senior Broadcast Journalist, interview, 16 September 2009

Hughes, S. (2010) BBC Defence and Security Producer, interview, 14 June 2010

Hughes, S. (2011) BBC Defence and Security Producer, email correspondence, 31 January 2011

Mann, N. (2011) Field Producer for Sky News, interview, 6 January 2011

## Note on the author

Daniel Bennett is a PhD candidate in the War Studies Department at King's College, London. He is writing his thesis on the impact of blogging on the BBC's coverage of war and terrorism. The project is funded by the Arts and Humanities Research Council in conjunction with the BBC College of Journalism. He writes *Reporting War*, a blog for the Frontline Club in London, which explores the use of new media to cover conflict.

# Battle of (t)wits? Using Twitter as a journalistic tool

**Judith Townend**

Newspapers love to talk about Twitter. A search for the word Twitter in national newspapers returns over 3,000 articles for the past year, too many for the Nexis® UK database to count – 1,696 in one month alone. Twitter has appeared in 900 national newspaper headlines in the last year, while 24 articles in the same period refer to "Twitter twits" (see, for example, the *Sun* 2010)[i]. "Twit" may be a milder term than the one David Cameron chose to describe users of the service (Siddique and Agencies 2009), but it is an unfair label.

Generalising about Twitter users is as pointless an exercise as uniformly describing all people who pick up the telephone, or appear on television. Twitter is a communication tool;[ii] it is the way it is used that defines whether it is a productive or daft activity. This chapter attempts to show the different ways Twitter is being used by journalists, both effectively and ineffectively, and argues that while Twitter does host a lot of trivial activity by "twits", it also gives opportunity to create good journalism and enables better communication with the world outside the newsroom.

## Part of the process

As Jeff Jarvis has outlined, journalism's product is not perfect, despite the popular myth, and blogging facilitates "beta journalism" in which writers admit what they don't know, as well as what they do, and invite collaborations that will help improve their work (Jarvis 2009a). "Online, the story, the reporting, the knowledge are never done and never perfect," he writes. In his view, that does not mean that bloggers "revel in imperfection" or have no standards:

> It just means that we do journalism differently, because we can. We have our standards, too, and they include collaboration, transparency, letting readers into the process, and trying to say what we don't know when we publish – as caveats – rather than afterward – as corrections (ibid).

Twitter is an ideal tool to use in this "beta journalism" process: it can be used to let readers and followers know what you are looking for, to receive tip-offs and ideas and to publicise your work once it is finished. Some journalists have also experimented with conducting interviews by Twitter (Townend 2009a) although this method has its limitations. Not only is it difficult to express an idea in 140 characters, it can be difficult to co-ordinate the timing of answers and questions and involve onlooker contributions.[iii] Newspaper columnists have frequently mocked the limits and triviality of Twitter updates – sometimes before reversing their opinion of the service (cf. Knight 2008 and Johncock 2010). However, the word limit is longer than many news headlines and subheadlines and photo captions. Furthermore, the information contained within one tweet can be far more extensive because hyperlinks to additional content can be included in the message.

There are many instances that demonstrate Twitter's usefulness as a reporting tool, as well as a means for research and publicity. Ben Kendall, crime correspondent for the *Eastern Daily Press* and *Norwich Evening News*, experimented with live "tweeting" a court trial in August 2010 (Kendall, B. 2010; Townend 2010). "One issue is whether you can present a balanced and accurate account in the 140 character limit of a tweet," he reflected several months later, when a judge gave permission for a national newspaper journalist to tweet during the appeal of Wikileaks' Julian Assange for bail at Westminster Magistrates' Court on 15 December 2010.

> I would argue than an experienced journalist should be able to do this. It takes a bit of imagination but it is possible. And in any event, we traditionally work on the basis that we provide balance in a court case over the course of our coverage, not just in one story. Why shouldn't the same apply to tweets? (Kendall op cit).

Twitter was used by the *Guardian* newspaper to live report events such as the UK student fees protests in 2010 and correspondents including the BBC News Channel chief political correspondent Laura Kuenssberg (@BBCLauraK) and Sky News' online politics producer Ruth Barnett [iv] (@ruthbarnett) have developed their own individual styles for publishing news updates. Live tweeting from the ground is becoming an increasingly commonplace practice among journalists (see, for example, how Channel 4 News reporters use the service[v]). The *Guardian* successfully uses comment from Twitter for its homepage live blogs that track rolling news stories, such as the UK general election 2010 (Sparrow 2010) and the Tunisia crisis in January 2011 (Weaver 2011).

Nonetheless, the limitations of the medium must be acknowledged: confusions often arise when a conversation on Twitter is only viewed partially; when the speed of the service can lead to legal foolishness; and when misinformation is spread with ease. As Richard Kendall, a regional newspaper journalist based in Peterborough, tweeted:

> Twitter needs to NOT be taken for granted in same way as Wikipedia > just another source that needs corroborating evidence (Kendall, R. 2011).

## Cautionary tales

The difficulties in correcting the error on Twitter became apparent when NPR News incorrectly tweeted that Congresswoman Gabrielle Giffords had died after being shot in Tucson, Arizona. The false information was also tweeted by other media outlets on Twitter, including Reuters (Reuters 2011) and the BBC (BBC 2011).[vi] Even though NPR sent out a subsequent tweet that said "UPDATE: There are conflicting reports about whether she was killed", users kept finding the original message and re-tweeting it, despite the broadcaster's correction, as documented by the site Lost Remote (Safran 2011):

> For hours after it was reported she was alive, people kept discovering the original tweet that she was dead, retweeting it to their friends without seeing the update. In several cases, the retweet of the incorrect report came three or more hours after the report first spread…(Safran 2011).

This led to some Twitter users and journalists suggesting the introduction of a correction feature to show that a tweet contained false information. Journalists and bloggers subsequently discussed how such a tool might work in a live chat session on the Poynter.org website (Tenore 2011) and whether incorrect information on Twitter should be deleted (Silverman 2011). Less than two weeks after this incident, "a fearful game of online Chinese whispers in central London" (McDermott 2011) spread via Twitter. Reports claimed it had started with an innocent tweet about a fashion event:

> The frenzy erupted due to a misinterpretation of an invitation on @candicecbailey [sic] to attend an advertisement being filmed in the area. The tweet read: "Street style shooting in Oxford Circus for ASOS and Diet Coke. Let me know if you're around!!" News of a shooting incident and possible terrorist attack then spread like wildfire across the site as workers and shoppers tweeted and retweeted the misinterpretation (ibid).

Adding to the confusion, information was leaked from an email about a police training exercise. A Metropolitan Police spokesperson confirmed that reports of a shooting were false: "We can confirm that there has been no firearms incident in Oxford Street today. It would appear that some information about a routine police training exercise being held today has inadvertently got into the public domain" (quoted in Prigg and Davenport 2011). On this occasion, it would seem that mainstream media outlets managed to report rather than repeat the error.

## Who is Twitter?
Twitter provides only a limited representation of wider society and a user is likely to create themselves a nest of followers who share similar political views and interests to themselves. But journalists should not fall into the

trap of making a straw man argument (Townend 2009c) or slaying imaginary dragons (Beckett 2009) to fill newspaper column space, as many have done when analysing the influence of the internet and Twitter. Many articles have been written about why Twitter won't save democracy or cause a revolution, when it is not clear who has said it will. More useful are balanced blog posts by working reporters and editors, discussing Twitter's role in the newsroom, such as this one by Richard Kendall, which argued:

> I think most journalists would (hopefully) view Twitter as an opportunity for two-way communication and newsgathering source, and as a key distribution tool in today's world of digital world...Plus, the next time you go for a media-related job interview, it may well crop up as a question...It is not, though, a guaranteed saviour of journalism, the answer to newsroom prayers or going to write a story for you, and as with any source information needs verifying (Kendall, R.op cit).

Observers should not assume everyone who uses Twitter sees themselves as a publisher. While Twitter users share information openly on the internet, they may see the social media service as a place for personal conversation. However contradictory that might seem to onlookers, as Hargittai (2008) has described, "individuals' goals and activities on SNSs [social network sites] are extremely varied". Additionally, many Twitter users might be classed as "lurkers": people who do not publicly participate but follow the activity of others for their own interest or research purposes, consuming rather than producing (see Muller et al. 2010).

**Commercial activity**
The distinction between editorial and advertising has a long history in the UK, but in a struggling economic climate, journalists are under pressure to help sustain the news operation (see: Jarvis 2009b; Picard 2009; Greenslade 2010). Newspapers are turning to Twitter as another way of marketing their content, and journalists, as well as commercial staff, are using the service to help increase audience size and promote their employer. Alan Rusbridger, editor of the *Guardian*, recognises its editorial value in helping transform media transmission to media communication (2010) and has argued for its potential to generate revenue. At a media event in 2009 he talked about the possibility of developing the *Guardian*'s

relationship with the followers of its technology Twitter feed (Townend 2009b):

> The question of how you monetise those 900,000 [followers] is deeply interesting, but that's not my job. I do think you've got those 900,000 people coming voluntarily – you've got to think what would they pay for?

Marc Reeves, who launched Business Desk West Midlands in 2010, has pointed out that the future of media is not just about sustaining journalism; news content is only one part of the "package" (Reeves 2010), a point also argued by Adam Tinworth (2009). Reeves argues that "it's never been just about journalism" (2010):

> The reasons readers bought newspapers in their millions were many and complex – and not always about the page three lead. What about the TV listings, the racecards, the what's on guide? The edges were coloured in by journalism, sure, but all the reader really wanted to know was what time to set the VCR. And, painful though it is for the proud journalist to admit, those reams and reams of jobs, property and car ads were as much a reason to buy a paper for most readers as that insightful analysis of last Tuesday's health committee meeting.

## Twitter used as a natural part of the process

It is natural, then, that Twitter can also be used in this part of the process. The *Financial Times* and the *Guardian* News and Media press teams both use Twitter to promote the commercial activity of the companies, as well as the journalism. Twitter is just another tool to use in creating and promoting the media "package".

Advertisers can now pay for a topic to "trend",[vii] for tweets to be promoted in Twitter search pages, or for their account to be a recommended "follow" on Twitter; these are marked clearly as "promoted" features, just as advertorial is labelled in a newspaper. Will the increasing commercialisation of Twitter damage the product and its place in journalism? Without a magic crystal ball it is difficult to predict: users will react if paid for promoted trends dilute the quality of the service, but they are unlikely to stop using Twitter until something superior comes along. A useful comparison might be made with the music service Spotify, which has experimented with different economic models, reacting and modifying their pricing and advertising options according to user and competitor reactions (see Andrews 2010).

New communication and information tools are on the horizon as people adjust their online behaviour patterns and new technology is developed. Recently there has been a surge in the number of signups to Quora [viii](Siegler 2011), a social service for posing and answering questions, which could be described as a cross between Twitter and Wikipedia. When the next stage in social technology arrives, it would be encouraging if the best journalists are flexible enough to experiment with it, rather than spend time setting up straw men to knock down for whiny newspaper columns.

## Notes

[i] Nexis® UK database, accessed on 27 January 2011
[ii] Twitter describes itself as a "real-time information network". See http://twitter.com/about, accessed on 26 January 2011]
[iii] I write with first-hand experience: I experimented with "Twinterviews" briefly in February/March 2009 before abandoning the idea
[iv] Former Sky News Twitter/social media correspondent
[v] Reporters' Twitter accounts listed at http://www.channel4.com/news/about-channel-4-news, accessed: 26 January 2011
[vi] It should be noted that the error was also made in television coverage (Adams 2011)
[vii] To "trend" means a particular topic, labelled with a #, is listed among the most popular discussions of the day on Twitter
[viii] Available online at http://quora.com, accessed on 26 January 2011

## References

Adams, R. (2011) Gabrielle Giffords's husband tells of hearing reports of her death, *Guardian*. Available online at http://www.guardian.co.uk/world/richard-adams-blog/2011/jan/19/gabrielle-giffords-mark-kelly-abc-interview /, accessed on 27 January2011]

Andrews, R. (2010) Spotify halves subscription cost as competitors gather, paidContent:UK. Available online at http://paidcontent.org/article/419-spotify-halves-subscription-cost-as-competitors-gather/, accessed January 26, 2011

BBC (2011) @BBCBreaking on Twitter. Available online at http://twitter.com/#!/BBCBreaking/status/23820114382028800, accessed on 21 January 2011

Beckett, C. (2009) Deluded dragon slayers: Why we need a better debate about the net, POLIS Director's Blog. Available online at http://www.charliebeckett.org/?p=1437, accessed on 26 January 2011

Greenslade, R. (2010) Journalists as entrepreneurs? That's fine, but not if they have to sell, *Guardian*. Available online at http://www.guardian.co.uk/media/greenslade/2010/oct/08/entreprene urs-digital-media, accessed on 26 January 2011

Hargittai, E. (2008) Whose apace? Differences among users and non-users of social network sites, *Journal of Computer-Mediated Communication*, Vol. 13, No. 1 pp 276-297

Jarvis, J. (2009a) Product v. process journalism: The myth of perfection v. beta culture, Buzz Machine. Available online at http://www.buzzmachine.com/2009/06/07/processjournalism/, accessed on 13 January 2011

Jarvis, J. (2009b) The future of news is entrepreneurial, Buzz Machine. Available online at http://www.buzzmachine.com/2009/11/01/the-future-of-journalism-is-entrepreneurial/, accessed on 26 January 2011

Johncock, B. (2010) Twitter and the book trade: The good, the bad and the ugly. Futurebook.net. Available online at http://www.futurebook.net/content/twitter-and-book-trade-good-bad-and-ugly, accessed on 24 January 2011

Kendall, B. (2010) Wikileaks, Assange and court reporting in the 21st century, EDP 24. Available online at http://services.edp24.co.uk/FORUMS/EDP24/CS/blogs/ben_kendall/archive/2010/12/15/2372259.aspx, accessed on 26 January 2011

Kendall, R. (2010) A local journalist's Twitter guide, A web editor's tale. Available online at http://richardkendall.wordpress.com/2010/02/16/a-local-journalists-twitter-guide/, accessed on 25 January 2011

Kendall, R. (2011) Twitter message from @richardkendall to @JTownend, 25 January. Available online at http://twitter.com/#!/richardkendall/status/29927564986286082, accessed on 25 January 2011

Knight, I. (2008) The twits taking intimacy a tweet too far, TimesOnline.co.uk. Available online at http://www.timesonline.co.uk/tol/comment/columnists/india_knight/article5375361.ece, accessed on 24 January 2011

McDermott, B. (2011) Twitter post causes false reports of terror alert on Oxford Street, Beehive City, 19 January. Available online at http://www.beehivecity.com/newspapers/twitter-post-causes-terror-alert-in-central-london-948512/, accessed on 21 January 2011

Muller, M. et al. (2010) We are all lurkers: Consuming behaviors among authors and readers in enterprise file-sharing service, IBM. Available online at: http://domino.research.ibm.com/cambridge/research.nsf/58bac2a2a6b05a1285256b30005b3953/24c94026ba65876f852577b4001b3500!OpenDocument, accessed on 26 January 2011

Picard, R. (2009) Journalism as charity and entrepreneurship, The Media Business, 25 October. Available online at http://themediabusiness.blogspot.com/2009/10/journalism-as-charity-and.html, accessed 26 January 2011

Prigg, M. and Davenport, J. (2011) Twitter sparks "shooting" panic over "Oxford Street gunman", Thisislondon.co.uk, 19 January. Available online at http://www.thisislondon.co.uk/standard/article-23915674-twitter-sparks-shooting-panic-over-oxford-street-gunman.do, accessed on 21 January 2011

Reeves, M. (2010) TheBusinessDesk.com really means business, Mark Reeves, 2 August. Available online at http://marcreeves.blogspot.com/2010/08/thebusinessdeskcom-really-means.html#more, accessed on 13 January 2011

Reuters (2011) @Reuters on Twitter, 8 January. Available online at http://twitter.com/#!/Reuters/status/23857113772072960, accessed on 21 January 2011

Rusbridger, A. (2010) Why Twitter matters for media organisations, *Guardian*, 19 November. Available online at http://www.guardian.co.uk/media/2010/nov/19/alan-rusbridger-twitter, accessed on 26 January 2011

Safran, S. (2011) How incorrect reports of Giffords' death spread on Twitter, Lost Remote, 9 January. Available online at http://www.lostremote.com/2011/01/09/how-an-incorrect-report-of-giffords-death-spread-on-twitter/, accessed on 21 January 2011

Siddique, H. (2009) and agencies. David Cameron says sorry for "twat" comment during radio interview. *Guardian*, 29 July. Available at: http://www.guardian.co.uk/politics/2009/jul/29/david-cameron-apology-radio-twitter, accessed 13 January 2011

Siegler, M. G. (2011) Quora signups exploded in late December then doubled from that this week, TechCrunch, 5 January. Available online at http://techcrunch.com/2011/01/05/quora-surge/, accessed on 27 January 2011

Silverman, C. (2011) To delete or not to delete? *Columbia Journalism Review*, 14 January. Available online at http://www.cjr.org/behind_the_news/to_delete_or_not_to_delete.php?page=all, accessed on 21 January 2011

Sparrow, A. (2010) Live blogging the general election, *Guardian*, 10 May. Available online at http://www.guardian.co.uk/media/2010/may/10/live-blogging-general-election, accessed on 26 January 2011

*Sun.* (2010) Twitter twit: I'm so sorry, *Sun.* Available online at LexisNexis database, accessed on 22 February 2011

Tenore, M.J. (2011) Chat replay: How should journalists handle incorrect tweets? Poynter, 13 January. Available online at http://www.poynter.org/how-tos/digital-strategies/114595/live-chat-how-should-journalists-handle-incorrect-tweets/, accessed on 21 January 2011

Tinworth, A. (2009) Our real problem: The death of the news package. One Man and His Blog 4 December. Available online at http://www.onemanandhisblog.com/archives/2009/12/our_real_problem_the_death_of_the_news_p.html, accessed 26 January 2011

Townend, J. (2009a) Live "Twinterview" with Channel 4's Krishnan Guru-Murthy. Journalism.co.uk. Available online at http://blogs.journalism.co.uk/editors/2009/02/27/live-twinterview-with-channel-4s-krishnan-guru-murthy-kicks-off-3pm/, accessed on 26 January 2011

Townend, J. (2009b) Rusbridger on funding news: Provide 900,000 Twitter followers with services they will pay for, Journalism.co.uk. Available online at: http://www.journalism.co.uk/news/rusbridger-on-funding-news-provide-900-000-twitter-followers-with-services-they-will-pay-for/s2/a535253/, accessed on 13 January 2011

Townend, J. (2009c) Sunday paper strawman: Web scepticism+flashy headline. JTownend blog. Available online at http://blog.jtownend.com/2009/05/17/sunday-paper-strawman/, accessed on 26 January 2011

Townend, J. (2010) Twilence in court! Judge allows reporters to tweet during Assange hearing. Meeja Law. Available online at http://meejalaw.com/2010/12/14/twilence-in-court-judge-allows-reporters-to-tweet-during-assange-hearing/, accessed 26 January 2011

Weaver, M. (2011) Tunisia crisis: Live updates, *Guardian*. Available online at http://www.guardian.co.uk/news/blog/2011/jan/19/tunisia-crisis-live-updates, accessed on 26 January 2011

**Note on the author**
Judith Townend is an MPhil/PhD student at the Centre for Law, Justice and Journalism, City University London, where she researches legal restraints on the media. From 2008-10 she was a reporter for the media industry site Journalism.co.uk. She blogs at http://meejalaw.com and has written for a number of online publications, including Inforrm, Index on Censorship and the Media Standards Trust blog. She is @jtownend on Twitter.

# Section 3. In the killing fields: Local journalism and the internet

**John Mair**

It used to be a position of some standing in the community – editor of the *Barchester Chronicle* or similar. Today, being editor of the *Oldham Chronicle*, the *Coventry Telegraph*, the *Leeds Evening Post*, or the *Lincolnshire Echo* must be like being a deckchair attendant on the Titanic!

The local and regional press are caught in the perfect storm with advertising haemorrhaging away to the internet in spades. News online is taking the readers' eyeballs away too; they are getting older, less loyal and fewer – and costs (and staff) are being scythed away. The sums no longer add up. Preston is the Passchendale of modern journalism, York the Ypres. It is a battle to survive. You need to be brave or foolhardy to edit the *Barchester Chronicle* in the internet age.

Darren Parkin has taken over the *Coventry* (no longer *Evening*) *Telegraph* in that storm. He faces it head on with a developed web site, popular blogs and by trying to reconnect with his community on the pages of the *"Tele"*. Parkin should ask Neil Fowler for help. He has edited a number of local and regional papers – including the *Lincolnshire Echo*, the *Derby Evening Telegraph* and the *Western Mail* – over a quarter of a century and is today the *Guardian*'s research fellow at Nuffield College, Oxford. His special subject there (and here in his chapter) is how the local and regional press have adapted to the internet. Have they faced the future or not?

David Hayward, now of the BBC College of Journalism, is (or was) their nemesis. He masterminded the BBC local TV pilot in the Midlands in 2005-6. That was strangled not long after birth and steered to the rocks by local newspaper interests in the Midlands and nationally. Hayward argues that the future for journalism and for democracy is actually hyperlocal but it won't be for the BBC. The Corporation is now pegged back to, at best, regional programmes with part of the new licence fee set aside to build local (commercial) television.

# How the snowball towards the social media is gathering pace

**Darren Parkin**

Thin columns of smoke rising over desks like a familiar Lowry painting. Half empty bottles of whisky – and cheap ones at that – on most desks. Banter and remarks that would, today, have anyone marched straight to HR. The shuddering sound of a typewriter being misused by a sports hack before he unleashed a torrent of foul-mouthed abuse at it.

That was the newsroom I remember from decades ago. No computers, no internet. It was a world away from today. It was a dreamy and intoxicating time to be a young reporter. Every noisy, smoke-stenched day was about the scoop – it was a quest for perfection in an imperfect environment.

I remember when the first computers were delivered. Green text on a massive monitor that looked more like a giant microwave oven than a computer screen. "It'll never catch on!" screamed the sports editor as he told the editor, the staff, the reporters, and even me – the tea boy –

exactly what he thought of this new-fangled technology. His assessment contained no less than 14 "f" words, a couple of "bloodies" and two "arses" before reaching a crescendo of two "c" words. I know, because I counted every shocking one.

Rant over, he returned to his seat. Calmly lit his pipe, took a swig straight from bottle on his desk and sat there radish-faced, beside himself with anger. Two days later he was in early, ready to embrace the modern age. I watched fascinated as he used his same aggressive typing manner on the computer keyboard as he had done with his typewriter – two fingers jabbing away like a heavyweight's fists against an opponent's flanks. That year, he went through four keyboards.

And so, there began the evolutionary transition from journalistic dinosaur to the modern, multi-media professional we see in every newsroom across the land today. What began with a cough and a splutter looks destined to flourish as the world becomes engulfed in its insatiable desire for instant news – live feeds from the scene, blogs, web-chats and all manner of bells and whistles vying for the honour of being the one which delivers the final blow to the printed press.

The internet, with all its accessibility, freedom and infinite space has become the fastest-growing media tool since the printing press was invented. And, because of that monstrous speed of growth, it's not far off being the biggest weapon against pure journalism.

**The internet's lack of control, rules and regulations**
The internet – and I point the finger at social media in particular – has a lack of control, rules, regulations and guidelines which I find most disturbing. The thing with newspapers is that we all adhere to the law. Well, most of us do, most of the time. You take that regulation out of the equation and you're tip-toeing across very thin ice.

Journalists are well-trained, highly skilled and highly intelligent individuals. Social media opens up the world of journalism to anyone. Anyone can now be a journalist – but is it being backed up with the academic badges that adorn our own people?

The simplified example I would use to demonstrate this point is the digital camera. Years ago, the world of the photographer was a strange and exclusive place. The manual settings on their tools were baffling to even the smartest of human beings. Along came the digital camera and bang! Suddenly, the whole world is full of photographers.

Although the art of photography may suddenly have become accessible to all, the problem is those who excelled enough to make it their profession are fast becoming extinct. Like an ancient South American tribe whose ancestors may have harboured a cure for all sorts of modern ailments, we are slowly seeing a great and undervalued skill eroded.

## Destroying the profession – guilty m'lud

But we're all falling into the trap – myself included. I'm as guilty to the charge of destroying the profession as anyone for, later this year, there will not be a photographer at my wedding. Instead, my future wife and I are taking the same route as plenty of other brides and grooms – friends and family armed with a great artillery of digital cameras will be filling the wedding album for us. After all, everyone is a photographer these days.

And that's from where my love/hate relationship with digital media is born. Whilst I firmly believe the digital world is where we will all eventually end up as journalists, I can't help but think we are doomed to fail unless we are allowed to do it at our own pace and ensure regulation is at the top of the agenda with every twist and turn.

And surely, we must be some distance away from that inevitability? Time and time again you hear the argument over what are we doing as an industry to attract younger readers. My answer is always the same – why? At what point in the last 20 years have newspapers enjoyed a wealth of young readers? I certainly don't recall any point in my career when I believed the average age of a reader of the regional press was below 55. And, if it wasn't for the fact I have been in the newspaper industry since I was a teenager, I seriously doubt I would buy my local paper.

There are painfully few of my friends under 40 who even know what their local paper is called, let alone purchase it regularly. They do, however, turn to the internet for their news. The minute they get to their desk, the computer is on and they are catching ten minutes of news online, then they'll check Facebook to see what the rest of us are saying about them before firing up Twitter.

### The "Miracle on the Hudson" and the rise and rise of Twitter

Twitter. Now there's a thing. It took me a while to catch on to Twitter. I simply didn't get it. At first I wondered what the point might be in having a Facebook-style piece of social media condensed into 140 characters. Then, suddenly, there was the "Miracle on the Hudson". When Captain Chesley Sullenberger III hit a flock of birds in his Airbus A320 on 15 January 2009 he had no idea he was about to change the media world for good.

As he ditched the plane into the Hudson River, saving the lives of all 155 on board, the "Miracle of the Hudson" was being filmed on countless mobile phones. Within seconds, the footage was uploaded on to Twitter accounts. This in turn was re-tweeted over and over again until, within ten minutes of the landing, nearly every man, woman and child on the planet who had access to social media had witnessed the drama quicker than it took rescue boats to get to the stricken aircraft.

What a truly mind-blowing reality check. Television had the event covered within the hour – mainly using the footage from Twitter. Newspapers would report the story the following day. It was a delicious feast of instant news feeding a voracious appetite for the instantaneous. Social media one, print media nil. And that was the moment when I knew the snowball towards social media was gathering pace.

Will it replace newspapers? An interesting question. But let me instead ask you this. Did television destroy the radio? No, it didn't. It actually focused it clearly at the audience it now serves. There isn't a newspaper circulation in the country that hasn't experienced decline during these difficult times, and much of that is at the blood-soaked hands of the internet. But as an industry are we to just roll over and die? Of course not. Instead, the future is in our hands and we must look to adapt rather than be destroyed.

### Newspaper circulations globally set to decline

Newspaper circulations throughout the world will, I suspect, continue to decline. It is the rate of that descent which we – with all the flying skills of the great Captain Chesley Sullenberger III – must arrest. I believe, just as radio did during the formative years of television, that circulations will eventually settle on their own level and thrive there.

Radio and television can sit cheek to jowl and serve one another's audience – newsprint and digital must do the same. And it will. We just need to ensure that we professionals of the industry are at the controls.

## Note on the author

Darren Parkin became the youngest editor of the *Coventry Telegraph* in November 2009, aged 37, having been editor of several weekly newspapers in the Midlands. He began as a runner on a Youth Training Scheme at the *Dewsbury Reporter* and went on to become the country's youngest newspaper editor at the age of 24 when taking over the *Wolverhampton News*. The winner of multiple awards and a dedicated champion of local news, he is a father, a husband-to-be, and fiercely passionate about the *Coventry Telegraph*.

# How the British regional and local press is dealing with the internet – or not?

**Neil Fowler**

## A passive sector

The regional newspaper industry has never been the most innovative of business sectors. Structurally it has not changed much over the decades. Since before the Second World War, newspapers have been owned by a mixture of larger groups and smaller individual businesses with the overwhelming majority operating under standard business rules and limited company methods.

Names may have changed, the generic term "media" may be in some company titles and the industry may be in the grip of a pincer movement of structural change and economic downturn, but essentially regional and local newspapers are still attempting to originate and distribute local news on the back of advertising sales and some circulation revenue. It was late to acknowledge the power of the web and has been struggling to catch up ever since.

At the start of 2011, the top 20 regional press publishers account for 87 per cent of all regional press titles and 97 per cent of total weekly circulation. There are 87 regional press publishers producing a total of 1,196 titles. This includes 39 publishers producing just one title. In 2009, there were 1,290 titles, so 94 were lost over the year, but of those 94 four were regionalised daily editions of the free *Metro*, 17 were weekly paid-fors and the overwhelming majority, 73, were free titles. There remain 93 paid-for daily titles. The major groups are Trinity Mirror, Johnston Press, Newsquest and Northcliffe and they account for 66 per cent of titles and about 70 per cent of total sales. It employs about 30,000 people including some 10,000 journalists.

It may be in trouble, but it remains a substantial industrial sector, with some 40m of the UK population interacting with it on a weekly basis. However, to understand how the regional and local press is dealing with the internet, it is useful to examine briefly its history over the past 50 years.

### Industry in slow decline since the 1950s
Arguably the industry has been in slow decline since the 1950s when the economy began to grow and the public had more to do than read contemporaneous ink on paper. This marked the beginning of the end of the age of the regional and local newspaper as a means of mass communication to the total audience of a particular community.

Those newspapers were not particularly well equipped to adapt and evolve in line with this societal change. Economically, they were stable but slow-moving entities, often run by unimaginative managers who were weighed down with dealing with the might of the print unions. From 1945 to the early 1980s the industry trundled along. Profits were solid but not spectacular. Innovation was rare, despite the introduction of bulk classified advertising from North America by Roy Thomson in the 1960s and the attempt to ring London by Thomson and Westminster Press with a circle of suburban evenings. Groups would often use surplus funds to invest in other sectors rather than in regional newspapers as healthy returns were not seen as an option.

Three Royal Commissions on the Press (1947-1949; 1961-1962; 1974-1977) did little to stimulate the regional sector and sales were generally (with some notable exceptions) in gentle decline from the late 1960s.

Newspaper paginations were meagre with smaller selling evening publications often producing just 10-page broadsheet or 20-page tabloid editions.

Free newspapers were introduced to the UK in the mid-1960s, generally by local, small-scale entrepreneurs looking to challenge the established order. But even this new concept did not spark too many worries. Traditional owners launched their own spoilers against the upstarts and hoped they would go away. Some did, others, like Lionel Pickering and Keith Barwell, did not and became multi-millionaires when they sold out to bigger groups a couple of decades later.

## Rout of the print unions

It is true that regional companies began the rout of the print unions, initially at Nottingham in 1973, followed by Wolverhampton and Portsmouth in the early 1980s. But it took minor player Eddie Shah in his dispute at Warrington in 1983, which then inspired News International to move its national titles to Wapping without its traditional print work force, to bring the regional and local sector to life. These businesses, and especially the big groups, had been happy to watch smaller, independent organisations take the risks, and then subsequently carried out their own reorganisations without any of the attendant confrontation. This has been a continuing theme for most of the industry over the years – never lead, always follow.

The industry then enjoyed its so-called golden years. Much of the initial investment in new computers was funded by the unexpected goldmine of the Reuters shareholding in 1982, a windfall again exploited by others for the regionals' benefit, this time Fleet Street being the benefactor.

But from the late 1980s some new titles were launched and there were some moments of joy when newspaper sales spiked, generally on the back of relaunches from broadsheet to tabloid, but sales still maintained their slow decline. Businesses did not seem too concerned as recruitment advertising, in particular, funded substantial returns, notably from 1992 through to 2005. But minds were concentrated on margins which were often reaching more than 30 per cent. So when a whole new world began to emerge in the early 2000s, the sector was not in the best position to respond.

## Structural change in the first decade of the 21$^{st}$ century

Readership and circulation had been declining for decades but profits were maintained on the back of lucrative classified advertising. Despite the advent of local free newspapers in the 1960s and the growth of specialist magazine titles, regional and local newspapers were still able to prosper on their staple diet of the classified advertising categories of motoring, property and jobs. These had been developed in the early 1960s and were, as Rupert Murdoch once said, "rivers of gold".

Although competition for property and motoring advertising was fierce, the "rivers of gold" view was especially true for situations vacant advertising where there was an unwritten (and arguably anti-competitive) rule across the whole print industry (including national newspapers and both trade and consumer magazines) that jobs adverts were never discounted. Never.

However, by the mid 2000s, all kinds of classifieds were haemorrhaging to the internet. Advertising revenue on UK sites quadrupled between 2004 and 2009. Online classified businesses such as Craigslist, which had wreaked mayhem on North American newspapers, began forays into the UK. But even where they were not as successful as on the other side of the Atlantic, others such as eBay and Gumtree came in to fragment the market successfully.

Many formerly valuable categories were now either free on the web or yielding much lower rates. Many of these had migrated to low cost new sites developed by start-up companies or entrepreneurs. Regional and local newspaper companies did not have an immediate answer apart from trying to set up their own sites and offer lower (or free) rates but without having a core goal in mind. Although the Fish4 classifieds website was set up in 1999 as a joint venture between the main regional groups, it was not able to establish itself as a serious destination for some time as different publishers did not all treat it with the same degree of seriousness.

In addition, retail advertising was diminishing even before the bank crisis-inspired recession struck, and readership was getting older while not being replaced by any inroads in to younger demographics. The sector's share of the total advertising pot was continuing to decline. Total revenue fell from £3.13bn in 2004 to £1.71bn in 2009. Market share also fell substantially, too. In 2004 the regional press took 20 per cent of the UK's advertising spend; by 2009 the share had declined to 11.6 per cent. The internet's share had grown from 4 per cent to 24 per cent and had taken percentages from every other advertising sector with the exception of cinema. The other two print sectors, magazines and national press, also declined markedly.

After advertising, the second source of publishing revenue was newspaper sales, an area also under pressure. Circulation was drifting at an industry average of 5 per cent per annum but aggressive cover price increases over the last five years have helped to soften circulation revenue losses and has meant that the imbalance between the two principal creators of income has been levelled slightly, although only generally with the financial support of older readers.

Younger consumers of news have been brought up with a different model. If they are interested in news they see it as free either through newspapers such as *Metro*, or online or via the BBC. Their desire to pay for access to a service that they understand to be unrestricted is inalienable (and, of course, this does not just apply to news but to many other online goods and services) and all evidence so far indicates that they are unlikely to accept any change in that right.

## A thirst and a need for regional and local news

Despite these structural changes, and the economic woes in the UK that struck from 2008 onwards, there were still many factors supporting the case for a regional and local news industry in 2011. All companies, especially the groups burdened with debt, had undertaken tough cost-cutting programmes, by centralising as many services as possible through improved communications technology and exploiting capital services, such as press capacity, and were attempting to reduce costs to the minimum. Editorial and adverting staffs were reduced in numbers too but they still understood that the regional and local newspapers stood by their abilities to maintain a presence in their patches, albeit at a reduced level.

And 2010 TGI (Target Group Index) data showed that 75.6 per cent of all UK adults read a regional newspaper at least once a week. This was down from 80.4 per cent from the previous year but was still a healthy penetration. It might be falling, but there still seemed to remain a fundamental and substantial public appetite for local news. Older readers, who are living longer, are maintaining that thirst for local news. They recognise the core value of these often long-established brands whose value cannot be underestimated. They understand the need for scrutiny and coverage of local institutions such as councils and courts and appreciate the need for context that news selection brings.

Regional daily newspapers (including the free *Metro* and London *Evening Standard*) were still selling and distributing some 5m copies every day. And there were still 8m Sunday and weekly paid-for newspapers sold and more than 24m free newspapers distributed every week. Ray Tindle, proprietor of Tindle Newspapers, was bullish in a speech to a conference in May 2010. "Our profits for the two years of this dreadful recession are as near as dammit the same as those of the normal pre-boom times of a decade ago. We were happy then and we are not unhappy now with both sets of figures," he said.

"I can tell you that the recession year 2009/10 just ended at March 31 and the recession year before that 2008/9 – taken together – had profits over half of the boom years of 2006/7 and 2007/8. So with recession results roughly equal to normal years before the boom and over half the boom profits, and with the recession now hopefully fading and revenue rising again, and Ernst and Young having just forecast strong growth next year – 2011."

## Are the tools in place to help the sector survive and succeed?
The basic tool of how newspapers cover their patches is clearly the reporter, regardless of what technology is to be employed. The Newspaper Society says that there are still 10,000 local and regional journalists working on some 1,200 titles. Clearly the reduction in journalistic staff numbers has had effects on coverage and there has been a growing concern that local government and some courts were beginning to lack scrutiny by regional and local newspapers, so producing a democratic deficit. However, research carried out for the Press Association in 2009 found this effect to be patchy and there are no examples yet of localities suffering a total absence of media.

After a hesitant start to how the sector should approach the internet, all newspapers have now worked out their web policies, drawn up their rate cards and most are generally writing in real time for their sites, when necessary. They are not always cutting edge sites, but most are trying to adapt their resources with the regional and local market's needs and desires to make some business sense out of it all.

The 1,200 newspapers in the Newspaper Society now account for 1,500 websites as well as 600 niche and ultra local titles, along with 43 radio stations and two TV stations. So there has been substantial investment. There is no consistency but most of the larger regional sites now include blogging, reader comments and live news as a matter of course. Video streaming is used by an increasing number of publishers and podcasts, apps, mobile services and e-editions are gaining ground.

Some have dedicated staffs but most have material originated by multi-skilled journalists with an overview from a specialist web manager. Some publish news online as it is written; others hold it until the print edition has hit the streets. Some hold back feature material off the site, others publish it all. Some offer free page turning e-editions, others charge for them. Most will publish regional and local major breaking news stories as they happen since they have the presence of the BBC to balance.

Recent innovations include iPhone apps being developed by newspapers as diverse as the *Bristol Evening Post* to the *Rotherham Advertiser* which even launched its births, deaths and marriages app. In these examples Bristol is part of the publicly quoted Daily Mail group while Rotherham is a family-owned business. Other newspapers are launching their own apps almost on a weekly basis.

Trinity Mirror now owns Fish4 in its entirety and aggregates its own group classified advertisements as well as those from other businesses. And all Trinity Mirror's daily newspaper sites now include hyperlocal sites, often linking to and from existing community sites that they had already established.

The *Manchester Evening News* blogs and tweets live from meetings of Manchester City Council while Media Wales, the umbrella company for the *Western Mail*, the *South Wales Echo* and the *Wales on Sunday*, produces its own weekly online rugby show.

Most sites use their original brand to attract visitors and to build numbers, while others using the material for more than one newspaper use more generic titles such as WalesOnline. All Northcliffe group titles use the "thisis..." prefix, generally followed by a county name (e.g. thisisleicestershire.co.uk) and using a templated format, with the aim of being seen to be encompassing all of a region.

Their usage is increasing. The *Belfast Telegraph*'s audited online figures shows it has more than 1m unique visitors, looking at more than 11m page impressions. Its jobs pages attract almost 100,000 unique visitors. And the desire to use these statistics more proactively has persuaded the Audit Bureau of Circulations (ABC) to develop a new cross-platform certificate which will include a transparent view of the circulation of digital editions, including those specially designed for tablets, alongside print circulation. The industry readership organisation Jicreg has also launched a new measurement tool called Locally Connected that will produce joint web traffic and print usage to indicate the spread of any newspaper brand.

## Whither, or wither, the sector?

Over the last 15 years many experiments have been tried. Paywalls of various kinds have been trialled but there has been little consistency across the sector. Some sites are completely open, some offer limited access until after publication of their print titles. But what is true is that there remains no consensus on what the optimum model for regional and local newspapers, or news organisations as they should be called now, is for the future. The big four groups are experimenting with hyperlocal websites but they are in their early days and there is no evidence that they can support a professional team of journalists, even in the background.

These existing publishers are trying all kinds of new-age methods. They all have websites of varying quality, they sell advertising and attempt to monetise their links with search engines, but they mostly give away their news for free. Blogs, tweets, hyperlocal sites and reader-generated content are all used and encouraged – but none brings in much revenue, yet.

It looks grim for them, but online revenue is growing, albeit at a much lower yield than in the days of print only. This, of course, is not just an issue for regional and local media. The quality nationals and trade magazines that have been subsidised for years by high end jobs advertising are in exactly the same position, if not worse. And viewing online is continuing to increase. The Newspaper Society claims that total readership of all regional and local titles is now at an all-time high when depressed print sale figures are combined with burgeoning online visits.

The trick is for news organisations to be able to monetise their sites to a maximum level. Costs, especially in the big groups, have been pared down greatly. This has been a painful exercise but puts them in a reasonable position to survive and prosper. Broadly in the main groups, if it can be centralised or outsourced, it has been. The only staff directly employed by the titles are frontline – reporters and advertising reps.

Monetisation has generally to be through advertising. That online free news was allowed to become a reality will always be rued by news organisations, but was always going to happen after the BBC was allowed to grow its online base so rapidly in the early days of the net. The development of the app and the consumer willingness to pay for it is a hopeful sign. But tablet use remains in its infancy and will be of marginal assistance initially to the regional and local press, though its importance will grow significantly.

As the regional and local press faces the future, equipping itself with the tools for the modern media age, it is in a relatively strong position. And structurally the businesses that are more debt free than others are better positioned to succeed.

The government is restricting local authority publications and encouraging statutory advertising back in to the sector; editors are more comfortable with a joint online/print presence in the market place; overall interest in regional and local news remains substantial; businesses have a greater awareness and understanding of the online and mobile world and have laid the low-cost foundations to try to exploit it. The tools are in place – but whether in this low-cost world there are enough resources to originate good local material that will retain readers remains to be seen.

### Note on the author
Neil Fowler is the Guardian Research Fellow at Nuffield College, University of Oxford, where he is researching the decline and future of regional newspapers in the UK. He has spent much of his career in the UK regional press, having edited two morning and two evening daily newspapers. He has also been publisher and CEO of the *Toronto Sun* in

Canada and has been editor of the UK's biggest selling consumer magazine, *Which?*.

# Why hyperlocal media is crucial for democracy

**David Hayward**

A strong local media is essential to a strong local democracy. It's vital to have a fourth estate, holding power to account at all levels of authority and government. But with increasing pressure on funding for local journalism there are very serious concerns about the level of scrutiny being placed on these powers.

In 1995, when I started my career at BBC Radio Leicester, my first position was the "civics reporter". The role was to cover council meetings, court cases, employment tribunals, NHS and Police Authority meetings – not the most glamorous but it was important.

Each week would begin with the news editor passing you great swathes of minutes to go through. This trawl meant you knew of all the important decisions being made in Leicestershire that week, you were the watchdog. It wasn't just local radio: the *Leicester Mercury* had three reporters covering the beat. The weekly papers would be at all the district and borough council meetings and Leicester Sound, Central East and East Midlands Today would all send to the big county council budget meetings. This was a core part of what the local media did: we kept the local politicians and decision makers honest.

I was one of the last regular civics reporters; in the late 1990s the shift was disbanded. This wasn't to the benefit of local authorities; in fact, I remember one respected Leicestershire County Councillor telling me the BBC and 1 were a disgrace for abandoning local democracy. In the last year the BBC has gone some way to redressing this, with local radio political reporters. But there is still too little coverage of the local democratic process.

### Stark assessment of the state of local media

This vacuum has, in part, been filled by councils doing the job of the local media, by putting information online – through their websites and newsletters. This was a source of worry for among others the Media Trust, which said in a recent report it was "....concerned about the emergence of local authority newspapers and 'news' websites. This direct control of the local news agenda is not only undemocratic but an unsustainable and ineffective use of taxpayers' funds". The report goes on to give a stark assessment to the state of local media:

> Research clearly establishes that the relationship between news and democracy only works under certain conditions. Local and regional news media are in crisis. The crisis is being managed by closing papers or shedding staff. These cuts are having a devastating effect on the quality of the news. Job insecurity and commercial priorities place increasing limitations on journalists' ability to do the journalism most of them want to do – to question, analyse and scrutinise. What we are left with is a contradiction between the democratic potential of news media and the pressures of a recession-affected market. [i]

A fairly pessimistic view. This along with my own – no doubt rose-tinted – reminisces of the golden age of journalism might suggest that we are entering the dark ages. There have been, and will continue to be, many articles written about this. However, what I want to do is look at a couple of areas which might suggest we are on the cusp of a new and fascinating era of local journalism. The rise of hyperlocal blogs and the proposals for local television, championed by the Secretary of State for Culture Media and Sport, Jeremy Hunt. In May 2009 Arianna Huffington, the founder of the internet newspaper, the Huffington Post, said:

> Let's not confuse the decline of newspapers with the decline of journalism...Journalism will not only survive but thrive in the new world, but the discussion needs to go from how do we save the newspapers, to how do we save and strengthen journalism...We are in the middle of a golden age for news consumers, of comment interaction and communities.[ii]

There is many an argument to suggest this is the case in local media in the UK. Newspapers are declining – but there is the potential for a halcyon age of local news. Jeremy Hunt has regularly spoken about the desire for just this hence his plans for local television:

> It is easy to be patronising about hyper-local services, but take a look at the evidence of what consumers truly value. Eight out of 10 consider local news important. Nearly seven out of 10 adults feel localness of stories is more important than them being professionally produced...People in Barnham don't want to watch what is going on in Southampton. People in Chelmsford aren't interested in what's happening in Watford. That is the system we currently have at the moment, so that is what we are trying to rethink.[iii]

## Anger greets BBC plans for local television

More than five years ago, the BBC announced plans for a local television service. I remember it well as I helped to run the pilot scheme, setting up six television stations for a nine-month trial in the West Midlands. The BBC's efforts were met with anger from newspaper groups. They claimed their ever-declining markets for local news were being ripped away from them. They were delighted in late 2007 when the BBC dropped its plans under pressure from the BBC Trust.

This is one of the reasons why I'm so intrigued by the Culture Secretary's plans for local television. If they work, they promise, once again, to radically change the face of local news.

A dedicated city television channel providing news, entertainment and information would not only affect newspapers but seriously challenge the BBC's dominance of regional television and replace the ITV regions, which have been in sad decline for many years.

At the Oxford Media Convention, in January 2011, Hunt announced the government was to invite bids to run local television stations. Licences will be awarded before the end of 2012 and the service will be up and running soon after that. This makes a reality of what Hunt has long been an advocate: a network, or spine, of local stations across the UK. "For consumers, what this will mean is a new channel dedicated to the provision of local news and content," Hunt said, "one that will sit alongside other public service broadcasters, offering a new voice for local communities with local perspectives that are directly relevant to them." [iv] He was echoing comments he made during a London School of Economics event in January 2011, filmed by the BBC College of Journalism:

> This is not a top-down [policy], it is bottom-up, driven by local groups. I believe that the leadership debates transformed politics. I think local democracy is as important as national democracy, but it is very weak. Local television, with Jeremy Paxman-style hosts, could play its part in holding town halls to account. [v]

## A question of realism
Set against this must be a question of realism and whether the proposals for local television can work. Roy Greenslade, the respected media commentator and former tabloid editor, gave this far from optimistic view of those plans:

> For his own sake, I hope that Jeremy Hunt doesn't view his ultra-local television proposal as the Big Idea of his tenure as Secretary of State at the Department for Culture Media and Sport. Clearly, he has a vision of Britain following the United States and various European countries with local TV stations. If we accept what Hunt says at face value, and I certainly do, then he means well. He believes that democracy will be enhanced by local political access to the small screen. Under some pressure on BBC Radio 4's *Today* programme, the Culture Secretary conjured up an image of mayoral candidates taking part in election debates on the lines of the general

election clashes between the main party leaders. I fancy I hear Nick Clegg, rather than David Cameron, applauding that thought. More pertinently, it is fair to ask what kind of output on local TV is expected in the lengthy periods between elections. Why should we believe that television would benefit democracy any more than print newspapers do already, even as they subside towards their eventual demise? I readily accept that there is no harm in trying. We cannot know until it has been tried, so why not ignore the opinions of veteran media cynics such as me? It's a new idea. Stop being so negative. Let 100 TV channels bloom. But then we face the real problem. There is a giant gap, an abyss, between the idea and the reality.[vi]

The initial plan is for ten to 12 city-based stations. If these are a success, more will follow. This falls short of the original ambition, which had been to create a network of up to 80 stations. It was revised following a report led by the investment banker, Nicholas Shott, which suggested a plan on that scale would be unsustainable.

Even with the current, more modest scheme, there are a number of questions which need to be addressed. Not least, if there is a business model and a need for local television, why isn't it happening already? Today, it would be relatively easy and cheap to set up an online video channel providing this service, whereas the infrastructure and running costs of a more traditional television channel will be hugely expensive. The revenue from television advertising is falling, so where will that money come from? Nicholas Shott calculates it would take in the region of £25 million per annum to run the service. In his report he gave this assessment of funding:

> Local TV is unlikely to be viable if it is dependent on local advertising revenues alone. The agreement already in place with the BBC will be helpful in both providing an additional source of revenue and ensuring an adequate level of quality. In addition, the government may need to help facilitate access to national advertising revenue through an existing agency that has a significant existing inventory – for example, a national PSB. An underwritten national advertising contract of £15m per annum for at least the first three years will be required to have confidence in commercial viability.[vii]

The BBC has agreed to give considerable support for the proposals, both in terms of technical and newsgathering resources. If the government has to underwrite an additional £15 million could these proposals really work in the long term? The technical issues are huge and at the moment far from ideal. The BBC local television pilot was on two platforms, digital satellite and online. It soon became apparent to most of us working on it, the online/broadband option was by far the best. Not only was it far more immediate and accessible, it was also multimedia; offering text, audio, video and the chance to interact with the audience. The television platform simply did not do that and seemed clunky by comparison.

**Super-fast broadband could hold the key**
These latest plans for local television face a similar problem. The channels would initially be created on the DTT (Digital Terrestrial Television) network, which seems rather quaint and old-fashioned. Nicholas Shott recognises this and says that, although the local TV network could start off on DTT, it is when IPTV (Internet Protocol Television) and super-fast broadband comes online that it really becomes feasible:

> Local TV could succeed on DTT when viewed as a transitional platform. Immediate distribution by DTT would give time to establish a brand confidence in local content, in advance of its eventual transfer to IPTV, once it becomes the primary distribution platform. This brand, though, could only be built if there are high quality standards underpinning the production of local TV and the content was professional, compelling, immediate and relevant. It was also noted that IPTV may take a number of years to fully develop within the UK, and the typical local news market demographic – typically older – is less likely to have access to, and slower uptake of, new (internet) technology. Distribution by DTT is therefore even more necessary and relevant. But, this does not mean that local TV can be developed in isolation without consideration of an online presence or of its future on IPTV. Local TV distributed by DTT could help to pave the way to IPTV, by establishing what works and building a viable and sustainable model.[viii]

There are also concerns about the quality of any local TV offering. If the service is going to appear on DTT is needs to be of a very high standard, which is always costly:

On DTT, local TV services must stand alongside very high production values, expensively collected news and high investment in presenters. It was further noted that user-generated content is useful only occasionally to support news stories and other small pieces; it is not good enough to rely on regularly. There remains a perception among many existing media players that local TV equates to poor quality content and a "home video feel". It is not to say that such content does not have a place, but the Steering Group believes that any viable local TV proposition will require high production standards in order to compete in a multi-channel world.[ix]

There are already a number of online local TV services. Witney TV [x] came to the wider public awareness in September 2010 when it secured an exclusive interview with Jeremy Clarkson about the mysterious Top Gear racing driver, the Stig, being sacked. And Saddleworth TV [xi] gained prominence during the Oldham East and Saddleworth by-election in January 2011. Even the most ardent admirer would not say these provide a high quality service, but they do offer something that Hunt's local TV plans do need to take into account. They are operating now, without the need for a government licence and they do work.

## The rise and rise of hyperlocal blogs
This success has been mirrored by the rise of hyperlocal blogs, which are charted in hyperlocal voices on Paul Bradshaw's Online Journalism Blog.[xii] Just look at Talk About Local,[xiii] Will Perrin's King's Cross Environment,[xiv] Pits 'n' Pots in Stoke on Trent,[xv] the Lichfield Blog,[xvi] SE1[xvii] and Saddleworth News[xviii]. These local news sites have been around for several years, they have a strong base and are becoming more and more important.

Media analysts often focus on the fact that these websites are not making money. Claire Enders, the founder of Enders Analysis, has highlighted this, saying the funding situation for hyperlocal websites in the UK remains seriously challenged and that means they will be run by unpaid "activists and enthusiasts" for some time yet. But surely this is exactly the point: these websites are a natural successor to the parish pump newsletters. They are at the heart of a local community and a genuine grassroots media.

The Link, a bi-monthly newsletter for my village in Leicestershire, is run by volunteers and vital part of the community. It provides the basic requirement of local news, the council decisions which effect Wymeswold, the planning issues, crime, births, marriages, deaths and events, both upcoming and past. It's a great source of information and local journalism.

Hunt has spoken admiringly in the past about US television with its tradition of local, city-based stations. If they work there, then why not here? Well, the US has a far more federal system of media and government which allows these channels to flourish. Can the media environment of Sheffield, Bristol or Sunderland really be compared with that of Miami, Chicago or Los Angeles? Why not forget about trying to replicate what's happening in the States and concentrate on what works here?

## Providing the essential scrutiny of local powers

The UK has a public service broadcaster, which could very easily – if only it were allowed to – put video on its 40 existing local news websites. There is a thriving hyperlocal news network which, with support, could only get stronger. Local newspapers, albeit in decline, still have a powerful base throughout the country. Why not help develop their multiplatform content to reestablish a strong independent local media? A combination of all of these could provide the scrutiny of local powers which is so essential.

The local media landscape is very broad in the UK and evolving and developing all the time. Jeremy Hunt has proved he is an advocate of a strong local media. He obviously recognises its paramount importance for local democracy. The investment promised for local TV will add to this, but only if it's done within a structure which is sustainable and in the current climate financially viable. There are still many questions around whether the government proposals are any of these. However, a combination of the grassroots media, hyperlocal blogs and TV, revitalised newspapers, the BBC and local TV could well be.

# Notes

[i] Fenton, Natalie (2010) *Meeting the news needs of local communities*, Research by Goldsmiths Leverhulme Media Research Centre. London, commissioned by the Media Trust. Available online at http://www.mediatrust.org/uploads/128255497549240/original.pdf, accessed on 12 January 2011

[ii] Arianna Huffington speaking to a US Senate Commerce Communications subcommittee, May 2009

[iii] Jeremy Hunt, speaking at the Oxford Media Convention, January 2011

[iv] ibid

[v] Jeremy Hunt, speaking at the Future of Media Policy event, organised by the Media Society and POLIS at the LSE, 12 January 2011

[vi] Roy Greenslade, No Minister, you're plan to boost local media is a non starter, 29 September 2010, *Evening Standard*

[vii] Shott, Nicholas (2010) *Commercially viable local television in the UK: A review by Nicholas Shott for the Secretary of State for Culture Media and Sport*. Available online at http://www.culture.gov.uk/publications/7655.aspx, accessed on 12 January 2011

[viii] ibid

[ix] ibid

[x] http://www.witneytv.co.uk/mainindex.shtml, accessed on 12 January 2011

[xi] http://www.saddleworthnews.com/?p=3724, accessed on 12 January 2011

[xii] http://onlinejournalismblog.com/tag/hyperlocal-voices/, accessed on 12 January 2011

[xiii] http://talkaboutlocal.org.uk/, accessed on 12 January 2011

[xiv] http://www.kingscrossenvironment.com/, accessed on 12 January 2011

[xv] http://pitsnpots.co.uk/, accessed on 12 January 2011

[xvi] http://thelichfieldblog.co.uk/, accessed on 12 January 2011

[xvii] http://www.london-se1.co.uk/blog/, accessed on 12 January 2011

[xviii] http://www.saddleworthnews.com/, accessed on 12 January 2011

## Note on the author

David Hayward is the head of the journalism programme for the BBC College of Journalism. It is a series of events, masterclasses, debates, discussions and conferences on journalism issues. He has worked for the BBC for 15 years. He began his career as a reporter, producer and presenter at BBC Radio Leicester before moving to Eastern Europe in the 1990s to work with the World Service Trust in Sarajevo, Bucharest and Tirana. He returned to the UK as a reporter at BBC East Midlands Today, in Nottingham, before moving to the BBC Radio Newsroom in London. He then took up a role producing *Midlands Today* in Birmingham and worked on the BBC Local TV pilot and as TV Editor in Oxford before joining the College of Journalism. He lives in Leicestershire with his wife, Jo, and two boys, Max and Alexander.

# Section 4. From the edge to the centre of the newsroom

**John Mair**

The geography of the modern newsroom tells you all. Look at any of those recently opened by the BBC or future-facing organisations. Online and digital is at the centre, the sun around which other moons rotate; the epicentre of the newsroom universe. All roads lead to and from new media.

It wasn't always so. New media used to be tucked away on a different floor or in a room far away. It was not the place to build careers. Today, digital, social and User Generated Content are a building block or *rite de passage* not to be missed. It's not just at the BBC either; both the *Telegraph* and the *Guardian* are ensconced in new buildings and newsrooms with new media at their centres.

Geography can lead to commercial success. The bible of Middle England – the *Daily Mail* – is an unlikely revolutionary in internet journalism. The

Mail Online is a rip roaring runaway success with more than three million hits per day. It is the second most widely read English language website in the world. It found its audience and a style very easily. Sean Carson analyses the success of Mail Online and later also the flight of the automotive press from (expensive glossy) paper to the internet.

Josh Halliday went from the internet to a newspaper. He now has a prize job on the *Guardian* as part of their media team. Halliday is less than a year out of Sunderland University. But there he conquered the net, learnt as much from it as in the classroom, set up a hyperlocal blog in the city and quickly grasped that personal branding – using the net – was everything in modern journalism. His rise is a lesson for all journalism educators and students.

Charles Miller runs the BBC College of Journalism blog on their site. Finally in this section, he examines how journalists past and present use the setting up of blogs as a way to independence both personal and commercial (sometimes).

# The secrets behind Mail Online's soaring success

**Sean Carson**

October 2010 saw the Mail Online top the magic 50 million unique views a month mark, an average of just over 2.75 million daily users, according to figures released by the Audit Bureau of Circulations Electronic (ABCe). The website now captures around 35 per cent of the UK's online newspaper traffic, reporting a 446 per cent growth in audience figures over the last three years (Robinson 2010).

With such figures prompting comment from Martin Clarke (2010) – the mastermind executive behind the Mail Online's landmark success – in a briefing to his team that "this shows that, firstly, I am a fucking genius, and secondly, that you are all doing really well", who can argue with him?

The Mail Online's generated revenue is small – industry estimates puts the digital arm's revenue at anywhere between £10 million and £50 million according to James Robinson of the *Guardian* (op cit) and Rebecca Thomson of online and IT information providers, ComputerWeekly.com

(2010). But with 1.8 million of those viewers visiting the site 10 times or more per month and the Mail Online firmly cemented in its position as the world's second largest newspaper website after *The New York Times* – according Martin Clarke's analysis of Comscore's September 2010 figures at the Society of Editors meeting (Clarke op cit) – what is the secret to the Mail Online's success?

According to Clarke, it is "because it does what newspapers have always done, it tells fascinating stories clearly with great headlines, punchy words and brilliant pictures" (ibid). A nice, simple formula then. But what differentiates the Mail Online from the plethora of other online media websites which make the same claims.

## Editorial independence of the online operation

Firstly, the Mail Online's editorial team are focused purely on online production. Although sometimes working in partnership with print journalists, the Mail Online conducts its operation independently of the *Daily Mail*. Conversely, the former market leader, the *Guardian*, uses an integration strategy for its editorial teams that sees plenty of cross-platform collaboration between print and online departments, a strategy also adopted by the Telegraph Media Group.

An analysis of ABCe's average daily viewing figures for September 2010 clearly suggests that, with a 54 per cent improvement year-on-year for the Mail Online compared to 21.7 and 13.5 per cent for the *Guardian* and the *Telegraph*'s websites respectively, online traffic growth for the Mail Online is far outstripping the established players (Halliday 2010).

The ballooning success of the Mail Online is not only down to a simple division of editorial staff, however. Clarke believes the journalist's instinct is key to producing marketable content to attract the readers and that the responsibility must remain in the hands of the journalist, not the techie's, when it comes to making a decision about what will work best online. According to Clarke:

> The stories that do best for us are the stories that have always sold newspapers. Human interest, crime, consumer issues, gossip, showbusiness and political stories that relate to people's real lives. I don't think we'll ever win any web design awards, we haven't come up with any great technological advances and we ignored

pretty much everything even our own techies told us we should do. We designed the site around the content and then built a web publishing system ourselves so we could edit it the way we wanted. Thanks to our website, the *Mail* now reaches millions more people in Britain and around the world than it ever could before. Our columnists see their words read by hundreds of thousands of people who would never have heard of them otherwise. And we get 12,000 comments a day from people around the globe (Clarke op cit).

The Mail Online has truly embraced the digital age – with its blogs and social media – over the last decade. Significantly, over a period of two hours in which Facebook.com was down around the end of October 2010, traffic to the Mail Online homepage rose by 25 per cent. Clarke comments: "Remember, we're dealing with a technology here, not a theology…while we are very different sites, it seems our bookmarks are probably pretty close together on people's screens. And that also shows us the great opportunity here – one that some people seem strangely terrified of" (ibid).

## Is showbiz coverage another key driver?
The most common criticism of the Mail Online is that "dumbed-down" celebrity and showbiz content has been the key driver in what Douglas McCabe, a media analyst with Enders Analysts, terms "the success story of recent times in terms of growth and traffic" (Enders Analysis 2010). Mail Online executives are quick to point out, however, that a little less than 25 per cent of traffic is generated by celebrity and showbiz content. Rather, cleverly written headlines generated for search engine optimisation coupled with the intelligent use of technology has seen the Mail Online rise to the top of the lists in the obligatory "Google search".

However, an analysis of the Mail Online homepage over the period of a week in January 2011 suggests these claims made by Mail Online top brass are open to question. An analysis of the stories appearing on the Mail Online homepage revealed that when broken down into the categories: news, sport, showbiz and celebrity, female, health, science and technology and money, showbiz and celebrity content comprises more than a third (36 per cent) of stories visible on the first third of the Mail Online's homepage – in other words, the most important, up-to-date and most-read stories as viewed by users.

This analysis provides a conservative estimate of the extent to which showbiz and celebrity news and features makes up overall content. The Mail Online homepage features a permanent "female" section. As a result, an individual story featured in the female section of the website, which was almost always a celebrity and showbiz orientated story as well, was recorded twice – once per category. If the female category were to be ignored or amalgamated into showbiz and celebrity, showbiz and celebrity news would comprise a massive 57 per cent of overall homepage content. With a readership consisting of 60 per cent female – far and away ahead of common internet use – the Mail Online clearly knows its market and is catering for it brilliantly, but it still raises the question of just how much of the success the Mail Online has achieved has been derived from showbiz and celebrity content? Still, the homepage features a healthy amount of news in the traditional sense – around 21 per cent of recorded stories – with the other categories making up the remaining 7 per cent of stories between them.

It must be noted that this analysis was a brief and shallow study of the content portrayed on the Mail Online homepage and is not without its caveats but, in some ways, is representative of how a user may view the content balance of the Mail Online – in that users often visit online news sites for fleeting periods only analysing the surface of a website in what they see before them.

### "Mail Online carries same brand values as the print version"
The Mail Online is not merely a digitised version of the print edition. The website may carry a similar or identical story to the print publication but it will not just be lifted straight from the pages of that day's paper. The Mail Online insists that the website carries the same brand values as the Mail's print enterprise, with both products having their own distinct targets, yet complementing each other.

The success of the website has not come at the expense of the newspaper itself, however, with circulation figures of the *Daily Mail* remaining steady around the 2.1 million mark in August 2010, according to ABC figures (Robinson op cit). Moreover, 60 per cent of the 1.2 million individuals who visit the Mail Online site everyday arrive there directly – around 30 per cent of traffic is generated by internet searches (ibid).

As Robin Goad, research director at Experian Hitwise, comments: "As the web has become more mainstream, the online market share is starting to reflect the offline market share" (ibid).

## Has the Mail Online been aggressively "flame-baiting"?

"Facebook users 'are insecure, narcissistic and have low self-esteem'" (Mail Foreign Service 2010) and "iPad users 'are the selfish elite' claims survey" (Bates 2010) are two Mail Online headlines singled out by online blog, the Media Blog, as "flame bait" – posts deliberately published to provoke strong reactions (Media Blog 2010). Indeed, these two articles both received around three times the average number of comments for a story. Most infamously, columnist Jan Moir's comments on 16 November 2009, following the death of pop-star Stephen Gately, provoked more than 1,600 responses on the website – though, surprisingly the Press Complaints Commission later ruled that the column did not breach its Code of Practice.

Regardless of the secret to the Mail Online's success, there is one overriding factor. With Rupert Murdoch's News Corp erecting paywalls for its online content, the Mail Online has continued with its strategy of making content free. As Peter Williams, finance director at DMGT, commented: "It is important to remember online does not require anything like the same |advertising| yields as the newspaper does" (Durrani 2010). Significantly, DMGT's half year report for the period up to April 2010 stressed that "digital revenues across the company for the period were up 13 per cent to £9m, although the company's overall revenue was down 7 per cent to £132m" (Thomson 2010).

With the Mail Online iPad app rumoured to be near completion and ready for launch, as well as 70,000 people signing up for the 60-day free trial of the Mail Online iPhone app, with a pricing structure of £4.99 and £8.99 for a six and twelve-month subscription respectively after the free trial has lapsed (Barrie and Hamilton 2010; Mail Online 2010), these new distribution channels for news could prove still more lucrative for the *Mail*.

## The multitude of factors behind the winning mix

In short, it is not just the free nature of the content that has contributed towards the success of the Mail Online. Many factors have gone into the mix: aggressive trafficking with good delivery from internet searches and social networking media, an editorial team dedicated solely to online content separate from their print journalist piers, a faith placed in the journalist and not accountants or techies and interesting and easily digestible content that provokes reaction, whether it be positive or negative.

## References

Barrie, D. and Hamilton, D. (2010) Winning online and in print, Society of Editors, Available online at: http://www.societyofeditors.co.uk/page-view.php?pagename=Winningonlineandinprint, accessed on 16 January 2011

Bates, D. (2010) iPad users "are the selfish elite", claims survey, Mail Online, 30 July. Available online at http://www.dailymail.co.uk/sciencetech/article-1298722/iPad-users-selfish-elite.html#ixzz1BIpJYRul, accessed on 16 January 2011

Clarke, M. (2010) Winning online and in print: Mail Online [Powerpoint slides]. Available online at http://www.societyofeditors.co.uk/page-view.php?pagename=Winningonlineandinprint, accessed on 16 January 2011

Durrani, A. (2010) MailOnline to turn a profit in 2011, Brand Republic, 28 Ju;y. Available online at http://www.brandrepublic.com/news/1019104/MailOnline-turn-profit-2011/, accessed on 16 January 2011

Enders Analysis (2010) In the news, Enders Analysis, 15 November. Available online at http://www.endersanalysis.com/news, accessed on 16 January 2011

Halliday, J. (2010) ABCe: Mail Online tops 50m monthly browsers, *Guardian*, 25 November. Available online at http://www.guardian.co.uk/media/2010/nov/25/abce-abcs, accessed on 16 January 2011

Mail Online (2010) It's the App you've all been waiting for... FREE for 60 days, Mail Online, Available online at http://www.dailymail.co.uk/home/article-1324833/MailOnline-iPhone-app-Download-try-FREE-60-days.html#ixzz1BIwgT4cx, accessed on 16 January 2011

Mail Foreign Service (2010) Facebook users "are insecure, narcissistic and have low self-esteem", Mail Online, 9 November. Available online at http://www.dailymail.co.uk/sciencetech/article-1310230/Facebook-users-narcissistic-insecure-low-self-esteem.html#ixzz1BF5yRDjc, accessed on 16 January 2011

The Media Blog (2010) Is Daily Mail "flame-bait" the secret of its online success? Media Blog, 12 September. Available online at http://themediablog.typepad.com/the-media-blog/2010/09/daily-mail-ipad-facebook-1843120910.html, accessed on 16 January 2011

Thomson, R. (2010) *Daily Mail* digital revenues boosted as Mail Online continues to grow, ComputerWeekly.com, 27.May. Available online at http://www.computerweekly.com/Articles/2010/05/27/241374/Daily-Mail-digital-revenues-boosted-as-Mail-Online-continues-to.htm, accessed on 16 January 2011

Robinson, J. (2010) MailOnline: What is the secret of its success? *Guardian*, 15 November. Available online at http://www.guardian.co.uk/media/2010/nov/15/mailonline-daily-mail-website, accessed on 16 January 2011

**Note on the author**
Sean Carson is studying for an MA in Automotive Journalism at Coventry University. He graduated from the University of Liverpool in 2009 with a BSc in Geography.

# Blogging for journalists: A route to independence?

**Charles Miller**

## Introduction

Journalists have traditionally only had access to an audience through a big organisation. Newspaper businesses needed printing presses and distribution systems; television and radio services needed broadcasting technology and the means to win licences. The internet has changed those dependencies, building a global distribution system that is effectively free to use for journalists and others. In the past decade or so, journalists have been experimenting with the possibilities that has created, and discovering the extent to which freedom from a large media organisation is or is not desirable.

For this chapter, I have interviewed and examined the work of four successful journalist bloggers, each of whom has made use of a blog as part of a media career. I am interested in the extent to which blogging has given them editorial and financial freedom, how it relates to and creates

122

other opportunities to pursue their careers and how they manage the writing and posting of material.

There are an estimated 153 million blogs online (Blogpulse.com, January 2011[i]), most of which are non-professional. The most common category is "Diary", outperforming all others, including "MoviesTV", "Politics" and "Sports" (ibid). In terms of volume of output, then, blogging is predominantly done by amateurs and for fun.

But it is the minority of professional blogs that attract the most readers. On the day of writing, the five most cited blog posts tracked by Blogpulse are all on Engadget[ii], a US advertising-supported web magazine. Engadget lists more than 30 editorial staff, including an editor-in-chief, associate editors, a reviews editor and even three interns. Organisationally and commercially, it resembles a newspaper or magazine.

This study examines opportunities that lie between the individual non-professional bloggers – the home diarists – and sites such as Engadget which are simply using the blog as a new form of advertising-supported journalism. In that space lie the blogs of individual journalists, for whom blogging presents a new form for stories and ideas, and a new publishing experience. Andrew Sullivan [iii], a prominent American print journalist who now also runs his own blog, has described his transition to the world of blogging:

> From the first few days of using the form, I was hooked. The simple experience of being able to directly broadcast my own words to readers was an exhilarating literary liberation…I'd often chafed, as most writers do, at the endless delays, revisions, office politics, editorial fights, and last-minute cuts for space that dead-tree publishing entails. Blogging – even to an audience of a few hundred in the early days – was intoxicatingly free in comparison. Like taking a narcotic.

## Blogging: Technology and editorial form

In common usage, blogging (a shortened form of "web-logging") refers to the creation of a particular kind of online writing. Bloggers build up a collection of short entries on a website which are updated frequently. If you look through the entries on Google's free-to-use blogging site, Blogger, [iv] the flavour of private blogs soon becomes clear:

Lately, I've been struggling to get Aaron to sit down at dinner with us. It seems he's been more interested in playing than eating - that is, until he's really hungry. Then all he wants is a bowl of Cheerios. Ah, the wonders of toddler nutrition.

Mia the post lady informs me that guitar classes start next week. Good. It will be nice to be in the group again although I think Raul is now running a sweetie shop in a nearby town.

No one at my office even noticed when I cut off half of my hair! (Granted, my hair is pretty short, so half of it isn't as much as some people's half, but it's a reasonable change.)

These blogs contain family photographs and come under titles that, again, reveal much about their authors, such as "the true story of a military spouse on the go, the man she loves, the dogs she spoils, and the life we lead [now with baby]". There are also blogs written around hobbies, sports, as literary exercises, and many started – presumably with high hopes – but were quickly abandoned. In this sense, then, a blog is a series of posts on a website, typically informal and personal.

There is another sense of the word, referring to the technological form. A blog is a particular kind of software that allows a user to update a website without technical skills. Since the advent of the internet, companies such as Moonfruit[v] or Geocities[vi] have offered members of the public the chance to create websites. These services were easy to use, creating pages from templates rather than requiring HTML coding. Free webspace was also often part of the sales package of Internet Service Providers, who encouraged their customers to create their own sites

Blogging software made the process easier still: it also allowed users to design a site, from templates or by uploading new design elements; but it made updating the site with new text or other content a separate, easier process. Instead of creating new pages, the user simply filled in a box and pressed "post". Blog software automatically created a page of entries with the latest post at the top and older posts below.

Journalist bloggers may or may not consider what they are creating to be a blog: some prefer to talk about websites than blogs, distancing themselves from associations with the amateur market. But technically, those I am including here all use blogging software – with the same advantages of simplicity compared to other kinds of online website software that amateurs enjoy.

## Blogs and individual authors

Does a successful blog, as it acquires readers and revenue, naturally evolve into a media organisation? To assess the relative strength of individual and multi-staffed blogs, I have analysed two published lists of "Top Blogs", one British and one American.

The British list is Cision's "Top 50 UK Bloggers".[vii] Cision, a PR and media intelligence service, lists British blogs according to "the levels of social media engagement of the blogs and their author(s) and the sites' visibility". Cision has excluded blogs from "mainstream publishing organisations" but includes both single author and multi-author blogs. *Time* magazine's "25 Best Blogs of 2010" is an "annual pick of the blogs we can't live without".[viii] I have divided the blogs from both lists into those written by a single author, and those with more staff:

| List | Individual blogs | Multi-staff blogs |
|---|---|---|
| Cision: Top 50 UK Bloggers | 30 (60 per cent) | 20 (40 per cent) |
| Time: Best Blogs of 2010 | 12 (48 per cent) | 13 (52 per cent) |
| Combined lists | 42 (56 per cent) | 33 (44 per cent) |

Combining the above lists shows that more than half (56 per cent) of the blogs are "one person" editorial products. From these figures, clearly the "one person blog" is holding its own against well-staffed and often well-funded rivals.

## Four prominent bloggers

Against this background, I have focused on four journalists who have made blogging a key part of their careers. Here I will give a brief introduction to each, and in the next section, compare their experiences of blogging in the areas I am examining.

Robert Peston blogs on the BBC website on Peston's Picks. Since February 2006, he has been the BBC's Business Editor, his first job as a non-print journalist. He had previously been Financial Editor and

Political Editor of the *Financial Times*, and City Editor of the *Sunday Telegraph*, among other roles. Peston's blog was launched on 29 January 2007 with these words:

> Here and now is the best time to be broadcasting or writing about business. The private sector and the unleashing of market forces across the globe is changing all our lives, mostly for the better, but also (if, for example, you are in the wrong job in the wrong place, or if you've been saving in many conventional pension funds) for the worse. It's an epic drama called "globalisation", with Tolstoyan themes.[ix]

Four years on, with a regular output of posts on top business people and stories, Peston's blog attracts two and a half million UK page views a month (BBC Press Office figure for final quarter of 2010) and is, as Peston told me, "absolutely central to how I work".

Nikki Finke is a Hollywood journalist, specialising in movie and television industry news. She started her website Deadline.com in March 2006 (originally as DeadlineHollywoodDaily.com) as an extension of her work for the Los Angeles free newspaper *L. A. Weekly*, where she wrote a show business column. Her background is in hard news. She worked for the Associated Press in a number of roles including foreign correspondent in London and Moscow before moving into show business reporting.

After losing a New York job, Finke started the column on *L. A. Weekly*. She persuaded the paper to let her have a blog to post news more topically than was possible in a weekly column. She retained ownership of the site, and as its traffic and reputation increased, received a series of offers for the blog from outside media companies. In June 2009, MMC (Mail.com Media Corporation),[x] a digital media business with a number of online brands, bought the site for an undisclosed sum. Under the deal, Finke continues to edit Deadline.

Iain Dale began writing his blog, Iain Dale's Diary, in April 2002. He became one of Britain's most influential political bloggers with an audience in the hundreds of thousands, a rightwing voice railing against the Labour administration but often equally unhappy with the Conservative Party. The tone was set by his invective against Cherie Blair, the Prime Minister's wife, on his first day of blogging:

In many ways she is all a modern day woman could aspire to, yet she is quite happy, as is her husband, to accept all that the trappings of power can offer her and her family…When the Princes (sic) of Wales died she was on holiday in Portugal staying with Cliff Richard and then the British Ambassador – wonder who picked up the bill for that one, fellow taxpayers?

Dale has a background in various commercial jobs, and had set up Politico's bookshop in Westminster, specialising in political books. He was the Conservative Party candidate for North Norfolk in the May 2005 general election but lost to a Liberal Democrat. He continued his involvement with the party as Chief of Staff to David Davis's party leadership campaign in October 2005. In December 2010, Dale announced in his blog that he was giving it up, disillusioned with the world it had become:

I hate the backbiting that goes along with it. I hate the character assassination that is permanently present. I no longer enjoy the pressure of feeling I have to churn out four or five pieces every day.[xi]

Sally Whittle is a freelance journalist and a single mother since her divorce, living in Lancashire. She writes several blogs from home, the most prominent being Who's the Mummy? in which she posts about life with her five-year-old daughter who, in the blog, she calls Flea. Whittle's blog was ranked first in Cision's list of "Top Ten UK Mummy Blogs" in 2010. At the time of writing, Whittle's most recent post is about how a film she watched on television had made her cry:

I never cry. I almost never raise my voice, and I'm certainly not comfortable with public displays of emotion – I try to avoid mixing with too many Southerners because of all the unnecessary kissing, for example. I am pathologically Northern.

But put me in front of a cinema or TV screen and I turn into a complete girl. After repeated viewings, I still can't get through Serendipity without embarrassing myself (I blame the Nick Drake soundtrack) and I had to wear sunglasses on the way home from Toy Story 3 and pretend I had hay fever.

Like all embarrassing personal weaknesses, I've decided to blame this entirely on Flea. Because before she came along I watched *Titanic* and didn't cry. Now? I cry at Coke commercials. [xii]

Before blogging, Whittle was a staff journalist on trade magazines in London, particularly in the field of computers. When she moved to Lancashire, she went freelance, but, as she told me, after a time, she realised features were not being commissioned by magazines, or they had been "paying the same rates for ten years". Today, she earns the "vast majority" of her income from blogging or blogging-related activities.

## Blogging as a route to editorial and financial independence

Talking to Robert Peston, Nikki Finke, Iain Dale and Sally Whittle, I have explored their use of blogs as a vehicle for journalism. Despite the obvious differences in their blogs, career paths and subject areas, common factors emerge, suggesting there are features of blogging that journalists can expect to encounter whatever their particular circumstances.

*Editorial freedom*

"I've always been, in all the media organisations, a pretty independent, autonomous individual," said Robert Peston. "I'm a difficult bastard basically. I just take the view that I'm going to follow what interests me." Peston's current BBC job was the first in which he had to work with microphone and camera. As a former print journalist, blogging drew more directly on his previous experience. And the blog allowed him, he says, to demonstrate the solid foundations of stories he was reporting.

It also let him expose more detailed work he was doing, the so-called "scoops of interpretation" as he calls them. He told me he loved "ploughing through Bank of England data, or accounts of companies". The blog "gives me an outlet when I just spot a trend or something hidden away in some numbers or accounts that I think carries some weighty implications. It gives me a way of taking the reader through the argument and coming up with a fairly startling conclusion".

So, in the Bank of England's Financial Stability report, he spotted a chart about the cost of funding the big banks: "When I delved into it, I discovered that what it was really saying was that banks were getting an effective subsidy of £100 billion in 2009…Now that £100 billion figure of taxpayer subsidy was huge news. And the vehicle for revealing this news, was some quite sophisticated analysis that I did on the blog."

For all the freedom the blog provides, everything Peston writes is run past a dedicated blog editing team or a senior editorial figure in the BBC. And he insists it is much more than a casual accompaniment to his television and radio output: "I don't cut corners with the blog. It is not just what I happen to fancy writing at any particular moment. Everything on it is well-researched; the same standards of verification that I apply to everything else, apply to the blog." In summary, for Peston, blogging within a large broadcasting organisation gives him the freedom to publish when he wants, at a length of his choosing. But his blog output is still fully integrated editorially with the more formal and collaborative parts of BBC News.

For Sally Whittle, blogging was a conscious alternative to dependency on media organisations. As her freelance writing for business-to-business publications was drying up, blogging looked like a potentially attractive alternative. In 2004, she began with a blog about journalism, Getting Ink, which ran for six years. During that time, Whittle developed multiple sources of income and launched her parenting blog, Who's the Mummy?

The popularity of the parenting blog quickly overtook her other enterprises. "I almost had an audience from day one. I did my first post, and the MD of a PR agency I knew sent out a link," she told me. By the end of the first month, she had 300 readers a day and 2000 followers on Twitter.

The price she paid for the popularity of Who's the Mummy? was a loss of privacy: "no longer would 'the work you' be separate from private life". She wrote about her daughter and posted family photographs. She says she's not worried about strangers reading about her life, but doesn't like anyone she knows to read it. And she imagines what her daughter will think when she reads the blog in years to come. She says, sounding like she's only half-joking, "I'm shamelessly exploiting her."

The blog has allowed Whittle to write on a subject of her choosing, without any editorial supervision. Being free of a large organisation was "half terrifying", but as a freelance, she was used to taking the initiative on ideas, and as a practised journalist, she could turn out a well-written story in the right tone for her audience.

For Iain Dale, blogging was not a liberation from media organisations, but rather, as for most non-professional bloggers, a way to give himself a voice: "I just saw it as a brilliant way to say what I wanted to say when I wanted to say it." When he started blogging, Dale's life was a mix of business, with his Politico's bookshop and associated publishing enterprises, and politics in the Conservative Party. After two or three years when he wrote more casually and intermittently, he dates the start of the most successful phase of his blog as December 2005.

That month, he wrote about dissatisfaction among Liberal Democrats MPs with Charles Kennedy's leadership: "Instantly I started to get a readership. The first few days I was getting several hundred people a day; by the end of the first month it was about 4,000 a day. I mean you get quite a kick out of that." When someone at the *Daily Mail* called him with salacious details about John Prescott's affair with his secretary, his readership spiked at 100,000 a day. Dale set his own editorial agenda under his masthead slogan "Politics, Humour, Gossip, Commentary". His only sense of editorial constraint was his awareness of his readers: "You are independent, but you're still accountable to your readers and you know that if you don't give them what they want, they will go somewhere else to find it."

In setting up her Hollywood blog, Nikki Finke created a unique arrangement which gave her the independence of a personal blog combined with the benefits of being part of a media organisation, the *L. A. Weekly*. But achieving that was a struggle. At first, posting on the blog was laborious: "I had to go through this whole rigmarole of my copy went to my editor, then my editor sent it to the copy editor, then the copy editor sent it to the tech people, and it posted. And literally, this was like a five hour process, which defeated the whole purpose." Eventually, it was agreed she could post copy direct to the site.

Finke insisted that the blog should be hers, even though the site was hosted by *L. A. Weekly*. It meant she could, as she says, "grow it under their auspices". *L. A. Weekly* did not have the status of the *L. A. Times* or the other trade papers such as *Variety* or the *Hollywood Reporter*. Finke has been quoted describing it as "the official paper of valet parkers". But with her blog, that no longer mattered to her. She had a call from a friend, and was explaining she was only at the *Weekly* because she needed a job, "and he said: 'Yes, but what you're doing is you're showing us that you can be working for any shitty little rag, and as long as they have access to the internet, everybody will see your stuff'". By using the blog, she had become an independent journalist in the eyes of her readers.

*Financial independence*

Finke's experience of blogging is the most dramatic example here of how editorial freedom can lead to financial independence. As the readership of her blog rose, so did its advertising revenue. Finke was not on a percentage; she did not want to be. Negotiating her contract with *L. A. Weekly* and later its parent company *Village Voice*, she told them that whether they sold ads on the site was "uninteresting" to her: "I don't want a percentage. All I care about is that I get a steady, monthly income for what I'm doing for the website. The advertising is your thing."

Having an arms-length relationship with the commercial side of the site increased her editorial independence: she was not tempted to adjust what she wrote about a studio's problems because they might pull their advertisements from the site. But, as the owner of the site, when other companies became interested in buying it, she increased her own remuneration by telling *L. A. Weekly* that if they failed to match external offers, she would sell.

Finally, she received what she calls an "insanely good" offer: "when we got into seven figures" *L. A. Weekly* didn't match the offer, and the site was sold to MMC (Mail.com Media Corporation), a digital media business building up a portfolio of online brands. Today MMC handles the advertising, leaving Finke to concentrate on her journalism.

Finke has never disclosed how much she got from the sale. At the time, figures of $10 million to $14 million were reported.[xiii] Finke declined to tell me the figure but did admit how astonished she still is at this turn in her fortunes: "I go to my accounts all the time – my bank statements and my investment accounts – and look at them at least once a day, and sort of go 'Oh my God, I can't believe I have this money'. It's an extraordinary feeling to go from at one point selling my car because I don't know how I'm going to live to suddenly being set for life."

Iain Dale's blog was never intended to make money. But he believes it could have, although not through advertising: "There's a great nervousness for advertisers being associated with a site they regard as party political. And however much I might say: 'Well, I slag off the Conservatives as well', everyone viewed me as a partisan Conservative blogger."

Instead, he thinks he could have had an income through voluntary subscriptions. He considered asking his readers to set up direct debits for £5 a month. Even with a small take-up, this would be lucrative: if 1 per cent of 100,000 readers agreed to pay, it would generate £60,000 a year. "I think I could have done it, and I think I probably still could, but hopefully I won't ever have to put that to the test."

For Sally Whittle, the blog is a source of income – about £500 a month – from the advertising deals she has negotiated on the site. She deals with specialist advertising agencies, setting prices and arranging payments. She found that the companies she deals with are surprisingly casual about it: she has never been asked about the traffic to the site (about 30,000 to 50,000 unique visitors a month) and speculates "it's a bit like asking someone's age, you just don't do it".

Negotiating a price for the first time, she asked for £60 a month, and settled for £50. Whittle's blog gets advertising from blue chip companies including John Lewis, Barclays and Microsoft. For her, this was better than chasing magazines for freelance payments: "Having Microsoft paying into my account gives me a real kick."

Robert Peston would not be allowed to make money from his blog within the BBC, and is not planning to take it outside: "Other people have done it. I assume, therefore, that there is something viable that could be done. I don't know whether it would appeal to me." If it did, there is little doubt that Peston's readership of wealthy businesspeople would attract advertisers, as surely as Finke's powerful audience has given her blog financial value in Hollywood.

*Creating and connecting with an audience*
Blogs which strike a chord can quickly attract a sizeable audience. This is what has drawn young mothers to Sally Whittle's mums' blog. Part of the appeal is the sense that the blog is "for them" in a more intimate way

even than a niche magazine can be. Whittle says she writes about three posts a week, and that it takes her just two or three hours: "I can sit down and just write it. As my first news editor used to say: 'Don't get it right, get it written.'" On the blog, Whittle recounts her daily experiences as if she is doing it for fun or for therapy. So when she writes about her daughter's reluctance to have a sleep-over with her ex-husband, she receives a stream of sympathetic comments from divorced mothers, sharing their experiences.

Her audience figures equate to at least a thousand visitors a day, so only a tiny proportion are leaving comments, but the impression is that the reader is joining a small, friendly community. A feature of the blog is that Whittle replies on the site to each reader's comment, with lines such as: "Hahaha. Sorry, that's hysterical."

The readers of Iain Dale's blog were more in number, and had less in common with each other than Whittle's readers. But he was acutely aware of their demands: he says half of them visited the blog more than three times a day. And that put pressure on him to produce: "They expected me to have written something new. And believe it or not, there were days when I didn't have a view on anything! But your readers don't understand that, they think: 'Well, what's he doing?' And I would get emails demanding extra copy." He would typically post around five times a day, often writing at home in the evening and setting his pieces to publish throughout the following day.

Robert Peston's blog is notable for the quality of comments left below his posts. He says they are "incredibly helpful", and can influence how he develops his ideas or a story: "They make you think about issues in different ways, which is educational for me. Also, quite often you get tips for stories. People come up with angles, and you think: 'Actually, there might be a story there.'"

For Nikki Finke, checking readers' comments before they are posted was an extra burden which she took on reluctantly after pressure from her newspaper: "I kept saying: 'I'm doing this myself. I can barely handle keeping up with the news. You want me to keep up with comments too?'" Finke was determined not to have inane comments or spam on her site. She would only allow an "intelligent dialogue". She goes through the comments herself, although she now has staff to help out as well: "It's horrible because sometimes we get slammed: you suddenly look at the site, and you've got 3000 comments in the space of 15 minutes. And it's a lot of work…you have no idea."

*Blogging as part of a career portfolio*
Iain Dale has used blogging to boost a conventional media career. Although he was busy as a writer and editor before the blog, he says it was important in getting him other work. There was a fortnightly column in the *Daily Telegraph*, and, following occasional appearances on the station, a regular evening show on the London talk radio station LBC: "I would not have got the *Telegraph* column had I not had the blog. I would certainly not have got the LBC programme."

When it came to his political ambitions, he believes the blog did not help: "It was a double-edged sword…when you write a blog, you are a bit like Marmite, people either love you or hate you. You get tremendous loyalty, devotion, but you also get a lot of people who can't stand you. They can't really articulate why they can't stand you, but they can't."

For Robert Peston, blogging is a part of a mixed journalistic output across different BBC media. "With a big story what I will try to do is time the blog to go out at more or less the same time as I'm appearing on the telly or the radio." Extra details in the blog supplement the story he tells on air; and his on-air appearance draws an audience to the blog, looking for more information.

Sally Whittle uses blogging as a shop-window for her other skills. So her mum's blog links to Blogger.Ed, where she writes about blogging as a business. From there, she can publicise her other activities, which include freelance journalism, copywriting, the MAD (Mum and Dad Blogger) of the Year Awards, sponsored by Butlin's, [xiv] and The:101, her public relations training business.[xv] Whittle has a genuine portfolio career, and, as she says, "the blog is the centre of my portfolio".

Nikki Finke is already building on the success of her blog brand, Deadline, producing her own Oscars magazine, and is developing other projects.

*Blogging as a journalistic lifestyle*

The blogger can work from anywhere, at any time, which can be both a blessing and a curse. Nikki Finke spends hours on the telephone from her West Hollywood home where she works. But she isn't always home, and says the executives who call don't know where she is: "I work all the time, so I'm there with the equivalent of a netbook in an aisle at Home Depot, and they think I'm sitting in my office. A friend gave me his house in Hawaii for several weeks and I was working from there for [two months], and nobody had a clue."

Finke admits she is a workaholic: "Even when I'm on vacation I post." The 24/7 nature of a blog fits happily with her attitude to work: "I've made a commitment. I do not have a family. I've been married…hated it. I never have wanted children. I have always been completely career-oriented." In place of the demanding boss, there is the demanding readership: "There was one day when I was really late with Box Office because my plane was late. But, you know, they have to cut me slack every now and then."

Finke has hired a couple of senior reporters to work with her on Deadline. They too live and breathe their work, but she told them she did not expect the kind of dedication she brings to it: "I said: 'Look, I don't expect you to work my hours, but I do expect you to be news junkies.'"

For Iain Dale, who also admits he is a workaholic, the non-stop demands of blogging became too much. When a three-hour nightly radio show was added to his schedule, alongside his publishing business, as he says, "something had to give". Like some other bloggers, he found the experience more like broadcasting than print journalism: "The way I was doing it, it was very much akin to a 24-hour news channel, in that whenever something happened, people expected me to comment on it…There's this huge pressure: you've got to feed the beast all the time. You've created this monster, and you're not quite sure how to handle it."

Sally Whittle has used blogging to pursue her career within a pattern that fits her domestic life. Of the four bloggers I spoke to, Whittle most strongly gives the impression of being able to handle "the monster" she has created. She admits there has been a price to pay in the mixing of her professional and private lives. But the efficiencies of using her own life as material for the blog are beguiling.

Robert Peston, the only one of these four who works inside a big media organisation, is also the most willing to close his laptop and let his readers wait: "I'm pretty ruthless that from time to time I'm just going to spend some time with my family and not think about it." But even without any kind of commercial interest, he feels the form itself makes demands that spur him back to work: "There is a sense in which it is a pretty hard taskmaster. If I've got the one blog up there for too long, I don't feel comfortable. So there is a sort of psychological thing, that there comes a moment when I think: 'Oh God, people are going to be really bored with this, I must do something else.' So there is a bit of being on a treadmill – but I chose to be on the treadmill, and most of the time I love it actually."

## Conclusions

These four bloggers, practising widely-different kinds of journalism, reveal certain characteristics of the blog itself as a form. The freedom to publish at any time makes for a sense of being permanently "on", like a live news channel: "It is absolutely more like broadcasting," said Nikki Finke. In reality, the worst that will happen if there isn't a new post is that some readers will be disappointed and will check back less often. But the idea of disappointed readers is a powerful motivator because of the intimate communication between blogger and reader, which the comment system creates. Comments give the writer a direct sense of their audience, and feedback on everything they write. Sally Whittle enhances the effect by replying to comments: although the blog is public, her communication with readers is more like an exchange of personal emails, particularly as her subject matter is domestic.

More than other journalistic forms, the blog is intensely personal: a journalist with a newspaper column, or a broadcaster fronting a programme is still mediated by a large institution and supported by colleagues. Whilst this can also be true of a blog (as Robert Peston attests, describing the editorial support he receives in BBC News), the form is one whose practitioners are typically non-professionals, writing for their own entertainment. This continuity with the home blogging world helps maintain the sense of personal authorship in professional blogs.

And so, despite the lucrative commercial opportunities the blogging platform offers, the single-writer blog looks likely to survive. Nikki Finke's sale of her blog to a digital media conglomerate required her to continue in her role. Although she has hired extra staff, she still has complete editorial and design control: "They can't touch that stuff without me. Nobody can tell me what to write, or what not to write." For the new owners, her voice was key to the value of the business they were buying.

Where these four writers differ widely is in their ideas about what kind of journalism works best on a blog. For Robert Peston, it is a mix of breaking news, "scoops of interpretation" and a light topping of personal comment. Nikki Finke brings hard news reporting to the world of entertainment, although she is happy to admit to being "snarky" when she thinks someone is out of order. Iain Dale's blog worked best when he could reveal a story from inside Westminster, but its daily currency was his pithy comments on the passing political scene. And for Sally Whittle, a good post is an elegantly-crafted anecdote about her daughter, the kind of story her readers would like to find themselves telling their friends.

For all their differences, what makes them successful is good judgement about subject-matter, and the ability to write succinctly and in an authentic voice.

Journalist bloggers also require an almost obsessive work ethic. In that sense, blogging does not offer an escape route to the burnt-out corporate employee dreaming of the freedom to earn a living by posting the odd thought when inspiration strikes: the only kind of journalist who can make a one-person blog successful is one with the energy and drive to succeed inside a corporate environment. Blogging can be a route to independence, but it will never be an easy ride.

**The four featured blogs**
Iain Dale's Diary: http://iaindale.blogspot.com/
Nikki Finke: Deadline Hollywood:
http://www.deadline.com/hollywood/
Peston's Picks: http://www.bbc.co.uk/blogs/thereporters/robertpeston/
Sally Whittle: Who's the Mummy?: http://www.whosthemummy.co.uk/

# Notes

---

[i] See Blogpulse: www.blogpulse.com, accessed on 10 January 2011

[ii] See Engadget: http://www.engadget.com/, accessed on 10 January 2011

[iii] Andrew Sullivan, Why I blog, *Atlantic Monthly*, November 2008. Available online at http://www.theatlantic.com/magazine/archive/2008/11/why-i-blog/7060/2/, accessed on 2 January 2011. Sullivan's blog, The Daily Dish, has evolved from a single author enterprise into a multi-staff operation. Like Nikki Finke, he has retained editorial control while the site is hosted by a bigger organisation, the *Atlantic Monthly*. He outlined its evolution on 2 August 2010 in the blog: http://andrewsullivan.theatlantic.com/the_daily_dish/2010/08/home-news.html, accessed on 2 January 2011

[iv] See www.blogger.com

[v] See Moonfruit: http://www.moonfruit.com/, accessed on 2 January 2011

[vi] Geocities (archive): http://www.geocities.ws/, accessed on 10 January 2011

[vii] Cision "Top 50 UK blogs 2010". Available online at http://uk.cision.com/Resources/Social-Media-Index/Top-UK-Social-Media/Top-50-UK-Blogs/

[viii] *Time* magazine's "25 Best Blogs of 2010". Available online at http://www.time.com/time/specials/packages/completelist/0,29569,1999770,00.html, accessed on 2 January 2011

[ix] Peston's Picks, 29 January 2007. Available online at http://www.bbc.co.uk/blogs/thereporters/robertpeston/2007/01/why_its_time_for_business.html, accessed on 2 January 2011

[x] MMC Mail.com Media Corporation: http://corp.mail.com/, accessed on 11 January 2011

[xi] Iain Dale's Diary, 14 December 2010. Available online at http://iaindale.blogspot.com/2010/12/time-has-come-to-stop-blogging-and.html

[xii] Who's the Mummy? 19 January 2011. Available online at http://www.whosthemummy.co.uk/2011/01/such-a-girl.html, accessed on 11 January 2011

[xiii] Daily Finance, 23 June 2009. Available online at http://www.dailyfinance.com/story/media/nikki-finkes-10-million-payday/19075932/, accessed on 12 January 2011

[xiv] See the MADS 2010. Available online at http://www.the-mads.com/index.htm, accessed on 14 January 2011

[xv] See The:101 training. Available online at http://101editorial.moonfruit.com/#/about-us/4533823928, accessed on 13 January 2011

## Note on the author

Charles Miller is a television producer who has made programmes for BBC1, BBC2, ITV and Channel 4. Most recently, he has produced business biographies for the BBC2 *Money Programme*, profiling Bill Gates, Lord Sugar, Warren Buffett and Donald Trump. He has a special interest in new technology, with films about Microsoft, eBay, Google and Skype and two series about the internet, *Inside dot coms* and *The future just happened* for BBC2. He has written about technology and media for *The Times*, the *Guardian*, the *Independent* and other publications. Alongside programme-making, he works for the BBC College of Journalism website, where he edits the blog at www.bbc.co.uk/journalism/blog.

# Personal branding now a key to getting that first foot on the ladder into journalism

**Josh Halliday**

Gliding up the Kings Place elevator for the first time, one nervous hand gripped to the side, everything felt wrong. The podcast, the interview, the interest — it was all meant to happen to someone else. It felt almost fraudulent to be joining the *Guardian*. But joining the *Guardian* I was.

And it was only weeks later, journeying back down to the capital from my graduation in Sunderland, that it began to settle in. Did I get the job solely because of Twitter? Would I have got the job without my journalism degree? Does it really matter? All of which are interesting questions, and ones which I will attempt to answer in this chapter, but they're all a diversion from an age-old truism — that hard graft pays off. And it's never been truer than today.

The backdrop to today's labour, of course, hardly needs spelling out. Journalism education is a growth industry unbridled by what even the optimists concede is a period of unprecedented uncertainty for news media. "The next wave of journalism picking through the communications revolution's entrails could be yet more fragmented, only available on certain devices, or totally networked through whatever social media phenomenon comes next," wrote Emily Bell, the former digital content director at the *Guardian,* in September 2010.[xvi] "But even those keen to read the last rites over journalism would find it hard to look at how things were 10 years ago, and the chaotic, vibrant mix of new voices now, and conclude the coverage is diminished."

Ten years ago, and the dawn of a fledgling millennium, doesn't sound so long ago. Yet changes in the predominant routes into journalism could hardly be starker. Students will get short shrift pounding the pavements of Fleet Street, but on Twitter – where access to senior media executives is but a 140-character burst away – a potential way in is just around the corner. And the stranglehold of wealthy, metropolitan postgraduates on jobs at national titles is, slowly but surely, being broken down. For these reasons alone, your foot has never been closer to the ladder. However, it takes work, a bit of self promotion and no shortage of determination to tell a story like it's never been told.

## Personal branding

Journalism students in the United States "got it" long before those of us in the UK. Personal branding is a concept that that doesn't sit easily with too many of the wannabe journalists that I've met. It is either seen simply as too time-consuming to bother with, or a practice that has no tangible immediate reward. The latter point is undoubtedly correct – but just as with slow-burning, off-diary news stories, the fruits only bear themselves with patience.

Trawling through the "Tomorrow's News, Tomorrow's Journalists" forum on Journalism.co.uk towards the end of 2008, it became clear to me that I couldn't rely solely on a printed portfolio and a stint on the university newspaper if I was to get a job in journalism post graduation. Even the local newspaper – the traditional first foot on the ladder – had abandoned its trainee scheme. These US students talked endlessly about brand alignment, domain names and networking. None of which, it was immediately clear, seemed to have much at all to do with journalism. If anything, they were a distraction from actually doing journalism. In fact, it was within four days, as 2008 slipped into 2009, that kick-started the online drive which just over a year later got me a job at the *Guardian.*

In two postings by Suzanne Yada, a twentysomething US j-student at the time, the mantra of doing new media as a journalism student was truly laid bare. Yada's two career resolutions for the year ahead amounted to: "Become invaluable" and "network like mad". [xvii] Her dispatches spread like wildfire across the web, with new media pin-ups Jeff Jarvis and Jay Rosen pointing thousands of people in their direction. While these may not seem earth shattering, what they spelt out was clear: it will be the extra-curricular work that gets you hired, not what you do inside university. And that's as true today as it was on the final day of 2008.

Getting off the ground in this brave new world is undoubtedly the hardest part. Where do you start? What do you want to be known as? The first job is to decide what image you want to project online. This is branding, and we already do it subconsciously everyday. Without wanting to sound too prescriptive – because we're not all self-aggrandising journodrones – the key is to map out interests, research the market, and remember that what you publish online could quite easily make it before the eyes of a potential employer.

## How a Lincoln graduate secured his dream job at the BBC

It's a first step into the right circles without being pushy, obtrusive or unnaturally self-assertive. Dave Lee, a 23-year-old journalism graduate from the University of Lincoln, says his online network helped land him a dream job at the BBC World Service. It was a guest lecture at his university by Phillip Knightley, the celebrated former *Sunday Times* investigative journalist, who inspired Lee to write a brash blogpost, challenging some of what the veteran newsman had said about the industry. Martin Stabe, then a reporter at *Press Gazette*, found Lee's post interesting enough to link to. That small gesture "essentially started my career", he says now. But Lee grabbed his fifteen minutes of fame with both hands.

He later wangled his way into the Sky News newsroom after uploading a clip of a small earthquake in Lincolnshire to YouTube and – again somewhat brashly – noting how late the BBC had covered it compared to its rival, Sky News. Julian March, the Sky News production editor, offering Lee £50 to use the clip. "Forget the £50. Give me a work placement," was his response. Lee, today sitting in Bush House at one of the most important news institutions in the world, crafted his crucial career steps with a combination of digital media nous, brand development and, most importantly, hard work.

Lee and many other determined student journalists around the world are learning cutting-edge online reporting tools from the comfort of their own home – and often courtesy of free advice by experts thousands of miles away. This should be seized upon. At university, I spent roughly the same amount of time heeding the words of Mindy McAdams, a leading teacher of online journalism at the University of Florida, as I did tutors at my own institution.

Her Teaching Online Journalism site is an indispensable resource for extra-curricular students. "Journalism is not rocket science," McAdams wrote in provocative post in 2008.[xviii] "You don't need a master's degree to know how to do it, and you won't do it well until you haul yourself out of school and into a working newsroom. Journalism is learned on the job, and if you're not prepared to go out and do it after four years in undergrad, maybe you should just give up on it and go to law school instead." Quite. As a friend once said to me: "The difference between those who make it into the industry and those who don't is that the successful ones were student journalists, as opposed to being merely journalism students."

## Entrepreneurial streak at *Guardian* is nigh-on essential

Editing the university newspaper or Students' Union magazine was the glittering highlight of any presentable student's CV less than a decade ago. Although still noteworthy, those in the industry today look for a little more imagination, initiative and bravado. At the *Guardian*, at least, where the newspaper's fondness for all things social media is in rude health, an entrepreneurial streak is nigh-on essential.

Dan Sabbagh, formerly the media editor at *The Times* and one of the leading media business writers in the industry, joined the *Guardian* as head of media and technology not long after I did. It wasn't so much Sabbagh's record on Fleet Street that brought him to Kings Place – accomplished though it was – but what he did on leaving the News Corp title in late 2009. Along with two former colleagues at *The Times*, Sabbagh set up his own media and entertainment news site, Beehive City, from scratch – and it quickly became an influential voice, competing with past employers and other "traditional media" outlets alike. It is this new way of doing journalism, a more maverick and less rule-bound way, that is beginning to appeal to longstanding news institutions.

"When it comes to online publishing you need to be more informal, you need to be a little less bothered about dots and commas, a little less bothered about writing a story in a traditional inverted pyramid kind of way," Sabbagh said on joining the *Guardian* to freshen up the paper's media and technology coverage. "You need to be able to express ideas creatively, entertainingly, wittily. You need to be able to play with ideas, scenarios, stories, that aren't necessarily true, or rumours that might be true but you're not quite sure, rather than sitting there waiting for two independent sources to run something. You need in short, I think, just a different kind of approach, quite a generic approach is what succeeds on a website."[xix]

## Revival of the hyperlocal

Those trying to get into journalism might find this the fast-track route. Fortunately, there's no need to spend months on end constructing a foolproof niche concept for your new site – one already exists, straight off the shelf: hyperlocal. Hyperlocal reporting is as old as the day is long, but the advent of "citizen journalism" has given it something of a modern revival. In the summer of 2010, it was the thing to do.

Which is why I set up SR2 Blog – a self-hosted WordPress site catering to a modest four-miles square patch in east Sunderland. For some reason, my curriculum didn't include hyperlocal reporting like this as standard. It should have done. A lot of universities do, simply because it is the bread-and-butter of storytelling, a real trade – good, honest journalism that has an impact on every one of our daily lives. To practise it is a true education, and to report outside the sterile confines of campus life often felt like a true liberation. Gather a group of your fellow students and don't be afraid of recruiting contributors from outside of the university, ex-councillors, residents' association members, or people who simply take an interest in what goes on outside of their front door.

As a route into the industry, it would be easy to underestimate this apparently less-than-sexy concept. However, while these hyperlocal sites continue to spring up around the UK, the local media industry and the Department for Culture, Media and Sport – tasked with breathing life into the struggling status quo – really do have one eye on the grassroots.

Community-run sites such as these will play a big part in the future of local media, if the government and media regulator Ofcom get their way. And any high-level interest in burgeoning ways of doing journalism should not go as opportunities missed by those trying to get into the industry.

## Data journalism: the crucial specialism

Data journalism warrants more than a fleeting reference in this vein. While for now will leave it to the experts, Paul Bradshaw being one, suffice it to say that if there is one specialism to envelope yourself over the coming years, it will be this one. Being as proficient and capable with a mass of impenetrable data as with masses of text is a real skill, being able to visualise it into a digestible package is indispensable. The world's most venerable news organisations, including the *Guardian* and *The New York Times*, will likely find themselves in a data journalism "arms race" during the next few years as tranches of public information, such as the MPs' expenses documents, is suddenly freed and there to be told as a story.

Sir Tim Berners-Lee, the British-born inventor of the world wide web, said in November 2010 that the future of journalism lay with journalists adept in spreadsheets, programming and visualisation. Asked who would analyse the avalanche of public data once "the geeks have moved on", Berners-Lee replied: "The responsibility needs to be with the press. Journalists need to be data-savvy. It used to be that you would get stories by chatting to people in bars, and it still might be that you'll do it that way some times. But now it's also going to be about poring over data and equipping yourself with the tools to analyse it and picking out what's interesting."[xx]

In sum, those at the front of the queue in this brave new world of journalism will have all the best traits of the "old school" journalist – the dogged determination, rat-like cunning and the ability to build stories from conversations – as well as a willingness to experiment with fresh storytelling enabled by the internet. Nepotism is giving way to social networking, and never has there been greater opportunity for your journalism to precede you. It won't always be straightforward, but doors will always be open for those who remain undaunted by the pace and scale of change.

# Notes

---

[xvi] See http://www.guardian.co.uk/media/2010/sep/06/mediaguardian-10-years-change, accessed on 3 February 2011

[xvii] See http://www.suzanneyada.com/2008/12/31/resolutions-for-journalism-students-part-i-become-invaluable/, accessed on 4 February 2011

[xviii] See http://mindymcadams.com/tojou/2008/advice-to-journalism-students-forget-grad-school/, accessed on 5 February 2011

[xix] See http://www.journalism.co.uk/news/-the-door-is-open--guardian-s-dan-sabbagh-on-a-new-approach-to-partnerships-online/s2/a541318/, accessed on 4 February 2011

[xx] See http://www.guardian.co.uk/media/2010/nov/22/data-analysis-tim-berners-lee, accessed on 4 February 2011

## Note on the author

Josh Halliday was hired as the *Guardian*'s trainee media and technology reporter in June 2010 – a fortnight before his graduation from an undergraduate journalism degree at the University of Sunderland. Social networking, not nepotism, is one of the prime reasons for this uncanny break of luck, he says. The rest is down to sheer hard work – most of it extra-curricular.

# How the internet has transformed automotive journalism

**Sean Carson**

Over the last ten years, the influx of automotive websites and blogs – covering all manner of subjects from Reliant Robins to rare automotive exotica – has forced established automotive publications to change dramatically in terms of both appearance and content.

The increased accessibility of automotive web-based media to the general public has empowered the automotive enthusiast to take up the challenge themselves and create their own journalistic outlet, with no formal training or technical skills required.

The growth of the blog has allowed the individual to take journalism into their own hands and maximise the ability to produce content on a plethora of topics. Now, one blog may only cover one area of content per se (no matter how in-depth it is). But with even the most computer-illiterate of us still able to perform a Google search, the ease and proficiency with which the average internet user can surf the web means the next topic, and therefore area of maximised content aimed at an unbelievably narrow market by print standards, is only seconds away. Something a print publication could never compete with.

As Frank Giovinazzi, of the American International Automobile Dealers Association (AIADA), outlines: "The new reality of always-on, instant information has changed everything – from the frequency and volume of information to the very identity of the major publishers" (Giovinazzi 2006).

## US blogs take on the mainstream

In America, blogs such as Autoblog and Jalopnik (although now commercial enterprises in their own right, they were once independent) have really taken the fight to mainstream titles such as *Car and Driver* and *Motor Trend.* The story is the same in the UK. There are plenty of forums and blogs that cover the same news and publish the same leaked photographs and rumours of the next German or Italian road-based royalty as the established print players and web-based magazines do; they just do it with more exclamation marks. So why do people visit the amateur blog-type sites if they can get the low-down from people in touch with the industry who make it their job to report such news? Unfiltered information, freedom of expression, what ever you term it as, it's a major factor in attracting users to the blogs:

> We can put our comments there, we can frame it any way we want, but we're going to give you all the information we get. When we go to an auto show, within two hours of the press conference our live shots are there, all of the press shots and the complete press release is there on the site. We're not going to sit there and pick out the information we think our readers want to read, they're going to get all of it and we can do that because we don't have to worry about what it costs to print on paper. We can put as much up there as we can stuff and it doesn't cost us anything (ibid).

John Neff, editor of one of the most prominent upstarts in online journalism Autoblog.com, believes the lack of constraints surrounding what content they can publish attracts the glut of readers his site manages to net. In conjunction with this, Neff believes the informal editorial style of the blog-based automotive journalism outlet has contributed towards the formats success. "Autoblog's editorial approach is interesting in that it is a blog, and while that scares a lot of automakers because they think we might be unprofessional…the advantages of being a blog is that you don't have to be a perfect writer – you don't have to write a magnum opus for every article" (ibid).

While this maybe true, it's fair to say that it has also become somewhat of a contentious point in the world of online automotive journalism. As Zgale (2010) highlights, the lack of formal training and professional practice can get the blogger into hot water, the point being that "basic journalistic practices of checking sources and not believing everything you hear should be considered when writing any story". A sacrosanct principle of any journalist worth their salt that is often ignored by the blogger sometimes resulting in a story based on incorrect fact.

Initially, blogs had the edge on the online derivatives of the reputable print publications. The constant flow of information to the end-user that made the blog what it is today was key to its success back in the early 2000s, and in Autoblog.com's case proved a successful model achieving well over 3 million monthly visitors within two years of the launch of the site in 2003.

## Transformation of automotive journalism over the last decade

Today however, interactivity, informality and raw information are not enough to steal the market share. "Automotive journalism has been transformed over the last decade thanks in part to web-only publications pushing mainstream magazines to redefine their print issues and web sites" (ibid). In the early days, blogs could trade on these factors alone but currently, with the market place becoming ever more crowded, the big print monthly and weeklies have also branched out into the world of online content. The empowerment of the bedroom journalist, along with the increasing role technology plays in everyday life, has forced the recognised names of the motoring press to broaden their horizons and re-analyse their brand's strategy and position in the market place.

*Autocar* magazine, the oldest and second most read motoring publication in the UK, according to National Readership Survey figures with an estimated readership of 265,000 between October 2009 and September 2010 (NRS 2010), is a prime example of how the established and respected names in automotive journalism have staved off the threat and embraced the tools for the modern media age.

The *Autocar* umbrella of publications including *Autocar,* Autocar.co.uk and the new for 2011 *Autocar* iPad app and digitised version of the print magazine (available from mag.autocar.co.uk) have brought the brand to the forefront of online automotive content. With the brilliantly diverse cross-platform strategy *Autocar* has lined up for itself, the brand exemplifies how the advent of the internet has changed the world of automotive journalism for the better.

## How *Autocar* has moved the goal posts

With *Autocars's* product line-up consisting of a successful magazine and website, as well as a branded insurance product, popular trackday programme and now two new revenue streams coming online in 2011 in the form of *Autocar's* iPad app (priced at £2.99) and the digitised version of the magazine (priced at £2.80 per issue or £89 for a 12-month subscription) (Haymarket Media Group 2011), *Autocar* has moved the goal posts of the automotive journalism world out of reach of the bedroom-blogger in terms of the ability to offer almost limitless specialist content through a variety of different media. The ability to generate revenue through associated products is a beneficial facet of the business brought by the onset of the digital age and is heavily apparent in automotive journalism. *Autosport* and web-based magazine Pistonheads.com have capitalised on this phenomenon with sponsorship of the *Autosport* International Show and the Pistonheads Car Show not only giving them another outlet to promote their cause but also generating huge awareness in the process.

The digital world and the internet in particular have also fuelled the relentless quest to produce new and interesting ways to develop and display content whilst conveniently relieving fans of their hard-earned. Primarily, however, it's the ability to maximise the output of content, facilitated by the growth in the online platform allowing in-depth audio-visual content, that has been the primary driver of change in automotive journalism – regardless of the size of the organisation. Mark Payton, digital editorial director at Haymarket consumer media, comments:

> I love the way that online I can become vertical in a way that I could never afford to in print. I could take your wildest fetish and exploit it to its absolute extreme. So if you want in our case a car buyer's guide, we can just keep on going and we can indulge you fully. No matter what type of car you're in to or what your outlook on

motoring is, we can take it to its logical extreme and as an editorial director I find that extremely exciting (Bull 2010).

## No replacement for journalistic technique

Underlining the success of the recognised publications in the automotive world, however, is a fundamental point of journalism that transcends all platforms of media. There is no replacement for journalistic technique. Plain and simple. Readers appreciate the research and thought that has gone into a considered piece by someone who makes it their job to research, review and write about a given topic. Without wanting to dismiss the work of the blogger, it's often seen that the blog-type outlet is long on enthusiasm and interest but short on grounded fact or technique.

This is not to say professional publications are upright and austere however, as many major websites also offer the musings of the motoring journalists in a more relaxed blogging style again giving that option to the reader in terms of content. Still, coupled to the fact that the big players with established links to the automotive world have direct access to new models and motor shows, giving first hand news and reviews on anything from the latest Ferrari to fuel-duty rises, the reasons as to why the online versions (or even solely online) of well-known motoring titles achieve such success are not hard to fathom.

There's always an exception to the rule though. Pistonheads.com was established by David Edmonston in 1999, and although recognised as a pioneer in the world of online automotive journalism, the website's original concept was rather vague:

> I was researching the web in order to get up to speed with developments for my day job. This was around about the same time as I bought a sports car. I combined the two interests for fun initially. As I experimented more I realised how little investment I needed in order to create a "publication" that could steal a march on traditional magazines and sources of motoring news. With an old PC and a bit of shared server space I set about creating a crude magazine that would bring news daily rather than weekly – quite a novelty in the motoring world even in 1999 (Loughane 2005).

## The rise and rise of Pistonheads.com

The website's popularity grew rapidly, not least thanks to extensive television coverage in 2004, owing to death threats made to road safety campaigners on the website. By January 2007, the online magazine and forum had been swallowed up by the motoring arm of publishing giant Haymarket and by 2008 was receiving more than 1.5 million unique visitors each month (Racecar.com 2008). The once small and crude online magazine had traversed the gap between the individually run enterprise and the global online outlet for automotive content that it is today. To many, it is *the* original automotive journalism website.

The fact that Pistonheads.com was eventually bought out by Haymarket highlights the extent to which the internet has changed automotive journalism. With online content in the form of Autosport.com, Autocar.co.uk, WhatCar.com and Pistonheads.com among others, Haymarket have clearly set out their stall for the future, and in complementing their print counterparts (Pistonheads.com excepted) firmly believe online content is going to play a large part.

The arrival of the information age, and with it a new and unique platform on which to display content, has also heralded a new type of automotive journalism. Automotive satire is here.

Sniffpetrol.com is a satirical take on the motor industry that has become an extremely popular haunt for many interested in automotive journalism. With its clichéd road tester and Executive Associate Editor-At-Large for DAB OF OPPO magazine, Troy Queef, is a character who embodies all those done-to-death, corny and unoriginal quips of the motoring journalist. The site also features Carcoat Damphands, the venerable used car salesman who seemingly only speaks in cockney rhyming slang and riddles as well as the hilarious "not advertisement" section that pokes fun at the sometimes unbelievable and tenuous marketing campaigns masterminded by the manufacturers. Sniffpetrol.com is a brilliant example of how the versatility of online journalism allows for a product that would never have been able to succeed in print.

## Online automotive failures

Online automotive journalism has not been without its failures, though. Founded in March 2008 by Steve Davies, Richard Meaden (co-founder of *evo* magazine), Jethro Bovingdon (former deputy-editor of *evo* magazine) and Chris Harris (former road test editor of *Autocar*), DriversRepublic.com was a successful digital motoring magazine and niche social network for drivers – very similar to Pistonheads.com – that published news, features, first tests, a usually twice-weekly digital magazine and video clips. However, the site was to disband by 11 August 2009 and in the process highlighted one of the major issues to face online automotive journalism. According to Steve Davies (2010):

> There has been plenty of speculation on other sites and forums about the reasons why this has occurred, and despite the first impressions that it must have been for financial reasons, nothing could be further from the truth. Thanks to your participation and the generous support of the automotive industry we were in rude health and looking forward to a bumper year, but differences in our vision about future priorities have led to a parting of ways.

The ability of the internet to allow almost limitless scope for the production of content in many different forms brings with it a potentially, massively more varied set of aims for any given publication. With content maximisation as a main aim, the potential for dispute within management over the editorial direction of a publication is a real issue, and one that obviously in DriversRepublic.com's case could not be solved, leading to the closure of the website.

### Content remains free

As is with the most successful online newspaper, the Mail Online, few web-based motoring sites have erected a paywall – content remains free. The big publications have followed the lead of the biggest online title in Fleet Street in adopting a no-paywall strategy; a business model which many believe actually increases revenue. With readers of the online arm more likely to buy a copy of the same newspaper and the ability to serve ad impressions to millions of viewers at a negligible marginal cost, why shouldn't it work for the large motoring periodicals?

### References

Bull, A. (2010) *Multimedia journalism: A practical guide*, Abingdon, Oxon, Routledge

Davies, S. (2009) Farewell to DR, DriversRepublic.com, 11 August. Available online at http://blog.drivers-republic.com/2009/08/11/farewell-to-dr/, accessed on 23 January 2011

Gionvinazzi, F. (2006) Auto journalism's new speed, Bloomberg's Business Week, 27 March. Available online at http://www.businessweek.com/autos/content/mar2006/bw20060327_9 44744.htm, accessed on 23 January 2011

Haymarket Media Group (2011) *Autocar* strikes twice with digital media, 21 January. Available online at http://www.haymarket.com/newsarticle.aspx?news=957, accessed on 23 January 2011

Loughane, E. (2005) Net success interviews, Lulu.com. See http://www.lulu.com/product/paperback/net-success-interviews/120752, accessed on 23 January 2011

National Readership Survey (2010) *NRS readership estimates: General magazines: October 2009-September 2010*, NRS. Available online at http://www.nrs.co.uk/site.html, accessed on 23 January 2011

Racecar.com (2008) PistonHeads Show live attractions, Racecar.com, 2.January. Available online at http://www.racecar.com/Motorsport/News/PistonHeads-Show-live-attractions/20094.htm, accessed on 23 January 2011

Zgale (2010) The changing face of online automotive journalism, 25 July. Available online at: http://www.journalistech.org/index.php/2010/07/the-changing-face-of-online-automotive-journalism/, accessed on 23 January 2011

## Note on the author

Sean Carson is studying for an MA in Automotive Journalism at Coventry University. He graduated from the University of Liverpool in 2009 with a BSc in Geography.

# Section 5. Using the net for social action

**John Mair**

Journalism was mainly passive. We told the readers and viewers, they read and listened and moved on. The internet has changed all that. Interactivity is king. Journalism is now a fluid not static process. The reader or viewer has become as much an actor and part of the process of creation as the writer or producer.

They call it "crowdsourcing" though, significantly, the professional is still in the van. Paul Bradshaw, Visiting Professor at City University, leads the way in this (as in so much else in net journalism). He – with Andy Brightwell – has set up the site, Help Me Investigate, to dig out stories using real people as his sources and to drive them forward. Here they describe how it works. Revelation in cyberspace.

The net can also aid the democratic process in other ways. Channel 4 News with its public face reporter, Cathy Newman, has set up its own

*FactCheck* site: bullshit-detecting helped by deep searching and testing of claims. Some of those political claims made in the heat of electoral or other battles are tested to construction or destruction by the *FactCheck* team.

Politicians, Prime Ministers even, sometimes have to withdraw their claims and apologise. The Channel 4 Commissioning Editor for this strand, Vicky Taylor, describes how it works to aid clarity. The BBC, too, has done democracy a great service on its site by creating Democracy Live. Citizens with a computer can access their democratic institutions all over Europe and past and present. The father of that innovation, Pete Clifton, the head of multimedia development at BBC news, describes how he did it and what it does.

One thing is certain: the internet has changed the dynamics of democracy in Britain and worldwide significantly. The scales are moving firmly towards the citizen.

# Help Me Investigate: Anatomy of a crowdsourced investigation

Paul Bradshaw with Andy Brightwell

In both academic and mainstream literature about the web, one theme consistently recurs: the lowering of the barrier allowing individuals to collaborate in pursuit of a common goal. Whether it is creating the world's biggest encyclopedia, spreading news about a protest or tracking down a stolen phone, the rise of the network has seen a decline in the role of the formal organisation. And that includes news organisations.

In 2007, as I was writing a book chapter on investigative journalism and blogs (De Burgh 2008), I was struck in particular by two examples of this phenomenon. The first was an experiment by the *Florida News Press* when it started receiving calls from readers complaining about high water and sewage connection charges for newly constructed homes. The newspaper, short on in-house resources to investigate the leads, decided to ask their readers to help. The result is by now familiar as a textbook example of "crowdsourcing" – outsourcing a project to "the crowd":

Readers spontaneously organized their own investigations: Retired engineers analyzed blueprints, accountants pored over balance sheets, and an inside whistle-blower leaked documents showing evidence of bid-rigging (Howe 2006).

The second example concerned contaminated pet food in the US and did not involve a mainstream news organisation. In fact, it was frustration with poor mainstream "churnalism" (see Davies 2008) that motivated bloggers and internet users to start digging into the story. The resulting output from dozens of blogs ranged from useful information for pet owners, to the latest news, and the compilation of a database that suggested the official numbers of pet deaths recorded by the US Food and Drug Administration was short by several thousand. One site, Itchmo.com, became so popular that it was banned in China (Weise 2007).

What struck me about both examples was not that people could organise to produce investigative journalism, but that this practice of "crowdsourcing" had two key qualities for journalism. The first was engagement: in the case of the *News-Press* for six weeks the story generated more traffic to its website than "ever before, excepting hurricanes". This was the sort of interest that most investigative journalists could only dream of for what are often worthy, but dry, issues.

The second quality was subject: the contaminated pet food story was, in terms of mainstream news values, unfashionable and unjustifiable in terms of investment of resources. And this is true of many issues (miscarriages of justice stories are just one example: popular subjects of investigation 30 years ago, they rarely justify a journalist's effort now). It occurred to me that the crowdsourcing model of investigation might provide a way to investigate stories which were in the public interest but which commercial and public service news organisations would not consider worth their time.

## Building Help Me Investigate

I spent the following 18 months planning a web platform that would make it easier for people to collaborate in this way: the news agenda would be owned by the users (who could be either members of the public or journalists), and the small website staff would support users in their investigations, rather than the other way around.

With proof of concept funding from Channel 4's 4iP fund and Screen West Midlands, we began building the site in April 2009 (by now I had been joined by community specialist Nick Booth and web developer Stef Lewandowski). On 1 July, HelpMeInvestigate.com went live. There was no fanfare – just a single tweet about the site the day after its launch. By the end of the week the site was investigating what would come to be one of the biggest stories of the summer in Birmingham –the overspend of £2.2m by the city council on a new website (for research on this see Jon Hickman 2010). It would go on to complete further investigations into parking tickets and the use of surveillance powers, as well as much smaller-scale questions such as how a complaint was handled, or why two bus companies were charging different prices on the same route.

## Research: when does crowdsourcing work?

In early 2010, Andy Brightwell and I conducted some research into one particular successful investigation on the site. I wanted to know what had made the investigation successful – and how (or if) we might replicate those conditions for other investigations. The investigation in question was "What do you know about the *London Weekly*?" – an investigation into a free newspaper which was, they claimed, about to launch in London (thus part of the investigation was to establish if the claim was a hoax),

The people behind the *London Weekly* had made a number of claims about planned circulation, staffing and investment which went unchallenged in the specialist media. Journalists Martin Stabe, James Ball and Judith Townend, however, wanted to dig deeper. So, after an exchange on Twitter, Judith logged on to Help Me Investigate and started an investigation.

A month later members of the investigation had unearthed a wealth of detail about the people behind the *London Weekly* and the facts behind their claims. Some of the information was reported in *MediaWeek* and the *Media Guardian* podcast Media Talk; some formed the basis for posts on James Ball's blog, Journalism.co.uk and the Online Journalism Blog. Some information has, for legal reasons, remained unpublished.

## Methodology

Andrew Brightwell conducted a number of semi-structured interviews with contributors to the investigation. The sample was randomly selected but representative of the mix of contributors, who were categorised as either "alpha" (more than six contributions), "active" (two to six contributions) and "lurkers" (whose only contribution was to join the investigation). These interviews formed the qualitative basis for the research.

Complementing this data was quantitative information about users of the site as a whole. This was taken from two user surveys – one conducted when the site was three months' old and another at 12 months – and analysis of analytics taken from the investigation (such as numbers and types of actions and frequency).

## What are the characteristics of a crowdsourced investigation?
Examples of crowdsourced journalism tend to fit into one of two types. The first can be described as the "Mechanical Turk" model (after the Amazon-owned web service that allows you to offer piecemeal payment for repetitive work). This approach tends to involve large numbers of individuals performing small, similar tasks. Examples from journalism would include the *Guardian*'s experiment with inviting users to classify MPs' expenses to find possible stories, or the pet food bloggers inviting users to add details of affected pets to their database.

The second type can be described as the "Wisdom of Crowds" approach (after James Surowiecki's 2005 book of the same name). This approach tends to involve smaller numbers of users performing discrete tasks that rely on a particular expertise. It follows the creed of open source software development, often referred to as Linus's Law, which states: "Given enough eyeballs, all bugs are shallow" (Raymond 1999). The *Florida News Press* example given above fits into this category, relying as it did on users with specific knowledge (such as engineering or accounting) or access.

Help Me Investigate fits into the latter category: users are invited to tag themselves so that it is easier to locate users with particular expertise (tagged "FOI" or "lawyer", for example) or in a particular location. One of our first tasks was to analyse whether the investigation data matched those patterns observed elsewhere in crowdsourcing and online activity. An analysis of the number of actions by each user, for example, showed a clear "power law" distribution, where a minority of users accounted for the majority of activity.

This power law, however, did not translate into a breakdown approaching the 90-9-1 "law of participation inequality" observed by Jakob Nielsen (2006). Instead, the balance between those who made a couple of contributions (normally the 9 per cent of the 90-9-1 split) and those who made none (the 90 per cent) was roughly equal. This may have been because the design of the site meant it was not possible to "lurk" without being a member of the site already, or being invited and signing up. Adding in data on those looking at the investigation page who were not members may have shed further light on this.

## What made the crowdsourcing successful?

Clearly, it is worth making a distinction between what made the investigation successful as a series of outcomes, and what made crowdsourcing successful as a method. What made the community gather and continue to return? One hypothesis was that the nature of the investigation provided a natural cue to interested parties – the *London Weekly* was published on Fridays and Saturdays and there was a build-up of expectation to see if a new issue would, indeed, appear. We were curious to see if the investigation had any "rhythm". Would there be peaks of interest correlating to the expected publication?

The data threw up something else entirely. There was, indeed, a rhythm but it was Wednesdays that were the most popular day for people contributing to the investigation. Why? Well, it turned out that one of the investigation's "alpha" contributors – James Ball – set himself a task to blog about the investigation every week. His blog posts appeared on a Wednesday. That this turned out to be a significant factor in driving activity tells us one important lesson: talking publicly and regularly about the investigation's progress is key. This data was backed up from the interviews. One respondent mentioned the "weekly cue" explicitly.

More broadly, it seems that the site helped keep track of a number of discussions taking place around the web. Having been born from a discussion on Twitter, further conversations on Twitter resulted in further people signing up, along with comments threads and other online discussion. This fit the way the site was designed culturally – to be part of a network rather than asking people to do everything on-site.

But the planned *technical* connectivity of the site with the rest of the web (being able to pull related tweets or bookmarks, for example) had been dropped during development as we focused on core functionality. This was not a bad thing, we should emphasise, as it prevented us becoming distracted with "bells and whistles" and allowed us to iterate in reaction to user activity rather than our own assumptions of what users would want. This research shows that user activity and informs future development accordingly.

The presence of "alpha" users such as James Ball and Judith Townend was crucial in driving activity on the site – a pattern observed in other successful investigations. They picked up the threads contributed by others and not only wove them together into a coherent narrative which allowed others to enter more easily, but also set the new challenges that provided ways for people to contribute. The fact that they brought with them a strong social network presence is probably also a factor – but one that needs further research.

The site has always been designed to emphasise the role of the user in driving investigations. The agenda is not owned by a central publisher but by the person posing the question – and therefore the responsibility is theirs as well. In this sense it draws on Jenkins' argument (2006) that "Consumers will be more powerful within convergence culture – but only if they recognise and use that power." This cultural hurdle may be the biggest one that the site has to address. Indeed, the site is also designed to offer "failure for free" (Shirky 2008), allowing users to learn what works and what doesn't, and begin to take on that responsibility where required.

The investigation suited crowdsourcing well, since it could be broken down into separate parts and paths – most of which could be completed online: "Where does this claim come from?" "Can you find out about this person?" "What can you discover about this company?" One person, for example, used Google Streetview to establish that the registered address of the company was a postbox. Other investigations that are less easily broken down may be less suitable for crowdsourcing – or require more effort to ensure success.

A regular supply of updates provided the investigation with momentum. The accumulation of discoveries provided valuable feedback to users who then returned for more. In his book on Wikipedia, Andrew Lih (2009: 82) notes a similar pattern – "stigmergy" – that is observed in the natural world: "the situation in which the product of previous work, rather than direct communication [induces and directs] additional labour." An investigation without these "small pieces, loosely joined" (Weinberger 2002) might not suit crowdsourcing so well.

One problem, however, was that those paths led to a range of potential avenues of inquiry. In the end, although the core questions were answered (was the publication a hoax and what were the bases for their claims?) the investigation raised many more questions. These remained largely unanswered once the majority of users felt their questions had been answered. Like any investigation, there came a point at which those involved had to make a judgement whether they wished to invest any more time in it.

Finally, the investigation benefited from a diverse group of contributors who offered specialist knowledge or access. Some visited stations where the newspaper was claiming distribution to see how many copies were being handed out. Others used advanced search techniques to track down details on the people involved and the claims being made, or to make contact with people who had had previous experiences with those behind the newspaper. The visibility of the investigation online led to more than one "whistleblower" approach providing inside information.

## What can be done to make crowdsourcing easier?

Looking at the reasons that users of the site *as a whole* gave for not contributing to an investigation, the majority attributed this to "not having enough time". Although at least one interviewee, in contrast, highlighted the simplicity and ease of contributing, it needs to be as easy and simple as possible for users to contribute in order to lower the perception of effort and time needed.

Notably, the second biggest reason for not contributing was a "lack of personal connection with an investigation", demonstrating the importance of the individual and social dimension of crowdsourcing. Likewise, a "personal interest in the issue" was the single largest factor in someone contributing. A "Why should I contribute?" feature on each investigation may be worth considering.

Others mentioned the social dimension of crowdsourcing – the "sense of being involved in something together" – which Jenkins (2006) would refer to as "consumption as a networked practice". This motivation is also identified by Yochai Benkler in his work on networks (2006). Looking at non-financial reasons why people contribute their time to online projects, he refers to "socio-psychological reward". He also identifies the importance of "hedonistic, personal gratification". In other words, fun. (Interestingly, these match two of the three traditional reasons for consuming news: because it is socially valuable, and because it is entertaining. The third – because it is financially valuable – neatly matches the third reason for working.)

While it is easy to talk about "failure for free", more could be done to identify and support failing investigations. A monthly update feature to remind users of recent activity and – more importantly – the lack of activity might help here. The investigators in a group might be asked whether they wish to terminate the investigation in those cases, emphasising their responsibility for its progress and helping "clean up" the investigations listed on the first page of the site.

There is also a danger in interfering too much in reducing failure. This is a natural instinct, and we have to continually remind ourselves that we started the project with an expectation of 95 to 99 per cent of investigations "failing" through a lack of motivation on the part of the instigator. That was part of the design. It was the 1 to 5 per cent of questions which gained traction that would be the focus of the site. (This is how Meetup.com works, for example – most groups "fail" but there is no way to predict which ones. As it happens, the "success" rate of investigations has been much higher than expected.) One analogy is a news conference where members throw out ideas – only a few are chosen for investment of time and energy, the rest "fail".

In the end, it is the management of that tension between interfering to ensure everything succeeds – so removing the incentive for users to be self-motivated – and not interfering at all – leaving users feeling unsupported and unmotivated – that is likely to be the key to a successful crowdsourcing project. More than a year into the project, this was a skill that we were still learning.

# References

Benkler, Yochai (2006) The wealth of networks: How social production transforms markets and freedom. Available online at http://www.benkler.org/Benkler_Wealth_Of_Networks.pdf, accessed on 2 January 2011

Davies, Nick (2008) *Flat earth news*, London, Chatto

De Burgh, Hugo (ed.) (2008) *Investigative journalism*, Abingdon, Oxon, Routledge, second edition

Hickman, Jon. (2010) Help Me Investigate: The social practices of investigative journalism, 27 July. Available online at http://theplan.co.uk/help-me-investigate-the-social-practices-of-i

Howe, Jeff. (2006) Gannett to crowdsource news, *Wired*, 3 November. Available online at http://www.wired.com/software/webservices/news/2006/11/72067, accessed on 3 January 2011

Jenkins, Henry (2006) *Convergence culture: Where old and new media collide*, New York, New York University Press

Lih, Andrew (2009) *The Wikipedia revolution*, New York, Hyperion

Nielsen, Jakob (2006) Participation inequality: Encouraging more users to contribute, Jakob Nielsen's Alertbox, 9 October. Available online at http://www.useit.com/alertbox/participation_inequality.html, accessed on 3 January 2011

Raymond, Eric S. (1999) The cathedral and the bazaar. Available online at http://www.catb.org/~esr/writings/cathedral-bazaar/cathedral-bazaar/, accessed on 1 January 2010

Shirky, Clay (2008) *Here comes everybody: The power of organizing without organizations*, London, Allen Lane

Surowiecki, James (2005) *The wisdom of crowds*, London, Abacus

Weinberger, David (2002) *Small pieces, loosely joined: A unified theory of the web*, London, Basic Books

# Notes on the authors

Paul Bradshaw is an online journalist and blogger, a Reader in Online Journalism at Birmingham City University and a Visiting Professor at City University's School of Journalism in London. He manages his own blog, the Online Journalism Blog (OJB), and is the co-founder of Help Me Investigate, an investigative journalism website funded by Channel 4 and Screen WM. He has written for journalism.co.uk, *Press Gazette*, the *Guardian*'s Data Blog, Nieman Reports and the Poynter Institute in the US. Books that Bradshaw has contributed to include *Investigative journalism* (second edition), *Web journalism: A new form of citizenship*; and *Citizen journalism: Global perspectives*. A book on online journalism, co-written with former *Financial Times* web editor Liisa Rohumaa, is due later this. Adrian Monck ranked Bradshaw second in his list of "Britain's Top Ten Journo-Bloggers" (2007) and NowPublic has named him the fourth most visible Briton online in its "MostPublic Index" of the UK (2008). He was placed thirty-sixth in the *Birmingham Post*'s "Power 50" list of 2009. He has been listed in Journalism.co.uk's list of the leading innovators in journalism and media and Poynter's most influential people in social media. In 2010, he was shortlisted for Multimedia Publisher of the Year and in 2011 ranked 9th in PeerIndexs list of the most influential UK journalists on Twitter Bradshaw is also a graduate of Birmingham City University (then the University of Central England), where he studied media from 1995 to 1998.

Andrew Brightwell is an online communities manager at Public-i and formerly a social media reporter at Podnosh. He studied the MA in Online Journalism at Birmingham City University when he assisted Paul Bradshaw with research into the Help Me Investigate platform.

# Face the facts: How the Channel 4 News website has forced more honesty into British political dialogue

**Vicky Taylor**

> The fact is that, despite its mathematical base, statistics is as much an art as it is a science. A great many manipulations and even distortions are possible within the bounds of propriety.

So wrote Darrell Huff in 1954 in *How to lie with statistics*. Huff, a journalist himself, had recognised the fact that numbers could be manipulated in various ways to make their readers reach a conclusion which may be far from the truth. For politicians who deal in statistics, this manipulation could, of course, be very handy when you had a policy to defend or promote.

Being able to spot when you are being given some figures which have gone through the sieve of manipulation is clearly a useful democratic service and one which goes to the heart of why *FactCheck* was launched by Channel 4. *FactCheck* first appeared on the Channel 4 News website for the UK 2005 election, taking its name (with agreement, of course) from the American organisation of the same name.

Factcheck.org in America states its aim is to be a "consumer advocate for voters. To reduce the level of deception and confusion in US politics. We monitor the factual accuracy of what is said by major US political players in the form of TV ads, debates, speeches, interviews and news releases. Our goal is to apply the best practices of both journalism and scholarship, and to increase public knowledge and understanding".

The Channel 4 News *FactCheck* shares those same ideals. Our mission statement was, perhaps, a bit less wordy. We wanted to hold those in power to account and put more honesty into British political debate. If a politician makes a claim, we want to know if it is true or not. If he or she suggests something costs something, or will take so long – we want to ask are they telling the absolute truth as most people would understand it, or is there a bit of poetic licence in there too?

## Helping people make informed choices

If the people who vote for the politicians cannot tell the fact from the fiction, how can they make informed choices when it comes to polling day or in their day to day understanding of policies which affect them? Also, if the politicians themselves believe that no-one will concern themselves with forensically examining their facts, then the temptation to spin a particularly story may get rather strong.

When in March 2009, the *FactCheck* team was expanded and the content launched as a blog on the Channel 4 News website, Cathy Newman, the programme's political correspondent, was appointed as its figurehead. Her tenacity in finding out stories and squirreling away at the truth of what is being said not just in Westminster, but around the country too, were just the right skills needed for the job. She works out of the Channel 4 News Westminster offices with a team of two producers (more during an election campaign) to dig away at the data which underlies every claim and to spot the fiction masquerading as a political fact. Often they call on expert help to decipher the data, but generally it is a question of patiently going back through figures and archives to collect the necessary information. Data mining has become an interesting and productive area for journalism in the new digital world.

## Scrutinising everything – from public spending to CCTVs

Since its launch, the *FactCheck* team have scrutinised claims on everything from public spending and the causes of the recession, to the number of CCTV cameras and whether the new UK university fees are the highest in the world (the answer to the later was yes, if you are excluding private American universities). *FactCheck* also encourages members of the public to tell them about claims they have heard which they want checked out or just by tipping off the team about anything they might have missed.

Having a blog encouraged this type of interaction with the public and allowed web readers to search for the claims we have checked – either through the topic itself or by political party. It also means commenting on a story is very easy, and over the past couple of years *FactCheck* has received hundreds of comments. Most complimentary, others less so!

As multi-media journalism, *FactCheck* has to promote its content on as many platforms as possible to make it available to as many people as possible, not all of whom will be avid followers of parliamentary speeches. *Factchecks* appear regularly on the Channel 4 News TV programme with Cathy Newman reporting her statistical revelations as a TV News report. The *FactCheck* Twitter account updates followers on the new topics and as always Twitter is an efficient and effective way to get your news messages out to a wider audience quickly. The topics are then re-tweeted and a wider audience reached.

Some re-tweets are often generous in their recommendations. For instance: "I've spent the last half hour reading the @factcheck blog. They check numerical claims made by politicians, mainly. Recommended follow."

## The most popular *FactChecks*

Finally you can sign up for email alerts to new *FactChecks* so as not to miss the latest fact-crime being committed by a British politician. The most popular *FactChecks* to date were around the General Election 2010, when the team had a remit to examine claims made by party leaders, ministers, MPs and others in positions of power right across the political spectrum If something smacked of spin, we promised to go back to the source of the claim and test it out against published statistics and official reports, ransack the archives and consult independent experts in the field to try to get to the truth. In the election, this proved a useful device to follow up stories as they came up on the campaign trail.

One such *FactCheck* was actually just before the election campaign, but had ramifications throughout it. In March 2010, Gordon Brown told Sir John Chilcot's inquiry into the Iraq war that defence spending was going up in real terms. He then repeated the figures in Prime Minister's Questions in the House of Commons. Cathy Newman and her team got on the case and showed that his figures had not included inflation, so could not be claimed to have risen.

Gordon Brown had to admit he had been wrong to claim that defence spending rose in real terms every year under Labour. He acknowledged: "Because of the operational fluctuations in the way the money is spent, expenditure has risen in cash terms every year, in real terms it is 12 per cent higher, but I do accept that in one of two years defence expenditure did not rise in real terms." David Cameron, then Opposition leader, said: "In three years of asking the Prime Minister Questions, I do not think I have ever heard him make a correction or a retraction." Gordon Brown then wrote to Sir John Chilcot to amend his evidence apparently.

After this, a reader, John Machin, wrote on the *FactCheck* blog: "This is why I subscribe to *FactCheck*. So that my instinctive suspicions about politicians' honesty can be either confirmed or dismissed by some good hard facts. In this case, utterly confirmed. Thank you *FactCheck*."

## Challenging Cameron on special needs
But David Cameron's claims too were the subject of several Election *FactChecks*. One such one was the question raised by a father of a son with special needs. Jonathan Bartley questioned him on the provision for special needs schools and Conservative promises in their manifesto. Mr Bartley felt that, wrongly in his view, the Tories were encouraging inclusion in mainstream schools to the detriment of special needs schools. David Cameron was sympathetic, but *FactCheck* proved that David Cameron could not have it both ways.

Cathy Newman wrote: "Cameron denied 'absolutely' that his manifesto suggested ending the bias towards educating disabled children in mainstream schools. However, that's exactly what it does say. The Tories subsequently briefed that parents should be given greater choice, allowing them to send their disabled children to a mainstream school if they wished. But that's not a subtlety contained in the manifesto, as Cameron should know. On the basis of what he said to Mr. Bartley though, he needs to do some homework on just what is contained within the smart hardback cover of his manifesto."

Ed Balls, as Education Minister in Brown's government, was also forced to accept the true facts when *FactCheck* pointed them out. During Education Questions in the House of Commons in March 2010, Michael Gove highlighted statistics that showed that, out of the 80,000 pupils on free school meals, only 45 make it to Oxbridge. Ed Balls disputed the figures at first. Two Channel 4 *FactChecks* had shown Balls to be wrong: "But as regular *Factcheck* readers will know, Gove is on the money...On the number of free school meals pupils going to Oxford, we fail Balls's rebuttal rather than Gove's claim."

Again *FactCheck* had helped the public find out the truth in a political debate. "Following our exchange in the House yesterday I have now had an opportunity to look in detail at the figures you quoted and I can confirm that they are, on this occasion, correct. I did not claim in the House yesterday that these particular figures about Oxbridge entry were incorrect, but instead that I was not able to confirm accuracy" (letter from Ed Balls to Michael Gove, 9 March 2010).

But with the swings and roundabouts of politics, Ed Balls, when shadow Home Secretary in December 2010, was happy to write on the social network Twitter about a *FactCheck* which was checking out his opponent's figures and finding them wanting. This was a *FactCheck* which proved that cuts to some police forces were, in fact, worse than originally forecast.

## Questioning Unite's claims over the deficit

*FactCheck* has served the purpose of checking out claims made on other broadcasters, not just in the House of Commons. In December 2010, when Radio 4's *Today* programme had a heated debated about the size of the deficit in the UK, Len McCluskey, the head of Unite, was asked to defend his claim that " the deficit is not high by either historical or contemporary standards".

So just how big is the deficit exactly and what are fair comparisons to make an informed judgement? Union boss Len McCluskey had qualified his claim by saying he was more interested in the national debt than the deficit. Radio 4 presenter Evan Davies challenged his use of figures – saying "that's the thing *FactCheck* can check".

Well, how could *FactCheck* resist? There were two issues here: how big is the deficit, compared to previous years, and how big is the national debt? After a day toiling with the figures, the *FactCheck* verdict came: "There are a lot of claims being flung around about the deficit – partly as the Labour Party and the unions try to get back on the front foot about the economy. But on this one Len McCluskey got it wrong. The deficit is the highest for nearly 70 years, and the national debt is the highest than for 50 years."

With all this scrutiny upon its members, it is no surprise that when MPs and Peers browse through their own House of Commons website, they will come to library page which suggests that when dealing with statistics, *FactCheck* is a good source for them to check out the figures. It may, with a bit of careful reading, save them from becoming the subject of a Fiction verdict in a future *FactCheck*!

## Holding politicians to account

Cathy Newman explains how the Channel 4 magnifying glass on policy claims is going down among the politicians and how the team have to maintain the highest journalistic standards to maintain its reputation.

She says: "*FactCheck* is about holding the politicians to account, and causing a bit of trouble. It's pretty widely-read in Westminster – and, in some quarters, feared! If a politician gets a *FactCheck* Fiction rating they never hear the last of it from their opponents. So I think my fellow *FactCheckers* and I are always conscious that the blog has to be really thorough and impartial, otherwise it would soon lose its clout."

If it forces a bit more honesty into that system and means that there will be fewer distortions and manipulations in future, then it will have served a valuable democratic purpose.

## Note on the author

Vicky Taylor is Commissioning Editor, New Media News and Current Affairs, at Channel 4. After joining Thomson Regional Newspapers as a graduate trainee from Edinburgh University, she worked for three years on the *Newcastle Journal* as a news reporter and feature writer. In 1986, she joined the BBC in the Current Affairs department as a researcher and over the next 20 years worked on most of the News and Current Affairs programmes; *Breakfast, Newsnight, On the Record,* the *Nine O'Clock News* and political programmes. For many years she was a programme editor of live political programmes at the BBC, which included the election, Budget and political TV and radio programming. In 2001, she joined the BBC News website as Editor, Interactivity, launching the User Generated Content hub and pioneering the audience participation strategy for BBC News. She joined Channel 4 in November 2008 and works on taking the television News and Current Affairs brands onto the web and digital platforms. This includes web content for *Dispatches* and *Unreported World* on channel4.com and a strategy for Channel 4 News to integrate the television and web journalism, and provide content for the Channel 4 News website and its other digital projects.

# Democracy Live: Shining a light on our democratic processes

**Pete Clifton**

The vision for Democracy Live was always very clear – a new, easy to use site that would open up our democratic institutions to the public. Giving them greater clarity on the work of their elected representatives, and more understanding of how the political process worked. And although we knew such a site would never attract the mass audiences of the BBC News and Sport online sites, it was hard to imagine any project fitting more squarely with the BBC's public purpose of shining a light on our democratic processes. Strip the BBC right down to its core, and you'd find Democracy Live.

The request for an innovative way to showcase our parliaments and assemblies came from the then-Deputy Director General and Head of Journalism, Mark Byford, at the start of 2008. It was short on specifics – that was my job, with the right people around me. Later in the month, the Director General, Mark Thompson, gave a speech in Westminster entitled "The trouble with trust". The wide-ranging speech looked at how the public's trust in broadcasters had been undermined by scandals including some flaky telephone-based competitions, and drew comparisons with the public's consistently low opinion of politicians.

The concluding section of his speech (still to be found on the BBC site http://www.bbc.co.uk/blogs/theeditors/2008/01/the_trouble_with_tru st.html) looked at what the BBC could do to "help begin a broader response to the challenge of trust". And one of his specific suggestions was to "transform the way we connect British democracy – and all its many democratic institutions – to the public". He went on:

> We've always known that a core BBC mission was, not just to report journalistically on Parliament and the wider democratic process, but to be the public gallery from which citizens could see and hear proceedings for themselves. And we've done that, year in and year out, across our services. Now we believe that the BBC has an amazing chance to bring this gallery to life, to make it real, to make it potentially relevant for every citizen and every secondary school child in this country.

> We want to take our coverage of Westminster, the Scottish Parliament, the Welsh Assembly, the Northern Ireland Assembly, the European Parliament, as well as local councils up and down the land and turn them into the most engaging, the most creative multi-media portal for democracy in the world, using BBC Parliament and our other television, networks, radio, the web and mobile. Direct access to information about your MP or representative: how they vote, what they stand for, how you can contact them. Survival guides and in-depth analysis of current debates and current legislation. Easy ways, for anyone who wants to, to plug into and take part in the debate. And all of it available to every secondary school in the UK as part of a strengthened commitment by BBC Learning to supporting citizenship and modern media literacy.

> We don't want to do all this on our own, but in partnership with some of the existing sites which are pioneering web democracy – and with the democratic institutions themselves. Parliament and its sister institutions already have powerful forms of scrutiny and accountability that, to be honest, very few people outside their walls know anything about. We want to work with them to change that.

So no pressure then.

## Making it exciting and innovative always a challenge

The hour upon hour of debate, often in sparsely populated chambers, can be pretty dry stuff. So making it exciting and innovating was going to be a challenge. Looking around bbc.co.uk, it wasn't as if there were no windows on our institutions – quite the reverse, in fact. Probably more windows than in your average stately home…

Profiles of MPs, numerous guides to institutions (some of them in Welsh, of course), glossary of terms (several of these), a BBC Parliament site, blogs here and there, and, if you searched hard enough, some examples of video streaming of some segments of the proceedings from our various parliaments and assemblies. But searching hard enough was the key point. You had to be Sherlock Holmes on a good day to find even a fraction of this stuff.

So that was a decent starting point. Address this sprawl of interesting but hard to find content by bringing it together in one place. We would then have a coherent home for our political guides, blogs, glossaries and the like, easily promotable from other parts of the BBC website to complement our politics coverage.

At this point, the idea was still firmly in the worthy but dull camp. I sat down and talked to Nic Newman, who in those days was the Controller of Journalism in Future Media and Technology. We had to be joined at the hip when it came to delivering new multi-media projects – if I was the Morecambe in the editorial camp, he was very much the Wise (in every sense) over at FM&T Towers.

## Video the missing ingredient

Video was the missing ingredient in this mix. Grainy, jumpy, buffering streams were a thing of the past, and bbc.co.uk was already offering pretty good access to video as part of its content mix. Placing video at the heart of Democracy Live (or "Digital Democracy" as it was known in those early days) was going to be the key to making this a genuinely distinctive, world class proposition. The window on our main institutions – the Commons, the Lords, Scottish Parliament, Welsh Assembly, Northern Ireland Assembly and European Parliament – would be a video window.

Between Nic and I, and we could probably still argue about who was holding the pencil, we sketched a very ambitious looking video wall on a piece of A4 containing numerous windows showing what we thought would be live proceedings from each of the institutions. Impressive, in a badly drawn kind of way, but with no proper idea of whether it was possible or not.

Getting things done at the BBC is not always a straightforward affair, and a few rain forests must have been felled down the years for all the business cases that are written, refined, critiqued, re-written, refined etc, as part of the approvals process. Democracy Live was no different, though it was clear that there was already some enthusiasm from the very top of the organisation for a project that could help underpin the BBC's commitment to its public purposes. Not least because the original idea had come from very close to the top in the first place....

But even so, we needed some momentum. By this time I had Vicky Taylor as the first editorial lead and a product manager, Matt Coulson, to help work out the detail. The people at the helm of a place like the BBC do not have much time to spare, there are far too many papers and presentations for them to wade through on their various boards, and sometimes it is more effective to plant a good idea in their heads by keeping it simple and just showing them something amazing.

I wanted to get a move on, and so Matt and I approached Tui, an interactive design agency in Soho, to help build a prototype. This involved a fair bit of head scratching and trips to wine bars, but within six weeks we had a working prototype on our hands. A front page with eight windows showing live video, and lots of complementary information and data.

It was all smoke and mirrors, of course. The videos playing in the windows were clips we had put together that were just going round in a continuous loop, and only a few links on the prototype that actually led anywhere. But that didn't matter, as long as we knew where to click when the heat was on.

**The prototype rules the day**
And it was certainly good enough for Journalism Board, which in those days was chaired by Mark Byford and oversaw all the workings and plans

of the Journalism Group. We probably took along a paper of some kind to outline what we were thinking, but the prototype ruled the day. Multiple videos running in the main window, leading to a much bigger video player for each institution, and a few carefully selected links to show how we could bring complementary information together under one banner.

The Journalism Board was dissolved in March 2011 as part of a BBC re-organisation of News. And, as far as I know, that Democracy Live demonstration was the only example in the board's history of a spontaneous round of applause from the very senior, often hard to impress board members. Job done. From that moment we had a dozen or more advocates at the top tables, and we had our momentum.

That would be a big lesson from the project. Exciting the right people, with a very clear, working demo of what we were going to do, was key. Drawing it out of the paperwork and making it real (relatively speaking). Of course, the danger of a slick demo was that it promoted a rampant expectation that a launch was imminent, but I'd take enthusiasm and wild optimism over blinding indifference any time. Then the hard work began. Who was going to deliver it, what could we deliver technically, what did the audience want and how would this fit alongside existing sites outside the BBC?

The audience research was certainly encouraging. We demonstrated the site to groups in Cardiff and Birmingham and, acknowledging that it would not appeal to everybody, we specifically chose either people who actively followed political news and opinion online or who were regular users of the BBC News site with some interest in politics. They were upbeat, though we were briefly sidetracked by a lady in Birmingham who said the thing she liked most about Democracy Live was "all the great entertainment stories". On closer inspection we discovered she had accidentally left the prototype and was busy reading the Entertainment section of the BBC News site.

Apart from that distraction, the core message was that the plan for the site was positively received, with three broad elements to its appeal. It was seen as:

- heightening the BBC's public service credentials, and something that the BBC should be doing;

- a valuable information resource, both for education in democratic processes and to be used on a professional level to track political decision-making;

- and a hugely detailed and rich source of coverage of political debate, including video coverage.

## Engaging with the political process

Looking around the web, there were good examples of engagement with the politics process. Plenty of well informed, highly readable blogs, for example, and sites that were already working hard to keep our elected representatives on the hook – such as www.theyworkforyou.com. But the video-rich proposition we now had in mind felt very distinctive, backed up by all the background information we already had, and there was no reason why our site could not work closely with existing services and link intelligently to them.

Making the most of the video content was vital to us. As the project developed this became the number one objective for an expanding team – launch editor Mark Coyle, chief technical architect John O'Donovan and his technical lead Phil Miller. It was one thing to be offering hours or debate from all the institutions and keeping it available for all time, but how on earth would a user avoiding drowning in this vast ocean of debate from all corners of the UK and beyond?

The answer was the most innovative element of the project, and – along with the prototype that got everybody excited – the key factor in the success of Democracy Live. We would run speech to text recognition software across all the debates we were streaming live, and when they were encoded for on demand consumption later, the text transcription would be sitting quietly behind them. And while we would not publish the transcript, if a user searched for a particular topic they would be searching across the transcripts. The search results would then lead them directly to a relevant piece of video and not only that, a point two seconds before the word searched for was spoken.

At a stroke, this functionality would open up hours of video so that even the most casual of political observers would be able to home in on their place, name or topic of interest. The audio transcription service powering Democracy Live would be built on the Autonomy Virage media processing suite, with an additional layer licensed from Blinkx to integrate with the BBC's own media publishing systems. Sounds quite techie, but this meant we would be offering – for the first time on bbc.co.uk – a way to search within video. Previously, a search for video could only be examining the headline or accompanying text on a piece of published video, not the content of the video itself.

### Content relevant and usable for the public

Here was the innovation the project craved, and here was the way to make the content genuinely relevant and usable for the public. The software had to be trained with hundreds of hours of audio to make sure it could understand various regional accents. It also had to be able to do it in Welsh, one of our key commitments in our coverage of the Welsh Assembly. And though we were told that had never been done before, and some doubted it was possible, after painstaking tuition the software also got the hang of that.

Getting all the pieces in place, building relationships with the institutions, putting a new technical infrastructure in place to support the site, was to be a complicated business. But in November 2009, Democracy Live was launched. Reaction was positive, and the site was soon near the top end of the "net promoter" chart, our regular survey of bbc.co.uk users that finds out if they would recommend a service to a friend. Among the comments from the survey:

> Overall I think this is a brilliant development in the BBC's coverage of our political institutions. Having all the different Parliaments/Assemblies in one place is a great idea.

> The fact that it exists at all!! Long overdue…A breath of fresh air!

> It is one of the best resources available and single-handedly justifies my licence fee. I work in democratic outreach and it is a fantastic site to direct people to and to use in my education sessions. Amazing work BBC!

> It is easy to use, everything is up to date, and I find coverage on it that I wouldn't find anywhere else, all this at no cost. I also like the in-depth coverage of the role and abilities of each parliament.

All very encouraging, but not exactly job done. Inevitably, some elements of the site were not ready for launch, so the following months would be devoted to refining and polishing the complicated workflows for an editorial team of 11 and keeping a close eye on our ground-breaking technology.

## Adding a layer of more local information

Looking ahead, there is more to do. The site will benefit from adding a layer of more local information, leading users to information about their councils and pushing them in the direction of video streams from councils if they are providing them on their sites. And we can expect closer integration with the main BBC News site. Democracy Live already relies heavily on the promotion it receives from the News site, and in the future that is bound to increase. More use of metadata will allow us to link from News content direct to relevant video and text on Democracy Live, and the Politics index of the main site will do far more to celebrate the extraordinary range of live and on-demand video we are making available.

We also need to do more to promote the game-changing search functionality. Our research suggests that too many users still do not realise how powerful the search facility is, so that means thinking about how we promote it more clearly on the site itself, and with imagination across the rest of bbc.co.uk.

Looking back, Democracy Live did a number of things that feel like good practice for the BBC – and lots of other sites, for that matter:

- We made sense of an extraordinary sprawl of politics information – bewildering and often unfindable for the audience – by bringing it together in one place. Easy to promote, and hopefully easy to engage with.

- The site made use of search technology to offer a genuinely innovative service that made a potentially overwhelming range of content relevant and accessible for its users.

- It did not try to do everything. The site includes scores of links to external blogs and other places to comment and engage with the institutions. Democracy Live is part of the picture, and confident enough about its role to promote the riches on the rest of the web.

- And from a BBC perspective, it also helped us develop technology that will help us elsewhere. It may always be a relatively small part of our bbc.co.uk service, but the work it did around the presentation of multiple video screens and search will doubtless prove invaluable elsewhere.

## Note on the author

Pete Clifton was the BBC's Head of Editorial Development for Multi-Media Journalism for three years up to March 2011. He began as a news reporter and cricket correspondent at the *Northampton Chronicle and Echo* in 1981 and also worked at the Exchange Telegraph sports news agency and the Press Association in Fleet Street. He is a former Editor of BBC Ceefax, and both the BBC News and Sport websites.

# Section 6. Maximising the money

**John Mair**

No media product exists without an audience to buy it and appreciate it. That's common and commercial sense. The digital survivors will be those who not only find and nurture large audiences (such as Mail Online, in the UK, or the Huffington Post, in the US) but also find ways of monetising that audience so that the digital journalism pays for itself – or even makes a profit.

The search engines, especially Google, determine the likelihood of being accessed for all. Malcolm Coles makes a living from advising publishers on search engine optimisation. Here he shows how to add "digital sparkle" to any website. Oliver Snoddy, the new media son of Raymond Snoddy and his personal digital guru, shows us how to brand in the new digital world.

# Writing the news that people are looking for

**Malcolm Coles**

Whatever your view on the big strategic questions about paywalls and online brands, there's no getting away from the fact that millions of people use the internet every day as their primary way to access news. As you can't move on the internet without someone tracking you, this means that there is a huge quantity of data available about what news stories people are looking at and looking for – often in real time.

As an individual journalist or site publisher you can use this data to optimise your stories for news searches. You can work out what news stories people are interested in and how they are searching the internet to find them. You can tailor your stories – what you write and how you write about it – to your desired audience. And this makes it more likely that people using the internet to find their news will read your story rather than a competitor's.

This chapter is going to explain the many free tools and methods you can use to do this. The URLs for the services talked about are listed at the end (or you can get them on my blog at www.malcolmcoles.co.uk/news-search-tools). But we are going to start with the story of Karen Gillan's underwear.

## The predictive power of Karen Gillan's underwear

This graph shows the number of visitors to the celebrity gossip site Holy Moly (www.holymoly.com) in the first 11 months of 2010 who had arrived having searched Google for the term "Karen Gillan underwear" (Karen being the current *Doctor Who* companion).

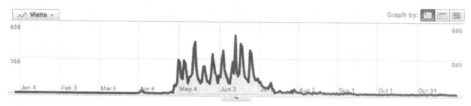

**Keywords**                                          Jan 1, 2010 - Nov 29, 2010

**Search sent 14,290 total visits via 61 keywords**
Filtered for keywords containing "karen gillan underwear"

It may not look like much. There's a little blip on 3 April – which turns out to be the date that the first 2010 episode of *Doctor Who* was transmitted and when people first started to search for Karen's underwear online. Holy Moly published a picture gallery of Karen Gillan at the end of April which included the word underwear – and promptly appeared at the top of the results in Google for a search on "Karen Gillan underwear". That's when the graph of visitor numbers took off. And you can see when *Doctor Who* finished on 26 June and interest tailed off.

The pattern between those dates is also interesting – each of those spikes is a Saturday and Sunday, The one spike that looks out of place is a Tuesday – this is when the programme was repeated. People watched that day because on the Saturday 12 June, England had been drawing with the USA in the World Cup. All this data reveals that British men on the internet are very predictable. When they are reminded she exists because *Doctor Who* is on at the weekend, they search for Karen Gillan in her underwear – unless the football is more interesting. When *Doctor Who* finishes, they forget all about her.

All of which meant that, predictably and depressingly, on Christmas Day 2010, the day of the *Doctor Who* Christmas special, visitors to the Holy Moly site using that search term went up 40-fold. These visitors each looked at six pages on the site on average as they flicked through pictures, taking 3 minutes and 16 seconds to linger over them. Nice. It's data similar to this – from your own site and other sites – that you can use to work out what people search for, when they search and how they search.

## Working out what people are interested in right now
There are a number of sources of information that will show you what people are currently searching for on the internet. With care, you can use these to work out what topics people are interested in – especially useful if you're a smaller publisher. Some of these are much better than others. Microsoft has fortunately shut down its Xrank site which thought the band Ash was enjoying an unexpected renaissance in 2010 when the Icelandic volcano erupted

Some of the main sites that work well in the UK are listed below, but there are all sorts of services devoted to monitoring real time interest in different ways. You can find a useful list, which is periodically updated, at www.adamsherk.com/seo/search-trend-tracking-tools/.

## Yahoo Buzz
Buzz is the Yahoo service where users submit and vote up interesting news sources. Yahoo has announced it is shutting it down. But while it's still going it's one of the better sources of accurate data on what topics people are searching for – though it has more of an entertainment than hard-news bias.

It's simple to see the data – there's a "top searches" box on the right hand side of most Buzz pages (but not the home page). This shows the 10 topics people are currently searching for (although Yahoo does not explain the time period it measures this over). The topics can be anything from a sportsman's name to a country (Egypt was in the top 10 during the January 2011 protests) to a financial term (VAT and income tax were both in the top 10 during January 2011) – and always seem to me to be a fairly accurate barometer of current news interests.

The best way to use it is to take the terms and type them into Google News, which does a better job than Buzz of showing you what the latest news is on a particular topic.

## Google Trends

Google Trends sounds good. It's not. The page is divided into Hot Topics (UK) and Hot Searches (USA). The UK list is based on news stories and mentions in Twitter and FriendFeed. However, it's often heavily polluted by American topics, especially American football. Hot Searches is based on real time search data but, obviously, is about America only. For a news or celebrity journalist, however, it can be good early guide to international or American news stories (although it's often influenced by American TV programmes and sport events). For everyone else, I would probably avoid it. It's not useful enough to be worth the effort of checking regularly.

## AOL Hot Searches

AOL Hot Searches are a similar concept to Yahoo Buzz – but the list is often very different to the topics that Yahoo suggests. The "Top searches" box in the top right hand side is more topic than personality-based, and so feels a bit newsier than Yahoo Buzz – but from my observations, it seems a little bit behind the times in terms of what's happening right now. But it's still a useful source of data. And further down the page are lists of top celebrity searches, top gadget searches and then, further down still, top TV, music and health queries. Again, the best advice with these is to type the names and topics into Google News to see what the current story is.

## Twitter trending topics

The news and questions that people tweet now is often what's searched for in a couple of hours' time. So by looking at trending topics on Twitter itself (and you can choose various countries and cities to narrow down this data) or services such as whatthetrend.com and trendistic.com you can see what's capturing people's interest.

On a day such as the one that the football transfer windows closes, trending footballers' names often reveal transfers that are about to happen before mainstream news sites do. The downside of this is that all sorts of rumours that are not true end up trending, of course...

187

## Surchur.com

Surchur describes itself as the dashboard to right now. It tries to aggregate signals from a variety of sources to give a league table of the current hot topics online. It has an American and entertainment slant but, despite that, often highlights interesting topics.

## Own analytics data

Most companies that run websites have some sort of analytics package installed – software which tells you how many people have visited your site, where they came from, what they typed into search engines to find your site, and even what they are looking for using the search box on your own site.

It's often a good idea to check this data for your own site first thing in the morning – as there are often valuable clues as to what people are looking for. Check for out-of-the-ordinary search terms – seeing what unusual phrases people are searching for (even if there are just a few visitors) can be a good guide to what new topics they are interested in.

## Other news sites

You can also make use of larger news sites' information. Many news sites show you what topics people are interested in on their site. The *Daily Telegraph*, for instance, lists "hot topics" under the main navigation on its home page. Many of the main section pages of the *Guardian* have a "hot topics" list along the bottom. BBC News has a section where you can see which stories are most popular by section – and hour by hour. Yahoo shows you which of their stories have been emailed the most and viewed the most. And NewsNow also has a list of hot topics.

## Working out how people search

One issue with many of the tools listed above is that they tend to deal in quite general topics. Most of them will tell you what subjects people are currently interested in – but they won't necessarily tell you the most popular phrases that people are typing into search engines around those topics.

It's important to find this out because of the way search engines work, especially news search services such as Google News. The key thing you need to know is that including the words that people search for in your headlines makes it much more likely that your stories will appear in the search results. For instance, if your headline had been "Wacko Jacko karks it", Google would not have shown your story to someone who typed "Michael Jackson dead" into its search box shortly after he died.

People often search like this – using a topic or person's name and then adding a more specific word or two (such as "dead" or "affair" or whatever) related to what they are interested in. It's those more specific words you want to find and include in your headlines. That way you have got more chance of your pages appearing in the results when people search.

So how do you find out that, for instance, people were more likely at the end of January 2011 to search for "Egypt protest" than "Egypt news", and for "Egyptian museum" than "Egyptian army"?

## Google AutoComplete

When you start typing words into Google, a box appears with suggested searches – showing what Google thinks you might be looking for based on popular previous searches and the letters you've typed so far. If you type "Kate Middleton is", then Google offers you "Kate Middleton is hot", "Kate Middleton is ugly" and "Kate Middleton is a commoner" as suggestions.

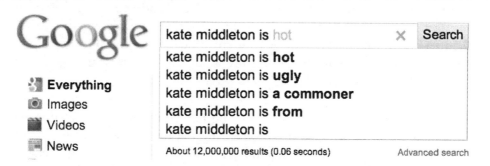

Putting famous people's names in followed by the word "is" is a good way to take the temperature of how well liked someone is. Try it with Prince Charles, Nick Clegg or Katie Price. When you start typing into the normal Google web search box, the suggestions Google gives are based on long-term data about what people are searching for. Do the same on a Google News page, however, and the suggestions are based on much shorter-term data – what people have been searching for in the last few days. Some experiments I did with unexpected events (such as celebrity deaths) show that the Google News suggestions will update within just a few hours for events that suddenly trigger huge numbers of searches.

You can use these suggestions to work out what words people are using to search for news stories. For instance, when Katie Price and Alex Reid were separating, if you typed "Katie Price A" into the Google News search box, it was the tabloid language of "Katie Price Alex Reid split" that Google showed as a suggestion – rather than separating or divorce.

This then becomes self reinforcing – when people start to type in a search term about Katie Price and Alex Reid, they will click on what Google suggests if it's close enough to what they had planned. So people who were planning to search for "Katie Price Alex Reid separation" end up searching for "Katie Price Alex Reid split". If you were writing about this, then to maximise the chances of your story being found in Google News and similar services, you should use the words people are searching for in your headline: in this case "split" rather than "separate".

It may seem a small thing – but choosing the right word and maximising your chances of being seen in Google News searches, can lead to 10s of thousands of extra readers. It just takes a few seconds work to do a check like this – I would recommend doing it every time you write a news story.

**Webmaster Tools**

If you have a Google Webmaster Tools account – which is free to set up – you can see data about which of your pages appeared in Google's results for which search phrases. The data is always a few days behind but if you are in the middle of a long-running story, it can be a good way to understand how people are searching. That is because the data shows you exactly how many people have searched for different phrases, even if a previous article of yours was on page three of Google's results and hardly anyone came to your site from it.

This data will show you search terms that you're neglecting to use – so look for relevant phrases with high search volumes and then use them in your headlines. Here's an example: this shows impressions for the Holy Moly site for search terms including "celeb" – an impression is when a page from Holy Moly appears in the results of someone searching. You can use data like this to decide that you might want to focus your writing on pregnant celebrities. Or that you need a new job.

| Query | Impressions |
| --- | --- |
| ☆ celebrity gossip | 60,500 |
| ☆ pregnant celebrities | 8,100 |
| ☆ celebrity penis | 6,600 |
| ☆ celebrity gossip uk | 1,600 |
| ☆ im a celebrity get me out of here 2010 | 1,600 |
| ☆ topless celebs | 1,300 |
| ☆ celebrity news | 880 |

## Experian Hitwise

The Experian Hitwise Data Centre is a good place to keep an eye on. It shows weekly updated figures on top search terms and sites in a few sectors, such as retail, travel and computing. The data is usually a week old but by monitoring it over time you will get a sense for how people search (as long as the subjects you're interested in are covered).

Similar to the Karan Gillan data earlier, it showed that one of the top 10 searches in the week that Kate Middleton announced her engagement was "Kate Middleton bikini".

## Google Adwords keywords tool

Google has a tool that shows you search volumes related to phrases you type in. There have been issues with the data it shows and, for most journalists, it's not a great tool to use, as it is not geared to news searches.

## Google Insight

Google Insight lets you look back at a defined period and compare search term popularity. You can check any time period from 2004 up until (almost) the present (you can't see data for the last few days – so you can't use it for real time). However, if you are writing about something that has happened before, you can type in some search terms and see how popular they were relative to each other last time an event happened.

So let's say you write about a reality TV show – by plugging in various combinations of likely search terms from last time the show was on you would probably discover that people tend to search for "show name + year" – they hardly ever search for "show name + series".

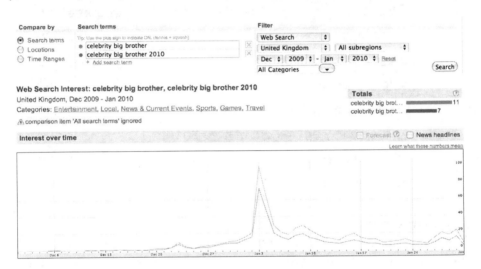

In the last couple of years, news organisations cottoned on to this and started to write their headlines as "show name year: the actual headline" (for example, "*I'm a Celebrity 2010*: contestants enter jungle"). This meant that until late 2010 (when television stations just about realised this) many news organisations would routinely appear higher in Google's results by doing this than the TV channels' own websites – which tended to talk about the series number rather than the year.

At the start of 2010, Holy Moly was the top Google result (above the Channel 4 site) when you searched for "*Celebrity Big Brother 2010*" and saw a huge increase in traffic as a result. Almost everyone has cottoned on to this particular trick now. But by mining the data like this, you can look for popular search terms that your competitors are not yet using and use them in your headlines. Google Insights also suggests top search terms related to those you put in, so it's another starting point for data about how people search.

And finally, you can use the data to see when people start searching – so if you are writing about a known event – the Budget, a TV show, a sports event – you can see how far in advance search-related interest started to build last time it was on. (You can see interest in *Celebrity Big Brother* started about two weeks before the show did from the earlier graph.)

## Promoting your content

At an individual journalist's level, optimising your content for search is about doing the two things I have discussed here: working out what people are searching for and working out how they are searching – and then writing about stories in a way that matches this.

Technical considerations can largely be left to those running the site (unless you are a small organisation when you should take an interest too). But there is one area where journalists, if they want to do well in search terms, need to concentrate: and that's social media. There are many attempts to "game" search results by people hoping to make a quick buck. And many of the quality signals that search engines have traditionally used – such as how many other websites link to a particular page – don't work for brand new news articles (as no one will have had a chance to link to them).

So search engines are increasingly turning to signals from social media – such as how many times a story is re-tweeted on Twitter or liked on Facebook – to help them decide which stories they should be showing more prominently in their news results. Exactly how the different search engines do this, and which ones do what, is still something of a mystery. But they definitely are doing it, and the use of social media signals is only likely to grow.

This means that, to promote your content in news search, you also need to promote it to humans via sites like Twitter, Facebook, Digg, Reddit and others. It will not be enough to use the right words to match how people search. The future of news search optimisation will be about getting real people to share your story so that the search engines can recognise that it's a valuable piece of content. The good news is that there's no tool that is going to make people want to do that – apart from good journalism.

## Data on search trends
uk.buzz.yahoo.com
google.co.uk/trends
http://hotsearch.aol.co.uk/
surchur.com
http://www.hitwise.com/uk/resources/data-centre

## Google tools
www.google.com/analytics
www.google.com/webmasters/tools/
http://www.google.com/insights/search/

## Other news sites' data
news.bbc.co.uk/1/shared/bsp/hi/live_stats/html/map.stm
http://uk.news.yahoo.com/popular/most-popular-most-mailed-all.html
http://www.newsnow.co.uk/h/Hot+Topics

## Note on the author
Malcolm Coles is a search-engine-optimisation and content-strategy consultant based in London. He has helped many large and small organisations with their digital content – one of which is Holy Moly, mentioned here. He blogs at www.malcolmcoles.co.uk and you can find him on Twitter as @malcolmcoles.

# The importance of real-time data to marketing and journalism

**Oliver Snoddy**

People often think that Hal Varian, Google's chief economist, is joking when he says that being a statistician will be the sexy job to have in the next ten years. He goes on to predict that "the ability to take data – to be able to understand it, to process it, to extract value from it, to visualise it, to communicate it – that's going to be a hugely important skill in the next decade".

Nowhere is this more relevant than in journalism, and mainstream news organisations have already taken note. From the *Guardian*'s Data Store, to excellent infographics and data visualisations from *The New York Times* and the BBC, "data journalism" is a hot topic. The Wikileaks saga may be the best current example of data journalism in action, but journalists are increasingly gaining access to a wide variety of large data sets, from governments, NGOs and whistleblowers alike. They are using this "new" data to create compelling visualisations about military casualties in Iraq and Afghanistan (such as in the BBC's reports on UK military deaths in

Afghanistan and Iraq), local incidents of swine flu (the *Guardian*'s swine flu data in the UK) and the unemployment rate according to demographics (*The New York Times*'s jobless rate for people like you), to name but a few.

New publishers such as Flowing Data and Visual Complexity are also developing this space. Journalists are both responding to, and helping to shape, an era of unprecedented data availability. We are, however, still at the very early stages of data journalism. Most data journalists would admit that they need to get better at telling compelling stories with data, rather than simply producing innovative and arresting visualisations that may or may not help their audiences understand a subject better. More fundamentally, the rise of "massive, passive" real-time data from almost 2 billion connected individuals around the world points to a new type of data journalism.

Journalists will increasingly gather and process data, in addition to making sense of data made available to them – investigative data journalism if you will. They will also need to be able to predict and represent the mood of the world at a variety of scales. In addition, they will need to leverage tactics for getting their stories distributed across the internet. Journalists will, thus, need to develop many skills. They will need to be entrepreneurial, multi-media storytellers, community builders, bloggers and curators. Some programming skills will also come in handy. Above all else, however, they will need two core capabilities: great editorial and storytelling skills – as they always have – and a new fluency in how real-time data can capture what is really happening in the world. Data journalism is going to be core to the future of journalism as a whole, and real-time data an increasingly important driving force.

## Considering marketing alongside journalism
I probably should have started by admitting that I don't know very much about journalism, not very much at all. As a director of New York ad agency Doremus, I do, however, have a keen interest in the future of marketing. While it may seem perverse to some to consider marketing and journalism alongside one another, I see technology driving them both in a similar direction and the necessary skills of each industry converging on one another. In the future, marketers will need to act more like journalists and vice-versa.

I hope to explain how technology is disrupting advertising and marketing, yet also creating significant new opportunities around "massive, passive" real-time data. Finally, I will make the case that these same ideas and tools are creating significant opportunities for journalism. Organisations such as the BBC, the *Guardian* and *The New York Times* may well be leveraging these tools as we speak. Mine can only be an outsider's view, looking in from the perspective of marketing. First up, how technology is disrupting marketing.

The internet, and technology in general, has had a big impact on marketing, but as the saying goes: "We 'ain't seen nothing yet." Websites, search engines, banner advertisements and more recently apps have caused marketing to restructure and demanded new skills and departments. The internet has brought with it new marketing skills, but hardly the overturning of the overall model. Compared to other industries – music, publishing, film – these impacts have been somewhat limited. The old model is not yet broken, but it is breaking.

## The key to Facebook's success
Facebook didn't invent real-world online profiles but it has been instrumental in driving a shift from an internet of imagined personas to one that directly reflects our real lives. This simple insight has been key to Facebook's success and central to the development of the internet over the past five years. Contrast the Facebook's, Twitter's and Foursquare's of today with the MySpace's and Second Life's of recent history. The internet is less and less a place to escape to – social networking only recently overtook porn as the key internet activity – and increasingly a very real part of our lives.

I remember being in a job interview aged 23 or 24 and being asked what my favourite website was. As an aspiring digital marketer, this should have been a simple enough question. I used more websites than most back then, but most performed a particular function. Few held the integral place Twitter or Facebook currently do. I made a hash of the question, much to my embarrassment, but that moment stuck with me and left me wondering what the internet really was.

The internet is no longer simply a place we go, or something we use, but a massive real-time connection of people and things, a "digital shadow" on reality if you will. And privacy concerns aside, this development path shows no sign of abating. We are sharing more and more information about ourselves and our experiences. At last count, Facebook delivers 60 million status updates each day, roughly one for every eight of its 500 million members. Add to that the more in-depth blog posts, and the quasi-active data sharing from applications such as Nike+, wifi-enabled scales and Google's PowerMeter data explosion.

CES 2011 was awash with connected devices from GE, LG and Samsung. A tweeting fridge anyone? 2011 will likely see the first persistent-location mobile apps, tracking our location continuously rather than prompting us to "check in" to specific locations. All of these actions are generating an exponential rise in the amount of data sharing and the existence of "massive, passive" data sets: data created from everyday, low involvement actions. Although some way off, we are converging on a situation where our every waking hour is captured and analysed, and we all become sensors in a hugely developed internet.

### Never has the internet seemed so relevant to so many
But only social media hipsters in East London share this much information, right? Wrong. It's surprising how quickly people get engaged when it's about their real lives. We are programmed to engage in these ways, and the technological barrier is falling. Only two years ago my dad thought I was crazy. Now he is connecting with long-lost colleagues on LinkedIn and tweeting about the media, Covent Garden and QPR, and telling other people to do the same. Never has the internet seemed so relevant to so many.

Social media marketing can be traced back to the origins of Web 2.0 in 2004. Marketers were quick to see the potential of social media: self-organising brand advocates; viral video hits etc. There were also high profile brand casualties, most notably Kryptonite's bike lock that was unlocked with a biro and became an internet sensation. Despite these opportunities and risks, most brands carried on largely as before, while dipping their toes in the social media water. It was additive, still often used as a broadcast channel, but by no means a new model for marketing.

There is a simple reason that most brands got away with the status quo and why now really is an inflection point: the connection between our offline and online lives was not yet strong enough. Most of our lives occurred offline and few people cast a big enough "digital shadow". The more people share, however, the more marketing is going to have to change, and the more journalism will also have to adapt to this new order. People will clearly argue this point, and also the demographic and regional variation in data sharing, but given that by 2020 the mobile phone will be the primary global internet connection device, smart marketers are investing in tools and new techniques now.

The future of marketing is in monitoring and analysing "massive, passive" real-time data – i.e. listening to what the masses are saying and sharing. This form of market research has never before been possible. It has already impacted on journalism more than marketing – citizen journalism – but has significant potential for all of the media. Increased data is enabling us to construct detailed network maps – topologies – of people in relation to brands and industries, and hence understand how ideas, perceptions and behaviours spread.

If marketing in the past was about broadcasting to individuals and looking for signs that brand ideas were taking hold, it is fast becoming about understanding the multitude of networks a brand is part of, and prioritising and targeting key individuals within these networks. Using network science to map networks of influence is helping us answer pertinent marketing questions. As marketing is concerned with the spread of brand perception and behaviour, this has relevance for the spread of ideas in general, and thus journalism.

Network science may be about to revolutionise marketing, but what has this got to do with journalism? Many would see journalism as the antithesis of marketing: the reporting on real events vs the creation of ideas to change real world events. If this ever was the case (doubtful), the rise of a more personally relevant, social internet will force marketing to change. It will simply be too difficult, and costly, to spread ideas that are not true or not relevant. Marketers will focus more on the reality of their products and services, and getting these experiences to be more contagious. As such, they will be investigating a multitude of brand experiences and aggregating and promoting them. In short, they will become brand journalists.

So what can we learn about the future of journalism and the new tools that will be required? Journalism has already been severely disrupted by the internet. The business model has been undermined, with a whole host of knock-on effects on media businesses and journalists alike. Citizen journalism has also forced journalists to justify their very existence. At the same time, micro-blogging platforms such as Twitter have been both a useful tool, and a competitor in breaking news coverage. However, the same growth in "massive, passive" data can plot a path ahead for journalism. Information is all good and well, but journalism is and always has been about perspective. "Massive, passive" real-time data is helping to answer a number of key questions for both marketing and journalism.

### What is really happening in the world?

There is a subtle but important difference between what people say when prompted and what they say independently. Marketing focus groups and reporters both experience this difference. Most brands are already monitoring what people are saying about them online. Tools such as Radian 6 and Brandwatch trawl the web for mentions of brand-specific keywords and estimate the combined sentiment of these posts – are they positive, negative or neutral? The ability to monitor buzz and sentiment in real-time is a big step forward in understanding what people really think about brands and how this changes over time. These tools are still limited in a number of ways, though, and require further development.

The biggest challenge is not in measuring these comments but in understanding what they actually mean. Grouping sentiment as positive or negative is a start, but natural language is still very difficult to interpret and clearly not as binary as "good" or "bad". For example, current tools struggle with comments such as "I love how terrible this product is". Secondly, all comments are not born equal. It is not always possible, nor necessarily desirable, to respond to every brand comment. How then to evaluate and prioritise? More about this later.

Just as real-time data can give brands insights into the mood of their customers and how best to engage them, so too can buzz monitoring tools giving journalists greater insights into the world around them. This is relevant to both breaking news stories and longer-term thought pieces.

At the short-term end of the scale, these tools are useful for quickly analysing and expressing trends that might otherwise be hard to understand. How quickly is an event unfolding, how is the mood of a nation shifting? At the other end of the spectrum, real-time data analysis provides a very real advantage in gaining deep insights and unearthing important trends. Citizen journalists may be able to break stories, but it is the journalist who can add perspective and evaluate what is really going on and tell stories of change.

www.wefeelfine.org is an early research project from Stanford University which records and maps people expressing their mood across the globe. Bubbles pop up as people express happiness, loneliness, fear and so on. While this is a beautiful and interesting data visualisation, it isn't a giant leap to see how similar analysis can better understand the mood of a nation six months after a general election, or how people's happiness is adversely affected by a terrorist attack, for example. Put simply, "massive, passive" data analysis can tell us what people really think and feel in real-time, which is highly valuable to a journalist and far harder for a citizen journalist to copy. Access to and mastery of real-time data is going to be a clear source of competitive advantage in journalism, as it is in marketing.

## An early warning system for ideas and news
Uncertainty creates risk in marketing and journalism. As already discussed, Kryptonite were taken by complete surprise when the video of their lock being picked with a biro suddenly went mainstream. Similarly, news services are increasingly surprised when stories "break" on Twitter first. I remember flicking between the BBC and Twitter, on the rumour of Michael Jackson's untimely death in June 2009. The BBC were quickly aware of the rumour, but did not know what to do without formal confirmation of Jackson's death. Buzz monitoring tools can highlight trends and mitigate against risk, but given the speed at which ideas, and particularly news, spread across the internet, it is still a huge challenge to respond quickly enough. What is needed is some form of early warning system, whether the advantage is minutes, hours or days.

Brand perception spreads through networks in an asymmetric fashion. Some people are key to spreading the idea, others are key "carriers" due to their location at the centre of influence networks. It may be hard to predict the key influencers for a given event, but the key carriers at the centre of a network can be monitored – sensors at the heart of the network. As ideas spread, this can give an early warning of an event. In healthcare, government departments are investigating how such an approach might give days or weeks of warning of an outbreak of H1N1 flu. This is like a more advanced version of looking at Google search tends, as it can help predict a spread of infection even before large numbers start searching for information. A similar approach can be applied to brand reputations, by using key individuals as "listening posts" within online networks. This kind of network would have benefited Kryptonite and also given them an existing network to push their response back out to.

The model also works well for breaking news. In the Michael Jackson case, perhaps an online monitoring network could have gained the BBC a few extra minutes and also signalled the likelihood that the story was correct, based on which individuals were confirming it. If nothing else, they would have been able to give a more detailed update on where the information was coming from and the chances of it being correct – like a real-time weather forecast perhaps. Just like early warning systems for tsunamis, smart news services are investing in network technologies that help predict events and their likely accuracy and momentum.

Beyond breaking news, the same models can help predict longer-term trends. From the popularity of political parties to the likely success of the Android mobile operating system, analysing key individuals at the heart of a network topology can give warning of the likely trajectory of events. This is again a source of competitive advantage for news organisations, which can increasingly report the news, but also the likelihood of future events.

This also has implications for the individual journalist. Being at the centre of a network topology is the virtual equivalent of being on the ground, the first to be in the know and an important propagator of information. Your own reputation is crucial, as is blogging and Tweeting your way to the centre of these networks. While low cost tools for accurately mapping personal networks do not yet exist, they will very shortly. Utilising these to maximise your online position and influence will be a key new skill of the data journalist.

### The world is not flat: whom to target for distribution?
A central marketing question is whom to target and why, both to promote positive stories and dispel negative ones. In an age of entrepreneurial journalism, knowing whom to target also becomes key. Both industries are, therefore, concerned with getting their stories distributed, at the lowest cost and effort. The rise of social media is

affecting how we make these decisions but also affording us powerful new insights into value and influence metrics.

Smart brands are increasingly focusing their efforts on the customers they already have, rather than simply advertising to acquire new ones. Online businesses tend to have a decent model for the lifetime value of their customers. Even in the offline world, store cards and apps such as Foursquare are beginning to fill in the blanks. This is a huge trend in marketing. Tools such as Flowtown enable brands to profile the email addresses of their customers and prospects to determine their social media presence and thus gain a handle on the value of people active in social channels. Knowing the business value of anyone who comes into contact with a brand is a key step towards prioritising and optimising communications through social channels. In a recent KLM initiative, brand ambassadors responded to people checking in to Foursquare at airports, found them in person and delivered a gift. This may simply be a nice and unscalable example of social CRM, but evaluating the potential value of brand interactions is an important trend in marketing.

What a person thinks about a brand is just as crucial. An individual who loves the brand but does not spend much and has little online influence is great, but arguably less important than a high value customer shouting about terrible customer service. We already have many of the tools for measuring advocacy levels, from buzz monitoring tools to simple measures from Facebook and Twitter. Similarly, understanding advocacy is important to journalistic distribution. An individual's level of advocacy is a key determinant of whether they will share your stories, and in a positive or negative light. Journalists can just as easily profile their email contacts for social networking activity and also separate advocates from detractors.

As noted before, networks come in all shapes and sizes – topologies. To understand the relative importance of a person in spreading ideas, simple measures such as Twitter followers and Facebook friends is not sufficient. We need to be able to map the whole structure of the network and pinpoint those at the centre, those with greatest influence.

**Measures of influence**
And so we come to one of the hottest and most controversial topics in marketing today: measures of influence. As the theory goes, increased

data about people and networks enables us to generate influence scores, as companies such as Peerindex and Klout have pioneered. As far as anyone can tell – they do not share their methodologies – these rather linear measures of influence do not map network topologies and are, thus, at best a measure of popularity. They miss one crucial element – relativity.

Justin Bieber is clearly influential to teenie boppers, and potentially more influential to this audience than Barack Obama. He is, however, clearly not more influential than Barack Obama *per se*, as Peerindex ranking would have you believe. By mapping specific networks of influence – e.g. tech bloggers – it is possible to more accurately measure relative influence. New social media research firms such as Dollywagon are pioneering this approach by mapping entire network topologies and the relative importance of every agent in the network. Such techniques are enabling us to understand trends in networks, key influencers and sentiment like never before.

Tools such as these will shift from offering custom research to models where individuals can map their own networks of influence. Companies such as DeskPro are working on universal customer support platforms which factor in elements such as influence. These emerging tools will be important for journalists keen to boost their own influence, and understand which of their contacts are key to the distribution of their stories. Whether you are a news service or lone journalist, getting your message to propagate is key. Having a television channel or column helps, but is not the only way. As with marketing, being able to highlight key individuals to target is crucial: people who are influential in particular networks; positive to your cause and central to networks. Similarly, established news channels can also leverage network models to extend their reach and influence online.

The rise of "massive, passive," real-time data as more people connect to the internet more often is a key result of technological development. It has begun to disrupt all the media, and is set to be a key driving force behind the development of marketing and journalism. Both industries are being challenged to gather, process, analyse, visualise and communicate complex data more efficiently. In marketing, one of the things we are researching at Doremus is the ability to understand the lifetime value of an individual by combining his/her business value, brand advocacy, network centrality and influence. Similarly, journalists of tomorrow will be increasingly interested in learning from real-time data.

This real-time data journalism will help news organisations predict breaking news events, tell more compelling stories about what people are thinking and feeling, and provide powerful new tools to understand how to get stories to propagate on the internet. While citizen journalism has wreaked havoc on news coverage, it is journalists and news companies who will be best placed to leverage these new tools and opportunities, and thus create competitive advantage. These tools will help journalists compete in a massively connected world, and tell stories with a perspective that citizen journalists will struggle to match.

**Note on the author**
Oliver Snoddy is the director, Digital Services, Doremus, of New York. See www.oliversnoddy.com; olisnoddy@gmail.com

# Section 7. Radical possibilities: Internet emerges as important site for media activists

**Richard Lance Keeble**

The internet is a site of enormous possibilities – both for states to extend their powers of surveillance and control over their citizens, for individuals (in certain societies) to extend their means of self expression and for radical political movements to bypass the constraints of the mainstream, corporate media and to communicate directly with their audiences.

There is not just one (dominant) public sphere – but many competing spheres. And the internet has certainly given an enormous boost to the alternative public sphere and its media both in the UK and globally. These are media committed, for instance, to confronting militarism, sexism, racism and those political and economic structures that are leading to environmental degradation.

Wikileaks has achieved worldwide fame for its unprecedented leaks of confidential, formerly secret data relating to international diplomacy and the conduct of states in the "war on terror". But there are many other sites across the globe promoting alternative forms of news and investigative journalism – and radical political debate and action.

For instance, in the United States, www.tomdispatch.com, edited by the celebrated historian Tom Engelhardt, offers extraordinarily detailed and authoritative investigations and analyses of American domestic and foreign policy. Significantly, many of Wikileaks "revelations" about the existence of assassination squads in Afghanistan, the massive expansion of US military bases in the country, the increasing use of drones in the "war on terror" had all previously been covered in tomdispatch.com.

Alternative, independent war correspondents such as Dahr Jamail also use the web to report on conflicts more from the perspectives of the local citizens and communities suffering under occupation than those of the military and political elites. Internationally Indymedia sites have been developed by radical, anti-war media activists. In addition, the sites of human rights organisations such as Amnesty International, Human Rights Watch, Liberty, Privacy International, Article 19, Reprieve and the Montreal-based Centre for Research and Globalisation, provide vast amounts of news and comment that feeds into the work of radical campaigners.

### "Democratising opportunities of internet mew media"

Here we focus on just a few – but significant – examples of radical internet activity. Firstly, I interview Marc Wadsworth, editor of a citizen journalism website, www.the-latest.com. Wadsworth has enormous experience as a reporter in the mainstream – such as with the *Guardian*, *Observer* and *Thames News*. But over the years he became disillusioned with the mainstream (particularly over its collusion in human rights abuses such as the jailing of the Guildford Four and over media racism "by commission or omission"). So rather than just whinge, he decided to be proactive and "take advantage of the democratising opportunities of internet new media".

His site is now able to tackle stories the mainstream ignores. For instance, one scoop led to the firing of the Mayor of London's chief political advisor and spin doctor James McGrath. *Press Gazette*, the trade journal and website of the British newspaper industry, headlined an article about McGrathgate: "Citizen journalism takes first UK scalp." After the 1 April

2009 G20 London protests The-Latest was the first news media outlet to question violent police tactics which resulted in several protestors being injured. It has also exposed a leading fascist party member writing a column for a national British newspaper (the *Daily Telegraph*), exposed mismanagement and corruption in the health service and art world and supported community groups to get their news published.

In addition, the site has formed the Citizen Journalism Educational Trust (CJET) to help train and resource people who would like to become journalists, producing educational material and offering specialist training for disadvantaged young adults in hard-to-reach communities.

## Exposing the bias of the corporate media system

Next Florian Zollmann interviews David Edwards and David Cromwell, of the radical media monitoring website, Media Lens. For ten years, the site has directed its critical gaze at Fleet Street and the broadcasting companies – particularly over their coverage of the "war on terror". Inspired by the theories of American intellectual mavericks Edward S. Herman and Noam Chomsky, they say their primary aim is to expose the "constant systematic bias of a corporate media system reporting on a world dominated by corporations". One of their methods is to engage in correspondence directly with the journalists involved. While they are always careful to remain courteous, the responses of journalists can be mixed: sometimes respectful; at other times downright rude.

Most of mainstream monitoring of the media certainly lacks a real critical edge – amounting very often to a form of insider gossiping – with little space given to alternative, radical voices. While such reporting persists, Media Lens operates as an important corrective to mainstream mystifications, propaganda and misinformation.

Finally in this section, Joss Winn takes an original, Marxist approach to Wikileaks arguing that while Wikileaks may be synonymous with freedom, like all aspects of social life, it is "*really subsumed* by the logic of property and capitalist work" as each of us remains (quoting Marx) "a living appendage of the machine".

# How The-Latest.Com is promoting citizen journalism for all – and uncovering the news

**Website Editor Marc Wadsworth in discussion with
Richard Lance Keeble**

**Tell us a bit about your background in journalism**
My stepfather, a working class man, from Salford, Greater Manchester, was a compositor for Associated Newspapers – the *Daily Mail* and *Evening News* group. He said I should become a printer like him. I became a journalist instead. My first paper was the *Surrey Daily Advertiser*. Contemporaries included current *Guardian* Editor Alan Rusbridger and Robin Elias, managing editor of ITV News. I went to school with sometime journalist and Gordon Brown's fabled spin-doctor Charlie Whelan.

My baptism of fire was the Guildford bombings of 1974. Just 19, I was the first reporter on the scene. I witnessed carnage. I remember remonstrating with my editor because alleged Irish Republican Army bomber Gerry Conlon appeared in court beaten up. Conlon's solicitor said police had attacked him. My editor said: "Police say they've got the bombers so there's no public sympathy for them." I felt so powerless as a cub reporter. Years later it was found that the "Guildford Four" (the jailed "bombers") had been framed by the police and were innocent. I joined the rival *Surrey Herald* and produced the newspaper's West Byfleet and Pyrford edition. I applied to do "shifts" at the *Evening Standard* and in 1978 news editor Stephen Clackson accepted me.

I worked freelance for the *Standard, Daily Mail, Daily Mirror* and *Guardian*. An avid socialite, I also supplied tit bits to Fleet Street gossip columnists. In 1982, I did a full-page investigative report "Race and jobs. Who comes off best?" for the *Daily Mirror* with reporter John Merritt, Alastair Campbell's best friend.

I spent three months in Memphis, Tennessee, freelancing as a foreign correspondent, getting pieces published in the *Guardian* and *Observer*, before returning to London, for a job as a "copy taster" on BBC *Newsnight* during the 1982 Falklands War. Later I became a reporter/presenter on BBC Radio London's pioneering *Black Londoner's* show. We produced peerless reportage of America's invasion of Grenada in 1983, but big media did not pick up the exclusive eyewitness accounts and our interviews with the key Grenadian political players.

I applied to Thames Television's *Thames News* regional programme and eventually became a reporter/presenter. During my ten years there, I got hate mail from white, racist viewers who told me they did not think a Black man should have my job. I was elected leader of the trade unions. I helped defend Thames journalists who dared to make a documentary, *Death on the Rock*, in 1988 questioning Margaret Thatcher sending Special Air Service troops to kill unarmed IRA members in Gibraltar. Thatcher unleashed a right-wing news media vendetta against Thames TV, with *The Sunday Times* being used as the main attack dog. In 1992, Thames TV failed to retain its London weekday franchise and the staff lost their jobs.

I have been freelance ever since. Backed by the NUJ, I fought the BBC when a "Deep Throat" producer friend of mine alerted me to an internal message circulated about me to staff on BBC World's press review programme, on which I used to appear, telling them: "Do not use." I was the leader of the Anti-Racist Alliance at the time and helped Doreen and Neville Lawrence set up the Justice for Stephen Lawrence campaign after their 18-year-old son was murdered by racists. I introduced Doreen and

Neville to Nelson Mandela and in so doing was able to lift the campaign to national and international prominence. That made my ostracism worthwhile.

**Why did you decide to set up The-Latest.Com?**
As you can see from my journalistic background, my eyes were opened early in my career to the injustices in the British news media at a local and national level. These injustices included journalistic collusion in human rights abuses such as the jailing of the Guildford Four (subsequently, the Birmingham Three and Tottenham Three, M25 Three etc as well) and – personal to me – media racism by commission and omission in print and broadcasting in terms of biased reporting and the under-representation of African Caribbean and Asian journalists. BBC Director General Greg Dyke may have criticised his own corporation for being "hideously white" in 2001 but little has changed as a quick glance at the newsrooms of today reveals.

Rather than whinge about the problem, I decided in 2006 to be proactive and take advantage of the democratising opportunities of internet new media to do something about it. My webmaster whizz friend Leonard McLaughlin encouraged me to register www.the-latest.com as a domain name. You know, "read all about it" the latest news – that was the theme. He said: "It's brilliant for its simplicity. Why didn't you, or someone else, think of it before? The thing about the internet is that it is news and content-hungry. If you can provide free news and other interesting content not available anywhere else on the net, this will be a big success." American Craig Newmark, of mega-successful website Craigslist, calls what we are doing "network journalism", the next stage after the social networking of Facebook, MySpace and Twitter – young people's conversations turning into news dissemination.

We owe so much to citizen journalism exposing truths about stories that big media pursued with a line driven by what the authorities want the public to believe. The "official" version of events peddled by the police about the death of innocent bystander Ian Tomlinson at the April 2009 G20 London protest attest to this. Before mobile phone footage recorded by a member of the public came to light, the police were able to get away with saying that protesters had prevented them from giving Tomlinson life-saving first aid. In reality, Tomlinson had been struck by a police baton and this contributed to his death. Big media had at first accepted the police version of events.

In the US, the frenzied beating by Los Angeles police of Black motorist Rodney King, in 1991, was also caught on camera and beamed around the world on news bulletins. 9/11; the Asian tsunami of 2004: 7/7; police brutality on the UK student protests of 2010. Mobile phone, digital camera and camcorder-armed members of the public have been empowered to make their own record of news, undistorted by billionaire media owners such as Silvio Berlusconi and Rupert Murdoch. Of course, big media has fought back by attempting to co-opt citizen journalism with their "Comment is Free" – yes, the *Guardian* doesn't want to pay for it – and appeals from user generated content units at print and broadcast media for news from the public. Big media will grab news content from the public (for free when, unlike us, they can afford to pay) but not cede editorial control.

## What initially were its special features?

The-Latest.Com was founded in January 2006 as Britain's first dedicated citizen journalism website, uniquely providing an alternative, open and mass participatory platform for members of the public to showcase their views, opinions, news and images. Through a series of website migrations since its inception, The-Latest has improved on its look and functionality so that technical features offered in its initial stages of development have been greatly enhanced to a beyond Web 2.0 standard.

The-Latest offers exciting opportunities to blog, be involved in video streaming and podcasts. The website has constantly updated scrolling national and international news, including Community Newswire content from charities and the voluntary sector. It features instant polls on topical subjects open to all of its visitors. Our wide-ranging text and image content provided by professional journalists and others who are member contributors, includes entertainment, music, world, general and community news, interviews, did you know?, funny and "Things to make you go ooh!" categories.

In addition, there are helpful events listings, as well as book and entertainment reviews. Details of events can be sent to The-Latest for inclusion on the site. You can upload music and other audio like podcasts. Members can take part in forum discussions and comment on stories. An "Image galleries" section is available where members can upload interesting pictures or even showcase photos in their own personalised gallery. Novice members are supported by professional journalists, who edit the content and provide portfolio-standard published material for contributors, many of whom have never before had this sort of creative opportunity.

Our members have gone on to work for a variety of news media organisations as a result of the skills that they have gained on the site. We would like to pay contributors for their work in the future. Either benefactors – Wikipedia-style – would help us do this, or we could sell on content to other media outlets.

### What financial hurdles did you have to leap at the start?

The financial responsibilities of operating a fully functional website such as The-Latest relate to overheads and remain the same today as they were at the beginning of our social enterprise project. The running costs include the retention of domain names, the dedicated hosting of the website and site overhauls, redesigns and migrations. These are met from the limited funds of The-Latest Ltd's two volunteer directors. We were greatly helped at the start of our project by the commitment of our Webmaster who dedicated his time and expertise for free along with me as Editor and the Deputy Editor, Deborah Hobson. We had to find a wealthy, progressive Black benefactor to pay thousands of pounds for the site's long over-due redesign. Had we not redesigned, the site would have fallen pitifully behind our competitors.

### How many staff did you begin with?

The-Latest.Com functions on a not-for-profit voluntary basis and therefore we don't have staff. We initially began with three workers who were Editor, Contributors' Editor and Webmaster. The present organisational structure for The-Latest consists of Editor, Deputy Editor, Webmaster and Picture Editor. These roles are complemented by the work of our volunteer Featured Contributors and the submissions of our wider membership.

### What criteria did you apply in recruiting them?

The editorial team and webmaster were recruited on the basis of their talent, expertise and skills as well as their enthusiasm for the concept of citizen journalism and their willingness to help grow the first citizen journalism news portal in the UK.

## Can you describe the development of the site over the years?

As part of the diverse opportunities that now exist for user participation and interaction on our citizen journalism website we offer a multimedia section which encourages members to upload videos, podcasts and music files of interest to the website which was not available in the early stages of the site's development. Video, on platforms including YouTube, is the fastest growing content on the internet. Unfortunately, we do not currently have a documentary making or short film capability that we would like largely due to the limited resources available to us for such endeavours. But we are working on remedying this in the future. We do have a prominent "Video box" space on the home page where footage of less than 10 minutes can be featured and this has been used to dramatic effect on several occasions.

We have enjoyed continued and steady growth in our membership that has enabled us to cover the full spectrum of citizen journalism. We give our members a genuine opportunity to set the news agenda by publishing their stories, blogs, comments, images and video. Our best content comes from the submissions of our citizen journalists. The same could not be said of big media.

## How have the number of hits grown over these years?

The numbers of people visiting The-Latest.Com each day, particularly from abroad (most hits are from North America!), have grown over the years. Any further discussion about this would veer into the arena of what we would regard as "commercially sensitive" information. However, I can say that the team at The-Latest are greatly encouraged and heartened by the progress made with the website in this regard although there is always room for improvement. A measure of the website's success can be gauged from Googling simply: "The-Latest" or "The Latest.Com" and seeing that the website is top of the list in the search results. Also, you can check the site's Alexa rating. News executives and other journalists bookmark the site and regularly browse it and use the website's stories. Look at the wonderful Testimonials to The-Latest from a range of news media and non-journalistic voices.

## How would you define as your typical reader?

The core of our membership consists of people in the age group of 18-25 who are university undergraduates or postgraduates, college students or those people interested in alternative media, the environment, anti-globalisation, internationalism, politics, human rights, anti-racism, anti-imperialism, peace, gender and sexual liberation, without being hung up on political correctness. We then have a diverse membership of mature professionals and others based in the UK, elsewhere in Europe, and abroad in places such as the US, India, other parts of Asia, and Africa.

## How would you define your typical contributor?

Regular submissions are received from our Featured Contributors, a number of whom are young people who have studied journalism and are now working in that field, like our correspondent in India. We also receive work from those who enjoy writing as a hobby and others who are "single issue" contributors.

## How much of the copy is provided by your staff and how much by citizen journalists?

At the very beginning of our project the Deputy Editor and I contributed significantly to the content published on The-Latest. However, as the site developed and the membership increased and became more active, the majority of articles, blogs and other content published are provided by our citizen reporters. We also, like the Seoul-based citizen journalism site OhMy News!, aggregate news from around the web. OhMyNews!, the most internationally famous citizen journalism website, has set up a network of international "curators" of news to provide guaranteed free content for its site – and this could be the most feasible way of sites like ours surviving.

## What do you regard as your major scoops? How did you manage to secure these ahead of your competitors in the mainstream media?

We have pulled off notable scoops, including the one that led to the firing of the Mayor of London's chief political advisor and spin doctor James McGrath that went global. *Press Gazette*, the trade journal and website of the British newspaper industry, headlined an article about McGrathgate: "Citizen journalism takes first UK scalp."

We scored well with our coverage of the 1 April 2009 G20 London protests. This resulted in the site getting text and photography from five writers and seven contributors taking photographs, a bigger news-gathering team than any other news media organisation. Deputy Editor Deborah Hobson was "kettled" by riot police who imprisoned demonstrators in a square near the Bank of England for eight hours. The-Latest was the first news media outlet to question violent police tactics which resulted in several protestors being injured. We also challenged their claim not to have attacked bystander Ian Tomlinson who died after being attacked by a policeman. Big media accepted the police version of events until a member of the public produced video evidence of an assault on Ian Tomlinson. We had exclusive, insightful coverage of the UK 2010 student protest which did not follow the national news agenda that took the police line in blaming demonstrators for violence. We have also:

- exposed a leading fascist party member writing a column for a national British newspaper (the *Daily Telegraph*): he was subsequently dropped;
- backed the families of murdered tourists Scarlett Keeling and Stephen Bennett in their fight for justice;
- exposed mismanagement and corruption in the health service and art world;
- uncovered city hall cronyism and sleaze;
- carried eyewitness reports and blogs from around the world;
- campaigned against a Jamaica-based cyberstalker hounding a British couple;
- supported community groups to get their news published.

## Do you regard yourself as being in competition with the mainstream or do you confidently follow your own agenda?

Citizen journalism sites such as The-Latest have been viewed as a threat by the mainstream media for some time. Broadcasters such as Sky and the BBC have reacted to the challenge of citizen journalism by incorporating elements of public participation, which they call "user generated content", in their set-up. However, this has largely focused on the submissions by the public for free of images and video exemplified by the content they used of the 7/7 London bombings of 2005.

Most of the major newspapers now have an online arm and Guardian.co.uk, in particular, has invested heavily in its blog section Comment is Free. Prophetic *Guardian* editor Alan Rusbridger describes print journalism as a "dead wood" industry and sees the challenge to traditional media coming primarily from the written word of citizen journalism and not just the "witness contributor"-originated images.

The-Latest is determined to break establishment orthodoxies by being journalism fuelled by opinion, wit, humour, compassion and commitment. We want stories that are off-diary and, more essentially, off the beaten track with non-mainstream news angles. We want to be the natural outlet for whistle-blowers and Deep Throats. Our contributors ensure that we most definitely have our own, alternative agenda of "news uncovered".

### How do you define "alternative" media?

Large sections of the public feel disillusioned with big media "churnalism" – a journalism based on the recycling of corporate and government press releases and news agency copy. This dissatisfaction has been followed by a thirst for a credible alternative which is being provided by citizen journalism in the relatively free, open and democratic environment of the internet.

Craig Newmark, who has invested in citizen-edited websites in the US, sums it up well. Speaking about these sites, he says: "The technology part is quite easy; what really matters is to talk truth to power. Although I want to change the world, I am tremendously lazy. So I see my participation more in helping other people help other people to change the world."

### I see today one of your lead stories is "John Travolta accused of "gay double life"". That seems to me to conform to the celebrity obsessions of the mainstream

Let me first set out The-Latest's stall in regard to celebrity stories. We deplore the shrinking of informative, unbiased political news and foreign news in the big media in favour of mind-numbing "celebrity news" and manufactured news about TV "reality" shows. It represents a terrible "dumbing down" of news and we set up The-Latest to act as an antidote to that kind of journalism. Having said that, we believe we must be where the discourse of the general public is at and not where ideally we would like it to be.

We will never be highbrow and ivory tower. We will unashamedly be in the realm of demotic journalism, like the Labour-supporting *Daily Mirror* when it was a proudly progressive, campaigning newspaper. But, even in its best incarnation, the *Mirror* covered celebrity news. It put serious, left politics in a sensationalist, populist news wrapping. So, The-Latest publishes stories like the one about John Travolta because it offered a fascinating insight into the life of a "celebrity". Why shouldn't a top Hollywood star be gay? A fellow star said it was widely known of "heterosexual" heart-throb Travolta. But it does not fit the construct of what heterosexual soap story-obsessed big media consider is a good story; denying a role model to young gay people struggling to "come out".

The story is about a high profile and popular actor whose apparent secret lifestyle is in direct conflict with his public persona and more importantly the perverse homophobic teachings of the Scientology cult of which Travolta is a leading member and advocate. It was right that we should expose the apparent hypocrisy of his behaviour as we did with Michael Jackson not wanting to be Black. (Note the way we covered the public deaths of reality show star Jade Goody and football icon George Best in a media-critical way.). Celebrity news on The-Latest can help our journalists talk about important issues such as cancer, death, race, sexuality and media propaganda aimed at maintaining the status quo by suppressing important news.

So, there are times when we will unashamedly cover some celebrity news since it can actually provide a critique of big media's news values. However, as much as possible these will be "public interest" stories as with the Travolta piece.

By the way, at The-Latest we like to print both sides of a controversy whether it be about the conflict over Palestine or white voters and the racist British National Party. We are unashamedly iconoclastic, thought provoking, trenchant, surprising, lampooning, like 19th century pamphleteers, and irreverent; but always on the side of the downtrodden and not the oppressor.

### What are the aims of the Citizen Journalism Educational Trust which you have helped set up?

The Citizen Journalism Educational Trust (CJET) has helped to train and resource people, particularly those who would like to become journalists, producing educational material and offering specialist training for disadvantaged young adults in hard-to-reach communities. Support for

CJET is widespread. Labour former Culture Secretary, the Rt Hon Lord Chris Smith, said: "In these times of public scepticism about politics, government and journalism, enabling citizens to find a better connection once again with the world of media and current affairs is incredibly important. This new Trust will help to do precisely that."

## And what has it so far achieved?

CJET successfully piloted a *Journalism for All* summer school course in 2009, funded by a London local authority and a grant from the Big Lottery Awards for All scheme. A key goal of future CJET courses is the removal of obstacles to participation faced by previously excluded people. All CJET student/learners are trained so that they can go back to their communities with a much-improved knowledge base and media and other skills that will help them to find employment and get involved in creative pursuits.

Other CJET courses will aim to increase involvement from young adults who faced social and educational barriers. CJET will help them come forward to take part in focused, work-related programmes and activities designed to assist in their development as adults. The Trust's training will help fill the gap where there was little on offer to previously excluded individuals in their locality – or where what was on offer was not relevant to them and their interests. Student/learners have been helped to get work experience in media organisations including *Time Out* magazine, the *South London Press* newspaper and *Community Newswire,* run by Media Trust and Press Association.

It should be noted that CJET has worked closely with other organisations whilst running its pilot Journalism for All summer school course in 2009. CJET has formed productive relationships with a number of media outlets including Sky, BBC, Media Trust, and the *Time Out* publication, the *South London Press*, Robust Training Ltd, City University and the London College of Communication, Kids Company and Morley College. CJET Trustees plan to work with similar organisations in the furtherance of its key goals.

## What are your major sources of news?

Our regular contributors, including those from abroad have ensured that The-Latest stands head and shoulders above big media in its diverse and off-beat coverage of first-hand news and views that, unlike so much of their output, is not churnalism. The editorial team at The-Latest also produce stories and investigative pieces from Freedom of Information requests to government departments and other public bodies, news tips received via our general "contact us" page on the site and from whistleblowers. We also source some stories from other outlets that publish under-represented opinion and news on the internet.

## How do these compare with the conventional sources of the mainstream?

A number of The-Latest stories have been followed up by broadcast media such as Sky News, ITV News, the BBC as well as national newspapers and others. We exposed a British fascist, Richard Barnbrook, newly elected to the Greater London Assembly, freely writing racially hateful blogs on the respected *Daily Telegraph* website and this was followed up by the *Guardian*, which publicised our story. Although the *Telegraph* editor responsible promised to comment to The-Latest, 24 hours later he had not. Yet he found time to attack the *Guardian*, with a blog on his newspaper's site, for publishing the story.

The editor was angry when The-Latest exposed his hypocrisy. But then that's what our site is about – citizens telling truth to power; making mischief, as long as it is not malicious, on behalf of the public.

Our slogan is unashamedly: "Citizen journalism for all." Our strap line is: "News uncovered." The key to citizen journalism is that it reverses the traditional dissemination of news, from a lecture to the public given by what Noam Chomsky calls the "white secular priesthood" of powerful journalists, to a democratic "conversation". No longer are readers' views consigned to a letters page buried deep inside a publication or a parish pump "local roundup" section of a newspaper. As the *Guardian*, which has trail-blazed on the subject, puts it, from now on the reader holds sway: "Comment is free". And instantaneous.

Readers, viewers and listener can set the news agenda, as never before, with their citizen journalism stories and camera phone's still and moving images. Let me quote the *Guardian*'s former website editor Emily Bell. She said that "the almost overwhelming possibilities that a digitally-armed general public presents for mainstream media can either galvanise or terrify".

## Which sites do you particularly admire?

I read and get alternative news from but don't necessarily admire: OhMyNews!, Huffington Post, Salon.Com, Counter Punch, The First Post, The-Week.Com, Gawker, Guido Fawkes, Radar, TMZ, UK Political Blog Feeds, Wikileaks, CPJ Press Freedom Online, What Do They Know, Committee to Protect Bloggers, The Drudge Report, Al-Jazeera, Pravda, Black Agenda Report, Journalism.co.uk, Press Gazette, Global Voices Online, World Development Movement, MediaLens, Put People First, MoveOn, Avaaz, Asian Times, African News Agency and Chronicle World. Take a look at The-Latest's Weblinks to see many more.

## How important are the Wikileaks?

Whistleblowers have been crucial to investigative journalism since time immemorial. The Watergate scoop of the *Washington Post*'s Bob Woodward and Carl Bernstein that brought down President Nixon in August 1974 is a famous example. Leaks from off-guard, disgruntled and dissenting officialdom can let the public know, through the optic of journalism, what politicians and their hugely influential advisors *really* think about issues and policy that affects them. In its own small way The-Latest has made its contribution.

The website revealed City Hall mendacity when it exposed the racist views of the Mayor of London chief political advisor James McGrath in 2008. The scoop was followed up by national media – print and broadcast – and McGrath was sacked as a consequence. McGrath's right-wing supporters, including *Sunday Times* columnist Rod Liddle, ex-Editor of BBC Radio's *Today* programme, unleashed a torrent of abuse on The-Latest editor and the website itself.

The publication in 2010 of the Wikileaks cables, of communications between US embassies around the world, was journalistically earth shattering. It was a bigger story than the leaking of details of British MPs' expenses to the *Daily Telegraph* that was also a huge story in 2009. Wikileaks, until then, had been a small but very useful website trawled by editors such as the *Guardian*'s Alan Rusbridger who waxed lyrical to me about it when I spoke with him about a financial scoop I had involving one of the world's biggest media tycoons.

The Wikileaks Cables catapulted the site and its boss Julian Assange to mega-fame status. This was alternative media's greatest moment – a scoop by the public for the public. It was so big that even Assange, Wikileaks' editor-in-chief, could not keep control over the dissemination of the highly damaging (to the US, other Western governments and their allies) material. Indeed, one of his media partners, the *Guardian*, ended up turning on Assange and biting the hand that had fed it. The paper published embarrassing evidence from Swedish police, obtained by investigative reporter Nick Davies, about the alleged rapes and sexual assaults about which they want to question Assange.

It is extraordinary but perhaps not surprising that Assange has faced death threats from US and other public officials. What has clearly come out of the affair is that the secrecy-obsessed masters of good, decent public officials cannot silence such people. The more governments and states strive to keep the lid on issues and policies about which the public have a right to know the more the whistleblowers will strike back with the help of brave journalists. And this will often happen via the democratising internet and social media outlets which are unfettered by the suffocating corporate interests that control big media.

The public has a new way of forcing uncovered news, news many editors previously wanted to ignore because it would offend their media owners, onto the big media agenda. Camera phones, camcorders, mobile phones, laptops with internet in the hands of the public have dramatically opened up news gathering and its distribution. Endangered big media have made valiant attempts to co-opt this citizen journalism. But the internet is too vast and unorganised for this attempt at colonisation to succeed. Governments, including the American, Egyptian, Saudi, Chinese and others, have attempted to block internet access, use of social network sites such as Facebook and Twitter (though their spies have access to all the content 24/7) and BlackBerry phone encryption, at times of mass protest. But, as Wikileaks has demonstrated, ultimately they will fail.

# Website relentlessly exposing the bias of the corporate media

**Florian Zollmann interviews David Edwards and David Cromwell,
editors of the media-monitoring website Media Lens, just
celebrating its tenth anniversary**

"Scoops are a side issue," say David Edwards and David Cromwell,
"what matters is the constant systematic bias of a corporate media
system reporting on a world dominated by corporations"

David Edwards and David Cromwell edit the British media monitoring
website Media Lens (www.medialens.org). For ten years they have
followed media coverage of crucial topics such as wars, foreign policy,
and climate change, publishing almost 500 media alerts. Media Lens'
dispatches meticulously challenge the accounts of British's most highly
acclaimed journalists. Edwards' and Cromwell's hard-hitting critiques
have been published in two books: *Guardians of power: The myth of the liberal
media* (Pluto Press, 2006) and *Newspeak in the 21ˢᵗ Century* (Pluto Press,
2009). And while the mainstream media has virtually neglected to write

about their work, John Pilger argues: "Not since Orwell and Chomsky has perceived reality been so skilfully revealed in the cause of truth."

## Tell us about your background in journalism?

We both worked in our spare time as freelance journalists in the 1990s. David Edwards wrote articles and book reviews for magazines like *Big Issue*, the *Ecologist*, *Red Pepper*, *New Internationalist*, *Z Magazine*, *Resurgence* and so on. David Cromwell was occasionally able to publish pieces in the *Scotsman* and in the *Herald* in Glasgow – on politics, science, the environment and travel – as well as book reviews, mainly in *Red Pepper* magazine. We published book reviews and articles in newspapers such as the *Independent, THES,* but both experienced difficulty in publishing pieces that seriously challenged the status quo and felt the very obvious pressure to become more "nuanced" and "measured".

Thanks to the influence of Media Lens, David Edwards wrote a biweekly "box" for the *New Statesman* for two years (2003-2005) and a biweekly column for *Gulf Today* for five years (2004-2009). We were credited as consultants in John Pilger's latest film *The war you don't see.* We had both worked in large corporations for several years, a key experience for understanding the way corporate journalism works. Rule one: don't criticise the company or its sponsors in front of customers!

## Why did you decide to set up Media Lens?

We met in 1999 when Cromwell asked Edwards to act as a "reader" for the media chapter of Cromwell's first book *Private planet* (having just read Edwards' book *The compassionate revolution* and seen his book reviews in magazines such as *Resurgence*). Inspired by the website Cromwell had created for *Private planet*, Edwards suggested setting up a media watch site together – he then came up with a name they both liked, *Media Lens.* The idea was to have something in the UK akin to the US-based *Fairness And Accuracy In Reporting.* There seemed to be a real need to challenge the omissions and distortions of the UK news media – not so much the tabloid press that most people can see is awful; but instead focusing on what is generally regarded as the best or most liberal: the BBC, C4 News, the *Guardian*, the *Independent* and so on.

## What initially were Media Lens's special features?

We had a *Yahoo* email group with a fairly short list of email addresses of friends, contacts and people we thought might be interested. The website had a homepage explaining who we were, together with our aims and underlying philosophy, a FAQ section, a few relevant articles by ourselves and others, a small "library" of quotes we culled from our collection, and statements of support from Edward S. Herman, Noam Chomsky, John Pilger and George Monbiot. Initially, there was no message board.

**What financial hurdles did you have to leap at the start?**
Virtually none. We just needed to pay for the registration of the domain names, medialens.org and medialens.org.uk. We were doing this entirely on a volunteer basis.

**How many staff did you begin with?**
The same as now – two editors plus one webmaster (now Olly Maw).

**Can you tell us about how you distribute tasks at your workplace?**
Our approach is fundamentally anarchistic in that there is no formal structure, no hierarchy – no-one gives or follows orders and yet somehow decisions get made and material is produced with minimal strife. Also, there is no workplace and we don't consider what we do work. We previously did what we did in our spare time because it was stimulating and fun – it's a luxury to get paid. There is also no organised or formal distribution of tasks – we tend to gravitate towards slightly different issues and angles according to our strengths and inclinations (balanced by the awareness that we should share the less thrilling tasks).

As soon as one of us finds a good subject for a media alert, we let the other know to keep clear to avoid duplication of effort. Again, differences are resolved without hierarchy – no-one has the power to make a final decision – through discussion and persuasion based on mutual respect and honest evaluation of the merits of the arguments. When you can't use power because none is available, you have to find another way. In our experience, the other way works better. Theoretically, if we ever fundamentally disagreed on something, we would come to a grinding halt because no-one has final decision-making power – so far that's never happened.

Olly built and maintains the website. There are also more admin-type tasks that we share, e.g. answering emails, responding to requests for interviews, paying in donations to our bank account, collecting mail from our PO Box, occasionally submitting bids for funding and so on.

## Can you describe the development of the site over the years?

Introducing a message board soon after we started raised public interest in our website. We have had some difficulty at times ensuring that it was not swamped by racists, conspiracy theorists and the like. We have had numerous discussions over the years with readers about the balance between freedom of speech on the one hand, and the problem of fanatics hijacking the site for purposes that are not ours – to promote hatred, even violence, and so on – on the other. It's been a difficult balancing act – we've learnt a lot. But we now feel the board is an invaluable resource for us and many other activists. The main development over the years is that we have built up an archive of media alerts now numbering almost 500. It really is the core of what we do.

The newly relaunched website (in November 2010) allows people to easily search through this enormous resource. There is also an improved broadcast system for sending out media alerts containing embedded links and with their own unique and immediate URL (previously, the webmaster had to archive alerts after they'd been sent out).

## How have the number of hits grown?

This isn't something we've really tracked. Last year, we had about 1 million hits. Visits can escalate considerably at times, e.g. in the run-up to the invasion of Iraq.

## Who would you define as your typical reader?

Typically they are "socially inadequate, pimpled, single, slightly seedy, bald, cauliflower-nosed, young men sitting in their mother's basements and ranting. They are very angry people" (see http://www.telegraph.co.uk/technology/internet/8053717/Andrew-Marr-attacks-inadequate-pimpled-and-single-bloggers.html).

That would be Andrew Marr's view! But seriously, we have no idea and we cringe at attempts to lump people together as "typical" types. Everyone is a unique individual. People write to us from every corner: Korean student protestors, Swedish pensioners, unemployed Canadians, BBC journalists, British army officers fighting in Afghanistan, activists in the Colombian jungle, Indian academics and others visiting the site and writing to journalists. To hear the concerns and perspectives from so many different people is one of the great joys of what we're doing.

## How do you define "alternative" media?

You have to be pretty gullible (or professionally biased) to believe that a corporate media system is willing and able to report honestly on a world dominated by corporate power. "Alternative" media are unconstrained by the internal and external pressures afflicting the corporate media. That means media not driven by profit, or indeed revenue; not beholden to wealthy owners and parent companies and advertisers; not dependent on elite centres of authority for subsidised sources of "news"; less vulnerable to powerful flak-wielding lobbies; less manipulated and cowed by pacifying "patriotic" ideologies that assume "our" suffering and happiness are of greater importance than "their" suffering and happiness, that we should bow down to "the flag", the nation, the President, the crown, or whatever (with these justifying a "war on terror", a "war on communism" and so on).

On a deeper level, an alternative press is one that is not motivated by self-interest, egotism or greed. Dissident journalists may write from a left perspective, but if their motivation is status, wealth and even power, they can hardly be said to constitute a genuine "alternative" to the mainstream.

## How do you define the approach of Media Lens?

In practical terms, our approach is to analyse print and broadcast media, mostly in the UK, but also in the US, with a critical mind. We invite readers to compare the mainstream version of events with alternative perspectives supplied by credible academics, dissident journalists, non-governmental organisations, the United Nations and so on. We compile regular, free "media alerts" that discuss important examples of media bias. At the end of each alert, we include a "suggested action" providing the email addresses for journalists and editors. We encourage readers to send polite challenges. Note that we strongly discourage the sending of impolite and abusive emails.

More fundamentally, we believe that media claims to "neutrality" are a deception that serve to hide systematic pro-corporate bias. "Neutrality" most often means "impartially" reporting dominant establishment views, while ignoring or marginalising dissent. In reality, it is not possible for journalists to be neutral: regardless of whether we do or do not overtly express our personal opinion, that opinion is always reflected in the facts we choose to highlight or ignore.

While Media Lens seeks to challenge some of the worst excesses of corporate media distortions as honestly as possible, our concern is not to affect some spurious "objectivity", but to engage with the world to do whatever we can to reduce suffering and to resist the forces that seek to subordinate human well-being to profit. We do not believe that passively observing human misery without attempting to intervene constitutes "neutrality". Nor do we believe that "neutrality" can ever be deemed more important than doing all in our power to help others.

## Could you tell us what kind of frameworks or analytical underpinnings guide your research?

We owe a particular debt to Edward S. Herman and Noam Chomsky, especially their wonderful book, *Manufacturing consent : The political economy of the mass media* (Pantheon, 1988). Herman and Chomsky's "propaganda model of media control" is a very sound basis for understanding how truth is filtered in the modern media system. A good introduction and overview is Mark Achbar's superb documentary from 1992, *Manufacturing consent: Noam Chomsky and the media.*

We are also inspired by approaches and philosophies that promote humanity and peace, and reject violence and hate. For example: the Buddhist contention that while greed, hatred and ignorance distort reason; compassion empowers it. But we don't believe compassion can be generated by force of will. Our aim is to increase rational awareness, critical thought and compassion, and to decrease greed, hatred and ignorance.

## At times, the mass media tends to criticise itself, in its media sections and columns, for example. What is your picture of media criticism by the corporate media?

Mostly it's a form of backhanded self-adulation – journalists are criticised for being *too* courageous and honest in criticising the powerful. Their critical reflexes are so overdeveloped that they risk actually *harming* democracy by spreading excessive cynicism. The claimed risk is that the public will end up believing no-one and nothing they see and hear. This is an exact reversal of the truth of the media's impact. What is so fascinating about the media is that it finds itself so uninteresting! It will talk about any weird subject under the sun, but the institutionalised problem of a profit-seeking corporate media reporting on a world dominated by profit-seeking corporations on which those media are dependent is – surprise

surprise! – of no interest. The problem is so obvious and so obviously important, but it is never discussed.

**What do you regard as your major scoops? Both, with regard to exclusive information you published and also with regard to exposing media bias.**

How tedious! What matters is not what is new and shocking, but what is true and humanly significant. We have had scoops: a serving British army officer fighting in Iraq emailed *Newsnight* with the real views of the British Army in response to our media alert (prompting a response by Mark Urban on the programme). Our exposure of the deep flaws in *Iraq Body Count's* database and methodology was a first, as far as we are aware, and so on. But scoops are a side issue. What matters is the constant systematic bias of a corporate media system reporting on a world dominated by corporations. This is the "bread and butter" issue of our work – it's not dazzlingly original or new, but it is crucial.

**From reading your alerts and diving through your message board it seems that you have constant interaction with readers and viewers who are also engaging with the media and with journalists who respond to your work. What kind of reactions have you received from the public, journalists and the media?**

When we started, the intensity of positive feeling really took us by surprise. We had numerous declarations of actual love: "WE LOVE YOU!!!!" (Carla T) and "I love you people!" (Jenny, Colombian jungle). There was clearly a desperate need for regular, uncompromised criticism of the mainstream media. The reaction of journalists, of course, has been mixed, but sometimes extremely positive. During the early stages of the Iraq war a media insider told us that our alerts had become a "rallying point" for dissent in the BBC. We currently have friendly insiders covertly helping us from inside the BBC's newsrooms and in several newspapers. A journalist at the *Observer* told us:

> It goes without saying, many thanks for providing the inspiration/facts and for all your and DC's good work. You are a constant needle, comfort and inspiration. Great stuff.

There have been many smears. Former *Observer* and *Independent* editor Roger Alton responded to one emailer: "Have you just been told to write in by those cunts at medialens? Don't you have a mind of your own?"

(email forwarded, 1 June 2006). Peter Beaumont's attack in the *Observer* was so far-fetched that it descended into a kind of slapstick:

> ... there is no conversation between them and their victims. It is a closed and distorting little world that selects and twists its facts to suit its arguments, a curious willy-waving exercise where the regulars brag about the emails they've sent to people like poor Helen Boaden at the BBC – and the replies they have garnered. Think a train spotters' club run by Uncle Joe Stalin.

Some journalists oscillate between support and antipathy. We have huge respect for the work of George Monbiot. When we began in 2001, he said of us: "... thank goodness for this brilliant project and the courage which has inspired it." After we challenged one of Monbiot's comments on Iraq in 2002, he wrote to us:

> Whenever a journalist takes a line at variance to your own, your automatic assumption is that he has stopped thinking for himself, and has been, wittingly or otherwise, coerced by dark forces. As a result, you are in danger of reproducing the very problems you criticise. You appear to me to be confronting one form of bias and intolerance with another. [i]

In 2005, he wrote:

> I know we've had disagreements in the past, but I wanted to send you a note of appreciation for your work. Your persistence seems to be paying off: it's clear that many of the country's most prominent journalists are aware of Medial Lens, read your bulletins and, perhaps, are beginning to feel the pressure. If, as I think you have, you have begun to force people working for newspapers and broadcasters to look over their left shoulders as well as their right, and worry about being held to account for the untruths they disseminate, then you have already performed a major service to democracy. I feel you have begun to open up a public debate on media bias, which has been a closed book in the United Kingdom for a long time (email to Media Lens, 2 February 2005).

Alas, after we asked Monbiot some difficult questions about his commentary on Iran in 2007 – again, it was nothing remotely personal, we just disagreed with him – he stopped replying to our emails altogether. The BBC's (then) *Newsnight* editor, Peter Barron, wrote:

> Another organisation that tries to influence our running orders is Medialens...In fact, I rather like them. David Cromwell and David Edwards, who run the site, are unfailingly polite, their points are well-argued and sometimes they're plain right. [ii]

**Is there anything you would like to have done differently. For example, do you think that some of your past criticisms have been too strong or too weak?**

We are sometimes surprised at how strongly our work has been vindicated by subsequent events. For example, on Iraqi WMD – we, of course, had no idea that we were being *conservative* in supporting claims that Iraq had been 90-95 per cent disarmed by 1998. It's frustrating to us that we weren't able to get these issues into the mainstream when it mattered, in 2002 and early 2003. Our main regret is that we haven't had sufficient resources to do more on issues like Haiti, climate change and Venezuela – we just haven't got the time or energy.

**I see on your website that you had written a media alert on the WikiLeaks. How important are the WikiLeaks to you? How do you think the mainstream covered the WikiLeaks?**

The leaks appear to be of potentially great importance, although US government insiders are privately saying they are "embarrassing" rather than "damaging". As ever, the importance to us revolves around the implications for media bias. The cross-spectrum media hate campaign directed at Assange has been a classic example of mainstream toxicity. An individual who, until recently, was completely unknown, is now a fully-fledged media cartoon: Assange the "sleazeball". It's amazing to consider that Assange has not even been charged, let alone convicted, of any crime. The media's depiction of him is entirely based on rumour and speculation.

**Could you describe the aims of Media Lens?**

To encourage people to think for themselves. To encourage people to challenge their own beliefs as potential Trojan thoughts manufactured and boosted by vested interests. To encourage people to question the idea that the happiness and suffering of some people are more important than the happiness and suffering of other people. To see how this moral prejudice is often built into media reporting that subtly identifies with a benevolent and superior "us" contrasted with an immoral and inferior "them". To encourage people to question the rights and rationality of authority: what is the basis of the claimed authority? Why should we defer to them? Who are they to demand our allegiance and even deference? Who designed that flag? Who decided it was virtually a religious symbol? Of what? Is there any basis to these rituals at all? How can we challenge them?

To question the true nature of human happiness: could the search for happiness in ambition, status and wealth be an answer to the human condition that best suits the needs of corporate politics and media, and their advertising dream-weavers? Is it possible that genuine happiness lies in a completely different direction – in working for the benefit of others? After all, the internet is essentially a giant expression of generosity. There is a continual race on amongst posters to our message board (us included) to post the latest interesting articles and facts on our message board – we all actually love to feel we are doing something for others, to feel we are responsible for inspiring and helping them.

To encourage people to consider the real aims of corporate power. How these aims impact on politics, media and the culture more generally. And, of course, we need to build and strengthen grassroots efforts to raise public awareness of the issues confronting humanity; to challenge the powerful elite interests that have driven us to the edge of the abyss. For instance, tackling climate change with the required radical action to avert climate chaos represents a very real threat to elite interests in the corporate, financial, media, government and military sectors. We need to challenge the mantra of endless economic growth and rampant mass consumption. We need to expose the myth that "our" leaders have essentially benevolent aims and humane priorities. What passes for a "democratic election" is a sham so long as people are immersed in a propaganda system of relentless brainwashing to promote state-corporate aims.

## And what, do you think, has Media Lens so far achieved?

We honestly have no idea and it's not something that interests us. Our focus is to be motivated to write material that we love writing, that we think is interesting, important, and helpful to our readers. The focus on goals inevitably means worrying about what other people think – "If I write this, will I alienate our key support base?" This creates the basis for compromise and self-censorship – technical term: "nuanced" journalism. What people think, our supporters included, is *not* a key concern – we have to write out of sincerity, out of what feels true and important to us, no matter how many bridges are left burning as a result. The key point is to do what we do because we love doing it, not because it will result in some great success or achievement in the future.

### Your work is based on factual evidence. What are your major sources of information?

We use many different sources, depending on the topic we're writing about. We both keep extensive files of quotes from books, articles, television, radio, etc. that stretch to several thousands of pages. We consult many different websites, let's choose some obvious favourites: Democracy Now! Just magnificent. Far superior to the BBC and on a shoestring budget. The Real News Network has wonderful interviews with the likes of Daniel Ellsberg and Gareth Porter. ZNet was one of our early inspirations. Eckhart Tolle TV is a current favourite source of "perennial philosophy" – the radical mysticism that inspires and informs our political activism and writing. Media Lens message board: now a wonderful resource from which we pinch many great nuggets for our media alerts.

We also spend time checking out Inter Press Service, IRIN News, Glenn Greenwald's blog, Chris Hedges, *Haaretz*, Craig Murray's blog, Palestine Chronicle, RealClimate.org, Tim Lambert's Deltoid blog, Ceasefire Magazine, Aljazeera English, Press TV, Russia Today, Israeli Occupation Archive, B'Tselem, *Financial Times*, Amnesty International, *Los Angeles Times*, *New York Times*, Neil Clark's blog, Venezuelanalysis.com, John Tirman's blog at MIT, *New Statesman*, *Morning Star*, Truthout, TomDispatch, chomsky.info, BBC News, *Guardian*, Electronic Intifada, Osho Online Library.

### How do these compare with the conventional sources of the mainstream?

The difference is really staggering. If you want to understand the "surge" in Iraq, the reality of Afghanistan, the US role in Haiti and Venezuela, the uprising in Tunisia and so on, it cannot be done through the BBC or the *Guardian*. We know – we sometimes come at issues from a position of almost complete ignorance in writing articles for the mainstream and our own media alerts. We simply *have* to go to Democracy Now! or ZNet, or a specialist website, to find out what is really going on. Time after time, we have found that the reality bears almost no resemblance to, say, the BBC version. If you want to understand WikiLeaks, you don't go to the *Guardian*, you go to Glenn Greenwald, and so on.

## What do you think of literary style in journalism?

It's important to remember that the whole idea of professional journalism is based on a conscious fraud. Schools of journalism were set up in the United States around 100 years ago just as corporations were achieving a monopoly over the mass media. The schools were intended to allay public concerns by supposedly educating journalists hired by wealthy media moguls to be impartial and objective. This bogus emphasis on neutrality has inevitably been reflected in the style of writing. The idea is that journalists should write in a coldly detached, unemotional style – they should keep their forbidden personal opinions well out of sight. In reality, the facts we choose to highlight inevitably reflect our personal opinions. For example, the BBC's Jim Muir recently wrote a report on the misery suffered by Iraq's refugees. He commented: "In one way or another, most of the factors that drove people here can be traced back to Saddam Hussein's rule and the chaos that followed." [iii]

Muir kept his personal opinions to himself, and he wrote not one word about his own government's responsibility for the catastrophe in Iraq. He made no mention of the role of the illegal 2003 invasion, of the earlier genocidal US-UK sanctions, or of the original long-term US-UK support that brought Saddam Hussein to power and kept him there. No matter how much Muir might like to believe he obscured his views, the facts he selected and ignored revealed everything about what he believes and about how he sees his role as a journalist.

Of course, the beauty of the best journalism is that it is humanly interesting – it comes from the heart as well as the head so that it reaches to the heart as well as the head. People aren't interested in some specious factual or emotional neutrality – they want to know what a journalist *honestly* thinks and feels is the truth of any given issue. They certainly don't want to read what a Zionist or Palestinian fanatic claims to believe is the truth. They want to hear a version of truth from someone who is sensitive to the suffering of both sides, someone who is interested in rational analysis and just solutions. In the case of the Israeli-Palestinian conflict, someone sensitive to the suffering of both sides will be appalled by the misery the Israelis are inflicting on the Palestinians – the balance of power, criminality, injustice and suffering all point that way. It makes no sense to be sensitive to the suffering of both and to then affect a version of "balance" that pretends the criminality and suffering are equal on both sides.

Journalistic honesty should extend to a writer's emotions: if a journalist feels appalled, outraged or grief-stricken by his or her government's role in causing human misery, he or she should express these emotions. If our government is responsible for the mass death of innocents in the name of realpolitik, that *is* horrific and disgusting. To suggest it isn't in the name of "balance" is a lie.

John Pilger is one of the finest modern journalists. He's not the best political analyst – Noam Chomsky and Edward Herman are in a league of their own – but he is a tremendous writer. Pilger's talent lies in a rare mix of intellectual acuity and emotional depth. He has the insight to cut through official lies to the truth of an issue in a few carefully sculpted sentences. But he also has the emotional sensitivity to know and express what he *feels* with great force. We have often felt that, in just one or two paragraphs, Pilger leaves the rest of the media exposed as shallow and compromised. He writes, not as a brain in a jar, not as a hired tool of a media machine, but as a fully human journalist.

## Notes

---

[i] See http://www.medialens.org/index.php?option=com_content&view=article&id=226:update-george-monbiot-responds-on-iraq-and-just-war&catid=16:alerts-2002&Itemid=43, accessed on 2 January 2011

[ii] See http://www.medialens.org/index.php?option=com_content&view=article&id=226:update-george-monbiot-responds-on-iraq-and-just-war&catid=16:alerts-2002&Itemid=43, accessed on 2 January 2011

[iii] See http://www.bbc.co.uk/news/world-middle-east-12266900, accessed on 2 January 2011

## Note on the interviewer

Florian Zollmann is studying for a PhD at Lincoln University's School of Journalism. He has recently written for *Ethical Space: The International Journal of Communication Ethics*, the Westminster Papers in Communication and Culture and *Z Magazine*. With Richard Lance Keeble and John Tulloch he jointly edited *Peace journalism, war and conflict resolution* (Peter Lang, 2010). He is also a contributor to the German independent magazine *Publik-Forum* where he is a blogger as well as a regular writer and editor for its supplement *Provo*.

# Wikileaks and the limits of protocol

**Joss Winn**

Facilitated by protocol, the internet is the most highly controlled mass media hitherto known (Galloway 2004: 243).

## Introduction
In this chapter, I reflect on Wikileaks and its use of technology to achieve freedom in capitalist society. Wikileaks represents an avant-garde form of media (i.e. networked, cryptographic), with traditional democratic values: opposing power and seeking the truth. At times, http://wikileaks.org appears broken and half abandoned while at other times it is clearly operating beyond the level of government efficiency and military intelligence. It has received both high acclaim and severe criticism from human rights organisations, the mainstream media and governments. It is a really existing threat to traditional forms of power and control yet, I suggest, it is fundamentally restrained by liberal ideology of freedom and democracy and the protocological limits of cybernetic capitalism.

## Social form: The administration of order

The purpose of the capitalist state is to maintain a class of poverty through the fabrication of social order (Neocleous 2004). This is achieved, first and foremost, through the separation of needs and capacities; that is, through the justification of private property and the imposition of waged labour. This separation is enforced through a variety of state institutions: domestically, through the legal system and the administrative role of the police, and internationally through diplomatic protocol, trade agreements and, at last resort, military force.

Since the emergence of liberalism, the administration of civil society has been undertaken through the fundamental necessity of wage labour and supported by a number of state institutions, collectively understood as "social welfare" or the "welfare state". The purpose of the welfare state is that of perpetuating the subordination of a person's labour to the overwhelming deprivation of property (i.e. maintaining order) through an administrative system of institutional control and social regulation (for example: education, health care, prison).

This system of "social security" with the police at its centre is the cornerstone of liberal thinking, the "supreme concept of bourgeois society" (ibid: xii). Through the fabrication of security lies the liberal illusion of freedom and liberty (i.e. individuality and self-interest). In fact, security at the level of society is an impossibility since it ignores the antagonism of the separation of needs and capacities (i.e. poverty) as the source of wealth. In capitalist society, the basis for security is that the working class must work (i.e. exploitation) and therefore the fabrication of security rests on the commodification of labour (i.e. discipline) and the capitalists' imperative to accumulate private property (i.e. insecurity).

"Terror" is the threat of the breakdown of civil society, the interruption of capital (i.e. value in motion). In response to the general and persistent threat of terror in capitalist society, the primary role of the police project is not the prevention of crime but rather the imposition and political administration of the class system. The real "war on terror" is "the permanent low-intensity warfare against the working class" (ibid: 82). To win this war on terror would entail the abolition of private property and, therefore, abolishing the state and its police apparatus. Thus, the state and the police cannot be understood apart from each other. A society based on the separation of needs from capacities is the outcome of a state formulated on the protection of private property and the regulation of wage labour through the all-pervasive political administration of its police project.

The logic of the internet is that of administration by protocol. As the social form of mass media *par excellence*, we have been tricked by the internet into confusing the abstract with the virtual. The "real-time" internet is not really real-time but a densification of space-time unlike any other technology. It is a factory of things where the space-time-unit is compressed to such a degree of abstraction that we refer to it as "virtual", unable to comprehend the violence of its abstract reality.

## Velocity: The internet and the densification of space-time

> Protocol is a type of controlling logic that operates outside institutional, governmental, and corporate power although it has important ties to all three (Galloway op cit: 122).

> Speed upholds institutions. Slowness cuts off flow (Tiqqun 2001: 74).

The internet is a concrete product of human labour and as such, a social form of abstract labour that compresses space-time (socially necessary labour time). It is a congealed form of value-creating-human-energy (labour) from which emerges a more dense space-time-unit, resulting in a flow of time and space encapsulated in the commodity form. The real-time internet is not simply synchronous, but compresses social labour time in space, constantly changing the magnitude of value with the velocity made possible by protocol. Standards, such as TCP/IP, HTTP, HTML, XML, etc. all increase the potential velocity of this networked social activity ("socially necessary labour time"). Speed is therefore relative, measured absolutely at the point-in-time of commodity exchange.

> For Einstein, the one constant was the speed of light and that was the measure against which all other movement is measured. In the social world Marx also provides us with a social measure: socially necessary labour time: the speed of life (Neary and Rikowski 2000).

The internet can, therefore, be understood as a number of standardised technologies which work to control and increase the velocity of socially necessary labour time, compressing the space-time-unit so that the normative standard of time becomes denser and the valorisation of value, and the expansion of abstraction, becomes the overwhelming logic which subsumes space, time, energy and speed.

These attributes of velocity, intensity and control are clearly revealed by Wikileaks. In the recent leak of diplomatic cables, the pace and discretion of diplomatic protocol has been met with the velocity and intensity made possible by the internet's protocological densification of space-time. The rhythm of diplomatic protocol has been interrupted by the rhythm of networked leaks. Wikileaks, is the exemplar social form of protocol becoming concretely manifest in capitalist society, revealing to us the logic of the expansion of abstraction, the violence of virtuality and the "terror of immateriality" (ibid).

## The violence of virtuality

> The first serious infowar is now engaged. The field of battle is Wikileaks. You are the troops!! #anonops #operationpayback #Wikileaks (anon_operation, Twitter, 8 December 2010).

> It takes networks to fight networks (Arquilla and Ronfeldt 2001: 15).

The "first serious infowar" is, in fact, an arms race of protocol to control the cybernetic "abstract machine" (Tiqqun 2001: 4). Extending the police project, this technique of governance is epitomised by "management" (derived from the Greek *kybernētēs* which means to "pilot"), that is, unlimited attempts at rationalisation which seek to support and defend the state through an unlimited flow and capture of information and its feedbacks.

Cybernetics is the theoretical and technological outcome and continuation of a state of war (i.e. World War Two), in which stability and control are the objectives. Developing with the emergence of post-war information and communication theory and corresponding innovation in computer software and hardware, intelligence is abstracted from the human population as generalised representations that are retained and communicated back to individuals in a commodified form (i.e. mass media). This feedback loop was originally conceived as a "system" and later as a naturalised "network" (i.e. "rhizome") which, drawing on the 19th century thermodynamic law of entropy, is at continual risk of disequilibrium and degradation and must therefore be reinforced by the development of cybernetics itself (ibid).

Since the 1980s, the dismantling of social protection systems has led to an attempt to make everyone bear the "risks" borne by capitalism. There has been a shift from the collective responsibility of the welfare state to the responsibilities of the individual toward society. In contrast to the mechanisms of control in the 19th century, which dissolved social bonds, cybernetic capitalism develops social bonds (a "nebulous citizen-community") through "the imperative of self-piloting and of piloting others in the service of social unity: it is the device-future of mankind as citizens of Empire" (ibid: 34).

The cybernetic logic of decentralisation through protocol extends and prolongs the centralised institutions of control (i.e. the police project) and in so far as this logic is intended to ward off events and organise feedback, it has a predictive purpose that "aims to eliminate all uncertainty connected to all possible futures" (ibid: 31). In this way, the velocity of protocol congeals past, present and *future* and with it, all spatial territory, too.

For cybernetics, total transparency is a means towards protocological and, therefore, social control in the face of risk. Because the removal of risk is never absolutely possible, citizens are understood as both presenting a risk to the system and a means to regulate that risk through *self-control*. Order in society is socialised through the control of public services that harvest information allowing for the fabrication of trends across time and space. In a sense, the control sector, now thoroughly socialised, is autonomous but in the hierarchy of control, the police, law and judicial system remain controllers of last resort. An awareness of risk (i.e. terror) brings with it an awareness of the vulnerability of a system that is dependent on an accelerated circulation/flow of information. Time and duration is an inherent weakness and their disruption is a disruption of value in motion.

## Wikileaks: A ZOO

> We do not want more transparency or more democracy. There's already enough. On the contrary – we want more opacity and more intensity (ibid: 40).

> Wikileaks needs to be completely opaque in order to force others to be totally transparent (Wikileaks 2010).

Operating under the strict rules of cybernetic protocol, Wikileaks submits the increasingly impotent protocols of government diplomacy to the "tyranny of transparency" required by the new cybernetic order. Transparency and openness are the inevitable outcomes of cybernetic capitalism in which the machines are in control and we are their mere appendages. Wikileaks naively assumes that with transparency follows democracy. It believes that when citizens are better informed and therefore more empowered, politicians act on the assumption that their actions are more visible and, therefore, accountable.

Thus the release of diplomatic cables is understood as a method of regulating the regulators. This view pre-supposes a liberal view of democracy but represents a clash in politics. As a capitalist political project, cybernetics is in the process of supplanting liberalism as both a paradigm and technique of government that aims to dissolve human subjectivity into a rationalised and stable (i.e. inoffensive) totality through the automated capture of increasingly transparent flows of information and communication (Tiqqun op cit). Wikileaks has revealed not only the invisible hand of diplomatic protocol but also the invisible hand of cybernetic protocol as it reproduces society. If state secrets can be exposed through the abstract machine of protocol, any aspect of public or private life in the liberal sense can be exposed by protocol, too. Thus, as Zizek, writing about Wikileaks, puts it:

> The real disturbance was at the level of appearances: we can no longer pretend we don't know what everyone knows we know. This is the paradox of public space: even if everyone knows an unpleasant fact, saying it in public changes everything (Zizek 2011).

On the internet, viruses, spamming and piracy are seen as methods to destabilise the operation of the communications network. Wikileaks is not in the same category. It serves mainstream media and hacks cybernetic protocol. It is the machinic protocol realising its full potential by harnessing hackers and cypherpunks who work at the avant-garde of cybernetics. In this view, Wikileaks is a rogue foot soldier of cybernetics, leaping over slow, diplomatic protocol to ensure the transparency and speed of the political machine. It is an audacious act (Giri 2010), an event only possible on this scale due to the guarantees put in place by protocological design.

Wikileaks operates through widely available cryptographic internet applications developed for military purposes (e.g. TOR, TLS/SSL, PGP, SSH). Due to this fundamental requirement of cryptographic tools, Wikileaks is arguably an example of Tiqqun's "zone of offensive opacity", a "black bloc of the cybernetic matrix from which an offensive will take place".

> The zones are at once small nuclei from where experimentation begins without being perceptible, a panic propagating cloud within the imperial system and spontaneous subversion at all levels. The proliferation of these zones of offensive opacity (ZOO), and the intensification of their interrelations, will give rise to an irreversible disequilibrium (Tiqqun op cit: 81).

According to Tiqqun, for a ZOO to be effective in provoking a change in the system, there must be a critical mass that fluctuates from a pivotal, local centre, and amplifies to contaminate the whole system. This "unassailable base" should be sheltered from attack and from fear of attack and must have independent supply lines. As the cybernetic system seeks to absorb/deaden the fluctuating autonomous zone, the base must grow larger as monitoring increases.

We saw this happen with Wikileaks. Contrary to Galloway's thesis, the horizontalism of the Internet Protocol (IP) could not be disciplined by the hierarchy of the Domain Name System (DNS). When Wikileaks' DNS service was taken down in December 2010, Google remained true to their mission to "organise the world's information and make it universally accessible and useful" and continued to provide shelter to Wikileaks' "unassailable base". This was a curious example of corporate interests (i.e. "information must be universally accessible") providing a "patch" for what appeared to be an error of protocol.

Here, the hierarchical structure of control of DNS seems to have shifted to the hierarchical control of Google, yet the loss of the wikileaks.org domain name led to the spontaneous creation of over 1000 mirror sites by Wikileaks' supporters across the internet, acting as distributed hosts to Wikileaks' publicity campaign. In these audacious acts, we caught a glimpse of a counter-world that uses the network to fight the network, a revolutionary "re-appropriation of the most modern technological tools, a re-appropriation that should permit contestation of the police on their own turf, by creating a counter-world with the same means that it uses. Speed here is understood as one of the important qualities of the revolutionary political arts" (Tiqqun op cit: 72).

## Real abstraction

> The formal complexity of society is the sign of its potential simplification – an index of the forces pressing against it (Kay and Mott 1982: 23).

Tiqqun sabotages speed with slowness. Wikileaks intensifies the feedbacks loops of information through transparency and opaqueness. Both are caught in the closed circuit of abstraction, mistaking the liberal face of capital for its ruthless body. Wikileaks uses the network to fight the network but remains a liberal attempt to restore order to representative democracy through the freedom of information and the tyranny of transparency. However, order in capitalist society is a fabrication that maintains a class of poverty, property-less and forced to work. People are no more free from the terror of the state and the necessities imposed on human life than before. Information, secret or free does not undermine the ecocidal logic of capitalist accumulation and the irrationality of property and labour that dominates us.

The actual social forms of capitalist society in all its complexity derive from abstractions based on private property and labour and the process and conditions of abstraction must be continually renewed, becoming increasingly novel and then naturalised as "common-sense". A condition of abundance is a threat to the motion of capital and increasing complexity through abstraction serves to frustrate such possibility (Kay and Mott op cit: 23). Assumptions, fundamental to liberal thinking, such as individuality and freedom, diversity and the reciprocity of rights, are abstractions that have achieved their own natural "logic" and impose an irrational order in society that is replicated through complexity.

## Conclusion
Wikileaks should be understood in the context of the real possibility of abundance and the violent imposition of order and security in the face of such "terrifying" potential. The architectural logic of the protocols of the internet are at once rational in that they reveal the possibility of the abundance of things (i.e. the meeting of needs with capacity), and yet disciplined by abstraction, in that they cannot escape the logic of capitalist work. The protocols upon which Wikileaks is built are thus a "management style" (Galloway op cit: 242) that privileges the freedom of things over the freedom of people, more so than any other prior technology.

This is the disappointing outcome of more than 40 years of intense effort to specify protological control (i.e. the internet). Protocol may be synonymous with the possibility of abundance, but this points to its limits. Wikileaks may be synonymous with freedom, but likewise this also points to its limits, too. Both protocol and its manifestation in Wikileaks are, like all aspects of social life, *really subsumed* by the logic of property and capitalist work and each of us remains "a living appendage of the machine" (Marx 1996).

## References
Arquilla, J. and Ronfeldt, D. (2001) *Networks and netwars: The future of terror, crime, and militancy*, California, Rand Corporation

Galloway, A. R. (2004) *Protocol. How control exists after decentralization*, Cambridge, MA, MIT Press

Giri, S. (2010) Wikileaks Beyond Wikileaks? Mute Magazine. Available online at http://www.metamute.org/en/articles/WikiLeaks_beyond_WikiLeaks, accessed on 1 February 2011

Kay, G. and Mott, J. (1982) *Political order and the law of labour*, London, Macmillan Press

Marx, K. (1996) *Capital, Volume 1: Marx and Engels Collected Works Volume 35*, International Publishers. Available online at http://marxists.org/archive/marx/works/cw/volume35/index.htm, accessed on 1 February 2011

Neary, M. and Rikowski, G. (2000) The speed of life: The significance of Karl Marx's concept of socially necessary labour-time. Available online at http://www.flowideas.co.uk/?page=articles&sub=Speed%20of%20Life%20-%20Part%20One, accessed on 1 February 2011

Neocleous, M. (2000) *The fabrication of social order: A critical theory of police power*, London, Pluto Press

Tiqqun (2001) *The cybernetic hypothesis.* First published in French by La Fabrique Editions; English translation (2010). Available online at http://cybernet.jottit.com/, accessed on 1 February 2011

Žižek, S. (2011) Good manners in the age of WikiLeaks, *London Review of Books*, Vol. 33, No.2 pp 9-10

## Note on the author

Joss Winn works in the Centre for Educational Research and Development at the University of Lincoln, where he undertakes research into the use and politics of technology in Higher Education. He also runs the Lincoln Academic Commons, a source of information for open source, open education and open access related projects. He holds degrees in Buddhist Studies (London, SOAS), Michigan (Ann Arbor)) and in Film Archiving (East Anglia). Previously, he worked for Amnesty International and the British Film Institute.

# Section 8. Out to the world: Challenging the power of the traditional media

**Richard Lance Keeble**

Globally, the internet is opening up extraordinary opportunities for challenging the political and cultural status quo. This section focuses on three important and under-reported examples. In Guyana, Denis Chabrol has set up the Demerara Waves online blog which bravely and directly challenges the government's near monopoly on the news. Particularly interesting is the way in which the site is aiming to extend its reach to the younger audience – who normally access their news via the social media, ipods, computers and mobile smart phones.

Chabrol explains: "Unlike traditional newspapers, Demerara Waves provides comparatively short text news reports with the basic details and some contextual background rather than extensive reports that are less attractive to most young people and people on the go!"

## Africa's rapid take-up of new social media

Next, journalism academic Fred Mudhai, in a ground-breaking study, examines the developments in internet journalism in Africa. The continent is currently registering the fastest growth rate in the take-up of mobile phones and Facebook, according to statistics from the International Telecommunications Union (see www.itu.int) and O'Reilly Research (see www.oreilly.com). According to Dr Mudhai, citizen journalism is alive and thriving across Africa, especially during electoral and other national crises as recent events in Kenya, Ivory Coast, Tunisia and Egypt have demonstrated. And blogs, Twitter and Facebook have become alternative sources of news and information.

## In China, social media "reshaping the modern media ecology"

Finally, in another important and original study, Chinese academic Homsom Shaw (Shao, Hongsong) examines the growth of internet-based media in his home country. He suggests new media are "completely reshaping the modern media ecology in ways people of two decades ago would never have imagined". He provides a number of fascinating case studies showing the ways in which the new social media are challenging the conventional news values and reporting routines of the traditional media.

He concludes on a positive note: "The public should not be pessimistic about the future openness of the internet. For it would be extremely difficult for the mass media in China to return to the days when the public were denied even the faintest hope of openly questioning and criticising mainstream viewpoints."

# Social networks at the heart of Guyana's sole online news operation

**Denis Chabrol**

Demerara Waves, a Guyana-based online news service, had its genesis in 2007 as a podcasting service aiming to provide an outlet for thought-provoking interviews.

It derives its name from the Demerara River on whose right bank sits the commercial and administrative capital of Guyana, a British colony until 1966. Moreover, Guyana's last privately-owned radio station was named Radio Demerara and was owned by the British company, Rediffusion that also had similar operations in Barbados, Jamaica, Trinidad. In tandem with the original plan of a news-talk formatted internet radio station, we added Waves in reference to terrestrial radio waves.

Central to Demerara Waves operations is the fact that Guyana's radio broadcasting landscape is still controlled by the government and the quality of news and current affairs programming has seriously declined in recent years. So the internet offers a medium which is both local and global in scope and reach, away from the tentacles of government, the private sector or other influences.

Those original interviews were mainly political in nature because the target audience was mostly the large Guyanese diaspora in the United States, Canada, the United Kingdom and to some extent the Caribbean who pay close attention to political and security developments in their homeland.

Undoubtedly encouraged by the positive responses to the podcasts on a free podcast site, Demerara Waves shifted gear and purchased its own domain and website – www.demerarawaves.com. And moves began to introduce a mixture of podcasts, live audio and text.

## Difficult early days

But the going was not to be easy. Having acquired my domain and tried, unsuccessfully, to build my own website I turned to a professional website builder. But then the new site turned out to be built with pirated content management systems. So I had to try again. All this proved to be an expensive experience: in fact, I spent more than US$2,000 on trying to make a difference in the Guyanese media!

With the website up and running again with little technical problems, the emphasis was on podcasting, live webcasting of current affairs/news events and a once-weekly live talk-show, "Periscope on politics". Considered Demerara Waves' flagship programme, "Periscope" attracted a growing audience among Guyanese in the diaspora. Efforts to formalise links with Caribbean stations were not greeted with a great deal of enthusiasm, mainly because of the unavailability of broadcast time and because stations hoped to acquire the content free.

But Demerara Waves' reputation as a credible medium has grown – particularly since it has been the source for several important exclusives in the local and regional media. For instance, when American, Katie Spotz was about to complete her Trans-Atlantic row from Africa to the Guyana, the power of the social media – particularly Twitter – was best demonstrated locally when people rushed to www.twitter.com/demwaves to follow the last few hours of her journey into Port Georgetown. Our tweets and photographs were used on a number of websites and newspapers, mainly in the United States.

Notwithstanding the growing popularity and interest, the operations of Demerara Waves could not be sustained on just good will. Turning to reputable companies for sponsorship of Demerara Waves' internet radio content was discouraging. In fact, one major regional business told Demerara Waves that its survey showed that returns from sponsorship were mainly secured from cricket, football and musical shows. So much for corporate citizenry in public education and information!!

## Exploiting the diaspora's thirst for news

Taking advantage of the thirst of the diaspora for news-as-it-happens, Demerara Waves decided to shift gear last year and become Guyana's only sole online newspaper to offer same-day news coverage of the most important issues and events. Our thousands of subscribers and visitors each day relish the idea that they can read today's news today rather than wait for one of the evening newscasts or tomorrow's newspapers. In fact, several people have already said they hardly read the newspapers anymore, relying instead on Demerara Waves.

The added advantage for Demerara Waves is that readers do not have to pay to access our content. Significantly, the number of comments on Demerara Waves' website has been increasing steadily ever since *Stabroek News*, a local independent newspaper, began charging for online readership. The reality is, nevertheless, that traditional newspapers have higher operational costs such as newsprint and related supplies, staff and electricity compared to the much lower costs of an online-only news operation such as Demerara Waves.

Our database of thousands of people is increasing in size each day. Rises in subscriptions have been seen particularly during major events such as the January 2011 grenade blast near a bus depot outside Guyana's largest public market in Georgetown.

Combining our website with social media such as Twitter and Facebook (www.facebook.com/demwaves), Demerara Waves has been able to carve a niche of its own. We push the news to people's email in-boxes and to their mobile phones. Surveys in the Caribbean and elsewhere have concluded that young people today hardly read books and newspapers. Their major sources of information are via the social media, ipods, computers and mobile smart phones and there, in part, is where demerarawaves.com is meeting them. Unlike traditional newspapers,

Demerara Waves provides comparatively short text news reports with the basic details and some contextual background rather than extensive reports that are less attractive to most young people and people on the go!

## Placing the emphasis on social networks
Much emphasis is placed on the social networks to tease people with a headline and a link to take them to www.demerarawaves.com. In a country where terrestrial radio broadcasting has been hamstrung by an almost 30-year-old monopoly, it is somewhat refreshing for not only the larger diaspora audience but the few Guyanese at home who can listen to a webcast on their mobile phones or computers.

Though some Guyanese still regard every website as a blog on which almost anything can be said about anyone, www.demerarawaves.com prides itself as a new media entity that holds the laws of libel, slander and defamation in high regard. Equal importance is given to fairness and balance in our coverage at all times, in accordance with time-tested journalistic principles.

Moreover, efforts are underway to re-design the website to make it more attractive and user-friendly to visitors and advertisers alike. The new website will be projecting itself as the South American country's hot-spot for both news and opinion as well as analyses.

Demerara Waves has been able to keep abreast of what's going on through a combination of sources and freelance contributors and tipsters across the country. With a new website coming on stream, the major challenge will, however, remain attracting and retaining a small but competent staff with the drive and passion to churn out the content as it happens. The staff must also have a good appreciation of the legal and ethical limitations while at the same time balancing those with freedom of speech and freedom of the media.

## All set for the general election
It is envisaged that with the increasing popularity of Demerara Waves as a source of text news, more people will gravitate to the internet radio broadcasts and podcasts when they recommence on a scheduled basis. With Guyana's general election scheduled for 2011, it means that audio-broadcasting equipment and webcasting time already purchased from a

United Kingdom-based server will no longer be left idle. They will be put to good and frequent use for direct internet radio streaming as well as link-ups with terrestrial stations in the Caribbean and North America that serve a large Guyanese audience. Panel discussions and the live coverage of campaign rallies are planned as part of the value-added content.

Demerara Waves, nevertheless, waits to see whether internet radio and podcasting will be governed by modern broadcast legislation that is expected from Guyana's 65-seat National Assembly before the end of 2011.

## Note on the author

Denis Chabrol formerly worked with the now defunct Guyana Broadcasting Corporation and the Caribbean News Agency/Caribbean Media Corporation. Currently he is a correspondent for the Caribbean Service of the British Broadcasting Corporation and Agence France Presse. The Publisher and Editor of Demerara Waves, he is a communications graduate of the University of Guyana and a United Nations Population Fund (UNFPA) Platinum Award-winner for radio production on HIV and AIDS.

# "Africa at 50" and the digital future: Implications for journalisms

**Okoth Fred Mudhai**

Investors in the mobile phone sector, fibre-optic cable infrastructure and related new media areas see opportunities in Africa's digital future. African governments and "local" private businesses, including banks, exploit money-making possibilities in modern technologies. Yet politicians dread the dispersal of communicative power into the hands of challengers such as civil society actors and social networks.

This chapter examines Africa's digital future in the context of the 50th anniversary of independence for many of the continent's states – with implications for mainstream and alternative journalisms. This was reflected in the wind of change, aided by a more open new media environment, blowing across North African nations such as Tunisia, Egypt and Libya in early 2011 – but varying contexts meant there was a limit on how far the message could spread to the rest of the vast continent, especially in the mostly ethnically divided sub-Saharan Africa. The extent to which the gathering, packaging and dissemination of news and information impact on the future depend on national and regional contexts.

## Brief background

Around 1960 (just before, during and three years after) a wind of change swept across Africa as various territories defined by colonialists several decades earlier gained "political"-governmental independence from developed nations. About a third of the continent's nations fought for, and achieved, self-rule in 1960 – and about two thirds gained independence between the mid-1950s and mid-1960s. It is for this reason that many of the more than 50 African countries celebrated their 50th anniversary of independence around 2010.

Various individuals and organisations helped Africa reflect on their past and celebrate a hopefully bright future. For instance, in late 2010, BBC Radio 4 ran a five-episode series titled *Africa at 50: Wind of change*. Such "revolutions" as witnessed in Tunisia and Egypt in early 2011 were partly spurred on by the new media technologies such as Twitter and Facebook. Indeed, as Berger stresses (Barratt and Berger 2007: 159), digital migration and convergence are key drivers in the development of Africa's media.

## Africa's digital future and journalism

Until 2010, most countries in Africa – especially in eastern and central regions – had been relying mostly on satellite technology for internet connections via European hubs. Three fibre optic cable companies-projects recently rolled out in eastern Africa – SEACOM (www.seacom.mu), the East African Submarine Cable System or EASSy (www.eassy.org) and the East African Marine Systems or TEAMS – joined similar infrastructure in other parts of the continent to improve connections to the rest of the world. "Africa's future *is* fibre," declares EASSy on its home page.

That digital future portends both opportunities and threats – economic growth and more open media-communication ecology on the one hand, and risks of instability on the other. Analysts such as Lyons (2011) argue that the "global growth-progress narrative is changing" to Africa as the new Asia and that the focus on "Chindia" (China-India) "may miss an even more exciting story in Africa" and mobile phone boom there. Recent estimates by the World Bank indicate that "improvements in

Africa's telecom infrastructure have contributed as much as 1 per cent to per capita GDP growth, a bigger role than changes in monetary or fiscal policies" (*Newsweek* 2010). In some countries such as Kenya, the World Bank reports that about a quarter of growth over the past decade is attributable to the information and communication technologies, or ICT, sector (Redfern 2010).

Political will is a key driver of ICT growth but control tendencies remain a problem. As in parts of Asia, some key North African countries exhibit the contradiction of both ICT boom and restrictions in expression – a paradox termed "controlled commodification" China-style (Weber and Jia 2007). Despite his strong-arm tendencies, landlocked Rwanda's President Kagame has put ICT at the centre of his socio-economic strategy.

## Fastest growth rate in mobile phone use

Africa's digital future involves increased penetration, registering the world's fastest growth rate, for instance, in mobile phones and Facebook use, according to statistics from the International Telecommunications Union (see www.itu.int) and O'Reilly Research (see www.oreilly.com). Amidst this growth, Africans are contributing to debates on their future which inevitably include digital aspects, off line and online, for instance, through such forums as Africa on the Blog.[i]

A number of Africans are defining, innovating, designing and exporting digital materials, products and resources. One example is Ushahidi (www.ushahidi.com), Swahili for "testimony", which was used to map the violence relating to the December 2007 Kenyan elections – and this was exported to South Africa, DR Congo, India, Pakistan, with Version 2, "Luanda", launched in late 2010.

Another is iHub (www.ihub.co.ke), describing itself as Nairobi's innovation hub with a focus on young entrepreneurs. Better known is mobile economy-banking solutions MPesa (mobile money, for low-cost transactions application) and associated M-Kesho (mobile tomorrow, a savings platform) launched by local Vodafone subsidiary Safaricom. In South Africa, youths have popularised a social networking site (SNS) MXit (www.mxit.co.za), created by Namibian developer Herman Heunis. It is South Africa's largest SNS, mainly used for chat and instant messaging, Java-based, mobile-based and practically free. The creators say on their website that it "turns any old phone to a smart phone" and the youths there prefer it to Facebook and Twitter.

## More African content online

The implications for ICT growth include more African content online, especially generated by journalists. Examples include such portals as All Africa.com (www.allafrica.com), a neat way to access most (but certainly not all) African newspapers' online content in one place. Through content agreements with 130 news organisations in Africa, the site boasts 1,000 stories a day and an archive of almost a million articles from 1997. Moreover, a number of newspapers have invested resources and personnel in online platforms. In Nairobi, the Nation Media Group, the Standard Group and Capital FM have created dedicated digital teams. In South Africa, *The Times* launched an online newspaper (with a free 120,000-140,000 circulation print version distributed as added value to subscribers of sister publication *The Sunday Times*). However, the future does not just lie in the mainstream journalism.

Citizen journalism is alive and thriving, especially during electoral and other national crises as recent events in Kenya, Ivory Coast, Tunisia, Libya and Egypt have demonstrated. Blogs, Twitter and Facebook have become alternative sources of news and information (see Becket 2008; Zuckerman 2009). "We can look forward to a raft of citizen bloggers (some of them doing journalism) around the continent..." (Barratt and Berger op cit: 167). Those behind Ushahidi and others used the new media effectively in reporting Kenya's 2007/2008 electoral crisis, and their use is likely to increase in future crises around Africa.

Another example is Voices of Africa, with its use of GPRS mobile phones to report on Nigeria and Kenya (Beckett 2008: 120). Other initiatives include the Citizen Journalism in Africa (CJA) project at www.citizenjournalismafrica.org which has trained 175 members from six countries, "especially in the use of social media, Web 2.0 and mobile technology" and Pambazuka News (www.pambazuka.org). These show that the future of journalism in Africa is alternative, digital, diverse and open-source.

That future, the subject of a 2008 special conference[ii] at the University of Oxford Reuters Institute for the Study of Journalism, is not restricted to the usual lamentations about restrictions on media freedoms. It is a future that has opportunities and challenges, and is intricately linked to socio-political and economic developments on the continent – locally and regionally. In this context, strengthening the pan-African approach will be a coping mechanism for the journalists – alternative and mainstream – and their outlets.

## Conclusions

Africa is not a monolithic whole; there are many "Africas". As most African countries celebrate the 50th anniversary of independence, the rulers and the ruled are re-examining and redefining their politics-governance and economies. Journalism on the continent is changing within the context of more pluralism and the demise of authoritarianism-militarism. There is movement from agriculture-based economies to oil and mining (not only in Congo and Nigeria but also in eastern Africa) and digital economies (such as in Rwanda and elsewhere in northern Africa).

Journalism and media businesses are cashing in on these economic opportunities. The embrace of alternative bilateral partners such as the Chinese, much to the chagrin of former colonisers, could be accompanied by further restrictions on media freedom.

Digital media offers many Africans beyond journalism more opportunities to communicate more freely and openly, and change the way they do politics-governance, business and social affairs at micro and macro levels. Is it making a difference? It is too early to be absolutely definite, but there are some indicators. Opportunities provided by growth in ICT with impacts in the economy are being exploited by journalism businesses such as Kenya's Nation Media Group and *The Times*, of South Africa.

In terms of content, the digital media has enabled a lot more content on Africa to go online. For Africans, government and politicos going online has resulted in some level of openness – though more needs to be done to enhance efficacy. For non-Africans, this has resulted in increasing knowledge of the continent, possibly reducing prejudices. The multi-direction information flow has thus partially reduced concerns about media or cultural imperialism.

The increasing ubiquity of new media – especially mobile phones – with attendant alternative journalism has reduced the dominance of mainstream journalism that often supports the status quo. The resulting networking and activism has challenged and countered governmental news and information controls. In particular, civil society organisations have played a key role in countering state propaganda.

Let's finish on a note of caution: African governments, while cherishing the economic benefits of ICTs, are reluctant to embrace its "open" nature. There, thus, remain enormous challenges for all those committed to media freedoms in many African countries, especially those with the highest internet access – including Egypt and South Africa.

## Notes

---

[i] See: www.africaontheblog.com/africa-what-will-the-next-50-years-look-like/, accessed on 2 February 2011
[ii] See Power of Journalism in Africa. Available online athttp://www.ox.ac.uk/media/news_releases_for_journalists/080923.html, accessed 2 February 2011

### References
Becket, C. (2008) *Supermedia: Saving journalism so it can save the world*, Oxford, Blackwell
Barratt, E. and Berger, G. (2007) *50 years of journalism: African media since Ghana's independence*, Johannesburg, Highway Africa
Blenford, A. (2009 Bold Rwanda takes broadband leap. BBC News, 21 September. Available online at http://news.bbc.co.uk/1/hi/technology/8266290.stm, accessed 19 November 2010
Lyons, R. (2011) Is Africa the New Asia?' Blog, 1 February. Available online at http://www.ronanlyons.com/2011/02/01/is-africa-the-new-asia/, accessed 2 February 2011
Mudhai, O. F. (2002) The internet: Triumphs and trials for Kenyan journalism, Robins, M. B. and Hilliard, R. L. (eds) *Beyond boundaries: Cyberspace in Africa*, Portsmouth, NH, Heinemann pp 89-104
*Newsweek* (2010) How Africa is becoming the New Asia, 18 February. Available online at http://www.newsweek.com/2010/02/18/how-africa-is-becoming-the-new-asia.html, accessed 2 February 2011

Redfern, Paul (2010) M-Pesa boosts war against poverty, *Daily Nation*, 22 November. Available online at http://www.nation.co.ke/News/MPesa%20boosts%20war%20against% 20poverty%20/-/1056/1058698/-/v2tybt/-/, accessed on 31 January 2011

Weber, I. and Jia, L. (2007) Internet and self-regulation in China: The cultural logic of controlled commodification', *Media, Culture and Society*, Vol. 29, No. 5 pp 772-789

Zuckerman, E. (2009) Citizen media and the Kenyan electoral crisis', Allan, S. and Thorsen, E. (eds) *Citizen journalism: Global perspectives*, New York, Peter Lang, pp.187-196

## Note on the author

Dr Fred Mudhai is a Senior Lecturer in Journalism and Global Media-Communication at Coventry University, UK. His publications include a chapter on internet and journalism in *Beyond boundaries: Cyberspace in Africa* (2002), a chapter on civic use of mobile phones in *Reformatting politics: Information technology and global civil society* (2006), a chapter on radio culture in *Popular media, democracy and citizenship in Africa* (2010) and a number of journal articles. He is co-editor of *African media and the digital public sphere* (2009) and was part of IT and Civil Society Network at the US Social Science Research Council (2003-2005). His journalism awards include two on ICT at global level. He was a full-time journalist at the Standard Group (Nairobi) in the 1990s, also contributing to outlets in Africa, the UK and the USA.

# Towards a new balance: The rise of new media and its balancing power in modern mass communication

**Homson Shaw**

### The old media facing the rise of the new

The influence of traditional media in China is being challenged and diminished by a fast-rising force as elsewhere in the world. The decline of such influence is caused partially by the internal structures and operational routines of traditional media, but more importantly by the rise of new media that are completely reshaping the modern media ecology in ways people of two decades ago would never have imagined.

The message flow in mass communication is typically one way, from source to receiver and feedback is more difficult than in the interpersonal setting (Dominick 2001: 16). When the sources of information and the channels for its dissemination are largely controlled by centralised governments and powerful media corporations messages would go through many filters before reaching the public (see Herman and Chomsky 2002). However the emergence of the internet has brought about a dramatic change to the traditional manner of message flow.

The new platform of communication has provided the passive audience of the past the freedom of choice. And where the reader or audience has a doubt about a story he or she can resort to other sources to check. The huge amount of available information also allows the media consumer to make comparisons and analyses. In addition, the new media provides audiences a space to publish their own opinions instantly, without having to pass the filters of traditional media that tend to block different or inappropriate messages.

New technologies have changed the living habits of both traditional and modern audiences by changing their environment and the reading and social tools they use. According to the 27th CNNIC statistic report on the development of China's internet network, there were 457 million internet users by December 2010, 450 million of them using broadband, covering 34.3 per cent of the total population, a 5.4 percent increase compared to the previous year's figure. Of the internet population 67.7 per cent use instant messaging and 66.3 per cent of them browse the internet via mobile phones. A total of 93.1 per cent of the internet users are aged from 10 to 49, in comparison to 5.8 per cent aged 50 and above, who are more traditional readers (CNNIC 2011).

A large number of new media entities emerged in China in response to the huge market opportunities. The network has, indeed, made today's world a completely different one. In 2001, several young editors of a local newspaper in the city of Hangzhou in eastern China started a BBS (Bulletin Board System) for convenient communication with their readers. They named it 19lou, as their office was on the 19th floor. Much to their surprise this humble single room, single PC-server-supported BBS soon became the most popular interactive social platform of the local readers. In five years they have grown into a middle-size firm working in an office area of 5,000 square meters serving more than one million citizens, with a mission to "become the most people-friendly and effective social network for the residents of cities" (Wang and Wu et al 2010).

Compared to the rapidly developing new media, the "old" media represented by television and official newspapers which are, by nature, semi-official institutions under the administration of the government, are still largely running in the traditional ways. Though they have been making efforts to make a smooth transition from the planned economy to a market economy, the top managers in these businesses are likely to take longer to adapt to the new technologies. There have been criticisms that the television screens in China are flooded by features made more to the taste and values of mainstream consumers than to the real and diversified needs of the public. Owing to their semi-official, semi-capitalist nature, the traditional media have to serve the mainstream values on the one hand and satisfy the advertisers on the other. As a result, they are constantly accused by media critics for "wooing the rich and ignoring the poor" and "straying away from their mission as a public instrument" (Wu 2008).

While the traditional media are trying to adapt to the changing era, new media are making a stronger impact, not only through developing new ways to cover news but in their operation mechanisms and market structures as well. Up to January 2011, there were 8,656,525 registered portals covering all walks of modern life (CNNIC op cit). The huge cyberspace they created challenged both traditional media structures as well as the dominant values in society.

Today's readers are more surfers than traditional readers of books, magazines and newspapers. They browse the internet for virtually everything. If a college student is asked how he finds news of the day he would almost surely tell you "the internet". The younger generation of readers not only read differently, but they react differently too. They post their comments if any news coverage or blog article interests them. Traditional papers that offer no feedback opportunities would be ignored by them.

That is why fewer younger people are reading the official newspapers than before. Their main interests have been attracted either to the web pages of leading portals such as sohu.com and sina.com, or specialised web pages of their interest. They are more interested in reading the blogs of celebrities and posting comments below their articles. The great majority of the modern day readers have diverted at least part of their time and energy to opening their own blogs and running their social networks. This means a shrinking world for the traditional media.

## The balancing power of new media: A few case studies

Perhaps powered by the public urge to access to uncensored contents, cyberspace often provides information the mainstream media would find inconvenient to publicise. One of the changes brought by the internet age is that people now have a much wider choice of what to read and listen, though such choice is still under different levels of control and interference. If one wants to know what the authorities want to say, read a mainstream newspaper or watch the news programme on CCTV1, or the web pages of dot-gov-dot-cn portals. For information hard to find on the mainstream newspapers and portals, go to the BBS spaces, blogs and countless other networks. Those who are interested in the political aspect of issues but are unable to find real insightful views from the mainstream sources can turn to portal-recommended blog columns, BBS space or specialist blogs.

Personal blogs are having the biggest impact on the traditional media. Click open sohu.com, for example, and you find 68 windows displaying all possible areas of interest. And among the three rows of menu windows at the top of its home page, "Blog" is sixth on the left in the top row. To many readers, this is the most exciting part of a web page because it often provides views and information that are hard to find in traditional newspapers or magazines. Typical blog articles may include insider analyses of a particular industry or of government policies, in-depth stories of unknown or ignored corners of society that mainstream papers might find inconvenient to reveal, or personal accounts or commentaries written by either specialists or grass-root individuals.

## A blog article on the real cause of bribery

Dr. Feng, Chairman of large real estate company in China, recently wrote a blog arguing that corruption was more a result of bad management structures than the moral downfall of the "corrupted" individual. He supported his argument by analysing the contrasting fate of two individuals, Mr. Huang, founder and Chairman of Gome Appliances, now convicted of bribery, and Mr. Wang, CEO of another real estate company, who is well known for his claims that he has never and would never bribe any officials (see Feng 2010).

## The 'My dad is Li Gang' case

On 16 October 2010, a car was in an accident with two girl students in northern China's Hebei University on a narrow lane on campus (Yigong 2010). Afterwards, the drunk driver youth did not stop but simply drove on to the dormitory and dropped off his girl friend. He was stopped by security guards on his way back and asked to take responsibility for his behaviour. He was said to have shown no sympathy towards the then seriously injured victims (one died later in hospital) and, in response to such request he yelled back at the surrounding people: "Sue me if you can, my dad is Li Gang!"

No official paper was known to have reported this accident. But on 17 October an account was posted on a forum of tianya.cn, a community-oriented social network, and triggered an earthquake on the net. Some 470,000 clicks were recorded soon after the story was posted. It was soon clear that the "dad" of the youth, named Li Qiming, a student of Hebei University and an intern at the local television station, was vice- director of a branch of the Bureau of Public Security, of Baoding City, Hebei Province, a northern province surrounding Beijing. It was not long before a myriad of details were revealed and spread to all the news pages of major portals in and outside China. This wave of exposure, controversy and accusation attracted enormous interest – and concerns – across the whole country. A famous catchphrase emerged: "My dad is Li Gang" to express the arrogance of those who believe they are protected from any criminal charges by their "official dads".

The huge public pressure soon brought out the "official dad" who made tearful apologies on television on 22 October. Soon afterwards it was reported that the victim of the accident was offered compensation of 460,000 RMB (about £45,000). *New Beijing Daily*, said to be the first corporately-run newspaper in China, reported on 16 December that Mr. Zhang Kai, the lawyer representing the victims of the Hebei University campus accident, who had previously been told not to represent the victim in the case, encountered three cars which tried to surround his car as he was driving out of Beijing. The licence plates of two of those cars had been deliberately removed. According to Mr. Zhang: "A dozen youngsters came out of their cars and tried to pull at my door handles, yelling 'You get out!'" And when he saw one of the youngsters pulling out an iron rod he immediately drove off at speed through the gap between the enclosing cars. The attackers remain at large.

There was a news item at new.qq.com (the largest online social network in China) on 26 January 2011 that the open trial of this case was about to begin at the local court, but the requests of journalists to sit in the court were declined for reasons of "limited space". A brief news item headed "Justness of Li Gang case questioned" appeared on jcrb.com, the Network of Justice, on 26 January 2011 reporting that only five media institutions selected by the authorities were allowed one journalist each to cover the trial as "an indication of a just trial", on condition that they would only use the scripts provided by the authorities (Wei 2010). Even then, the news report was removed in less than 24 hours. And despite a directive from high propaganda authorities to "stop the hype" the openness and justness of local court was widely questioned in China.

## Balancing the official and grass roots media

News coverage such as this would rarely appear in a traditional mainstream newspaper, particularly in local papers under the immediate administration of the local government and Communist Party of China authorities. But one can find many such examples on the news pages of internet portals. Countless other stories can be found on personal blogs, with more details in words and photographs, and more radical comments. The internet and the service it provides have blurred the boundaries between mass communication and interpersonal communication thanks to the insatiability of the internet, which is impossible for any authorities to bring under their control.

Any message sent by an individual can quickly catch the attention of the mass media and become widely circulated. This vast space provides the public a convenient access to a myriad of outlets for the sharing of information and opinions despite the attempts by the authorities to control its contents. It is believed by many that this will help bring about more openness, fairness and justice to society. At the same time, whenever the authorities detect controversial coverage they post comments on their own blog sites to offset the influence of blogs which express non-mainstream views. Such measures are officially referred to as "the correct leading of public opinion" and they are likely to expand in the future. However, the public should not be pessimistic about the future openness of the internet. For it would be extremely difficult for the mass media in China to return to the days when the public were denied even the faintest hope of openly questioning and criticising mainstream viewpoints.

# References

China Internet Network Information Center (CNNIC) (2011) 27th Statistic report on the development of China's internet network, 19 January. Available online at http://research.cnnic.cn/html/1295343214d2557.html, accessed on 1 January 2011

Dominick, Joseph R. (2001) *The dynamics of mass communication: Media in the digital age*, Boston, MA., McGraw Hill

Feng, Lun (2010) Bribery: Not a moral issue but one of administration structure. Available online at http://blog.sina.com.cn/s/blog_46f42eca01017n6i.html?tj=1, accessed on 17 December 2010

Herman, Edward S. and Chomsky, Noam (2002) *Manufacturing consent*, New York, Pantheon Books

Wang, Kan and Wu, Chongsheng et al (2010) Transition from traditional media to new media: The rise of 19Lou, *Press*, April

Wei, Hongqian (2010) Court session to begin today for Hebei University campus accident case, jcrb.com. Available online at http://news.qq.com/a/20110126/000028.htm, accessed on 16 December 2010

Wu, Xiaoying (2008) Current situation of China's TV and the challenges it faces, *Tian Fu New Ideas*, June

Yigong, Heda (2010) "Appalling!" Two new students of Hebei University knocked in the air. Commentary column, Tianya.cn, 17 October. Available online at http://www.tianya.cn/publicforum/content/free/1/1998737.shtml, accessed on 15 December 2010

# Note on the author

Homson Shaw (Shao, Hongsong) is Associate Dean International of Zhejiang University of Media and Communications and an executive member of the Council of Directors of Hangzhou Translators' Association. Awarded his first degree in English literature by Liaoning Normal University, he became a teacher of English at Yingkou Teachers' College in 1986. In 2004, he began to teach bilingual broadcasting at ZUMC School of International Cultures and Communications and started his studies of mass communication. Shaw is a translator of Edward Herman and Noam Chomsky's *Manufacturing consent*, which is scheduled to be published by Peking University Press in the spring of 2011. He also has a number of articles published in the journals of colleges and universities in China.

# Section 9. In and out of academia

Richard Lance Keeble

With almost 27 years of teaching in higher education (following 14 years as a hack), my own academic career has taken in all the extraordinary technological changes of recent times. When I started at City University, London, in September 1984, my teaching of production skills involved subbing copy by hand (carefully marking the fonts and measures on each page), drawing the designs on layout sheets – and then travelling to the printers to see the clanking, noisy presses spew out those many metal lines of print.

We then shifted to Amstrads. A massive room was full of them – and we felt very proud and cutting-edge. Yet it would take me a whole term of weekly workshops to explain the computer to the students – with a special session devoted to printing out! The PCs (remember those limbo files?) would produce columns of text which we would then stick on to broadsheet-type sheets. And then these would be fixed to the wall for the feedback sessions.

Ventura was the first desktop computer publishing program I had to master. And what a nightmare it proved. Ventura was, in fact, so complex I would need three sessions simply to explain to students how to create a file! But there was one distinct advantage in being a production teacher at this time. It was all strange and somewhat daunting to the students – so if you appeared to have mastered its mysteries (and, as always with teaching, there was a lot of "theatre" involved) you were admired as some techno-genius!

Then along came the QuarkXpress (and its many versions) and I grew to love its fiendishly logical and intricate layout facilities. In the early days, I somehow managed to keep two weeks ahead of the students – though, with the servers and computers constantly crashing, a lot of my time was spent calming tearful students for whom, say, a whole day's hard work was lost.

Over all these years, of course, I'd had not one bit of training: it was all learned "on the job". I remember spending an entire Easter "holiday" with my colleague, Bob Jones, attempting to master the intricacies of Ventura – by laying out a magazine for the department.

Over the last ten years, journalism, it hardly needs to be said, has gone through a technological revolution. And journalism teaching in universities has inevitably undergone radical changes. All programmes now have to be multi-platform – from day one. But courses do differ on the extent to which sites such as Twitter and Facebook, YouTube and Flickr are integrated into newsroom routines.

Former *Guardian* executive Emily Bell, now director of Columbia's Tow Center for Digital Journalism, has certainly provoked considerable debate amongst hackademics after arguing in her inaugural lecture in October 2010 that the journalism graduates of the future will "know how to glean and interpret data and marry it to compelling narrative. They will understand the capacity and limitations of software, and how to optimise its use for journalism". A much-hyped new MA programme at Columbia will lead to a joint journalism and computer science qualification. Could that be increasingly the road taken by universities in this country?

In this section's first chapter, Ian Reeves, former editor of *Press Gazette* and currently director of learning and teaching at the University of Kent's Centre for Journalism, certainly follows the cue provided by Emily Bell and stresses the importance of programming skills for today's journalists. Reeves interviews a number of practitioners but finds no consensus over the necessary knowledge and skills for the PJ (programmer-journalist).

So Reeves suggests his own: "a familiarity with HTML and CSS, the basic building blocks of web pages; a familiarity with url structures and the organisation of web pages; and an ability to set up and manipulate a simple MySQL relational database. From there, you could pick a framework such as Ruby on Rails, Python or Django – Ruby on Rails is the friendliest for the newcomer – and dive right in". He adds: "The good news is that there is a huge amount of help available online in the shape of tutorials, networks and forums."

Finally in this section, John Mair (the ebullient joint editor of this book) and his colleague Peter Woodbridge report on the extraordinary series of lectures (dubbed the "Coventry Conversations") held regularly at the city's university. Open to the public, the speakers have included all the main movers and shakers of the industry – from the Director General of the BBC to the founders of Channel 4 and on to famous on-screen faces – Jon Snow, Jeremy Paxman, Kirsty Wark, Jeremy Vine to name but four. Mair and Woodbridge write: "The Conversations have turned Coventry into a cutting edge centre for media discussion. The Conversations have become part of the institutional fabric – the DNA – of the university and of the city too. They are the best known brand in CU and affectionately known by students as the 'CovCons'."

All are published in their entirety online. Sometimes they are also "broadcast" live via Twitter and blogging. The result of this open approach has been wide-ranging, with more than 5,000 bums on seats each year, much attention in the local, national and press and a swathe of professional opportunities opening for students. The university podcast site had 65,000 plus downloads to date (March 2011); the most popular a *Panorama* reporter on how she uncovered the truth about Ritalin and ADHD which had been downloaded 2,000 times. The university's *i*tunesU site has had three million hits to date on the Coventry Conversations, the most popular about the games industry but a surprising success is a conference on the reporting of Afghanistan.

While universities are facing appalling cutbacks and student fees are set to rise to unacceptable levels, there are still spaces in HE in which innovative teaching and learning can flourish: the "CovCons" (with their clever exploitation of the web) are proof enough of that.

Ext 884 .

To Renew
Books.

# University Centre Barnsley

Telephone: 01226 216 884

Class No: ...................................

**This book is to be returned on or before the last date stamped below.  Thank you!**

| | | |
|---|---|---|
| | | |
| | | |
| | | |
| | | |
| | | |
| | | |
| | | |
| | | |
| | | |
| | | |
| | | |
| | | |

# How I learned to stop worrying and love the code

**Ian Reeves**

Late in 2006, Professor John Naughton, of the Open University, delivered a memorable address to the Society of Editors' annual conference. The journalism industry, he felt, was woefully disconnected from the new generation of media consumers who would be its future customers, and to prove his point he requested a show of hands.

How many in the audience, he wondered, had their own account at a social networking site? Around half a dozen arms crept into the air. How many had ever uploaded a video to YouTube? Three of those arms came down. How many had used BitTorrent? No hands remained. How many knew what BitTorrent was? Silence. Embarrassed coughs.

It was a telling moment. The room was full of influential journalists from national and regional newspapers and broadcasters. These were the decision-makers who were working to plot their industry's escape from the darkness that they could already feel was falling across the mainstream media landscape. And yet hardly any of them had experimented with the technology they hoped would play a major part in their salvation. But, as Prof. Naughton went on to tell them, these tools that most of them had so far avoided were being seized upon with untrammelled enthusiasm by their future consumers:

> These kids have been socially conditioned in a universe that runs parallel to the one inhabited by most folks in the media business. They've been playing computer games of mind-blowing complexity forever. They're resourceful, knowledgeable and natural users of computer and communications technology. They're Digital Natives – accustomed to creating content of their own – and publishing it. They buy music from the *i*Tunes store…use BitTorrent to get US editions of *Lost*. They think "Google" is a synonym for "research" and regard it as quite normal to maintain and read blogs, use Skype to talk to their mates and upload photos to Flickr. Some write entries on Wikipedia. And they know how to use iMovie or Adobe Premiere to edit videos and upload them to YouTube. These are the future, my friends. They're here and living among us. They're not very interested in us, and I'm not sure I blame them. The best we can hope for is that one day they may keep us as pets.

For an industry with a long, proud and profitable tradition of editorially-led technical innovation, this was a worrying state of affairs. The line of editors that could be traced from W. T. Stead – whose pioneering new journalism owed much to his development of new typographic techniques for designing and presenting journalism – through Arthur Christiansen, Kelvin Mackenzie and Paul Dacre, was populated with men who were technically adept at developing new ways to present their journalism to the mass market.

## Digital natives reshape the future of journalism

But as the consumption of news moved away from the printed page, their successors, as Naughton illustrated, could no longer make the claim that they were at the technological cutting edge. More worrying, those Digital Natives whom he identified were doing more than consuming and creating content. Some of them were creating entirely new digital products that would help reshape the future of mass communication and storytelling.

They not only understood the technology as end users. They knew how to get under the bonnet. They were developers, programmers and coders – hackers – who were already developing the digital tools that have multiplied and expanded at dizzying speed even in the four years since Naughton's speech. And while the journalism industry has been happy to exploit new technologies these hackers have created – tools and services such as Wordpress, Dipity, Vuvox, Yahoo Pipes, Scraperwiki – it has been conspicuously absent from their development. Worse, it has even been reluctant to set its more technically-enthusiastic journalists free to innovate.

I was one of the print editors in the audience without my hand in the air at the end of Naughton's 2006 address. Since then I have had the opportunity, on various projects, to explore the underlying technologies that make digital journalism possible. In this chapter I will try to explore whether the technological divide between hacks and hackers is narrowing and examine whether current journalists, editors and their managers feel that the emerging role of journalist-programmer has an important part to play in their industry's future. The role of BJ – broadcast journalist – is well established. We've since seen the rise of the VJ, videojournalist. Is now the time of the PJ, the programmer journalist, to stake a claim? I'll also try to unravel the tangle of technologies and to identify whether there is a core set of fundamental technical skills that an aspiring journalist-programmer might need.

## Early reluctance to integrate programmers into the heart of the business

There existed in many news organisations a profound early reluctance to integrate developers, programmers and coders into the heart of their businesses. Yes, they were employing some of them to build their web sites – usually in a basement room remote from the editorial floor. But often they were eyed with suspicion and, occasionally, contempt. The journalist who dared show an interest in creation of content for the web risked unique opprobrium. Digital journalism pioneer Kevin Anderson (2010) blogged in January 2010:

> I have spent most of my career developing unique digital skills while producing content for broadcast and print. I have often felt that I had to work harder than traditional journalists to prove that I'm not just an "expert in cut and paste". I work very hard to know my

beats, work across platforms and produce high quality journalism that meets or exceeds the industry standards of print, broadcast and web journalism. I am not the only digital journalist who puts this sort of effort in. Yet the industry is still rife with the same anti-digital prejudice I witnessed ten years ago. It's long past time for senior figures in journalism to publicly state that demeaning digital staff is not acceptable. Prejudice towards digital journalists needs to stop. It sends a message to digital journalists that they are unwanted at a time when their skills are desperately needed by newspapers. Digital staff should not be the convenient whipping women and men for those angry and upset about economic uncertainty in the industry.

Perhaps that explains why even those journalists working within the industry who had developed skills in programming and who had their own ideas of how the future might develop, tended to leave in order to bring them to fruition.

Take the example of Joe Weiss, a photojournalist and picture editor who developed Soundslides, the Flash-based tool that lets visually-minded journalists create audio slideshows without having to learn a complex software package. A self-taught programmer, Weiss had worked as a multimedia producer, and had been director of photography at the *Herald-Sun*, in North Carolina. He worked on Soundslides in his own time, and released it commercially in 2005. It has since become widely used in the industry.

Then there's Adrian Holovaty, perhaps the most famous advocate of "journalism via computer programming". A journalism graduate who worked for the *Atlanta Journal Constitution*, the *Lawrence Journal-World* and the *Washington Post*, Holovaty developed ChicagoCrime.org as a personal side project. It was a trailblazing interactive online "mash-up" of map and crime data that allowed the city's residents to identify reported crime in their neighbourhood by keying in their zip code or by clicking on the street where they lived. He also recognised the industry's reluctance to embrace digital specialists, in a 2006 interview with the Online Journalism Review:

> Newsrooms need to welcome technical people with open arms and give them an environment in which they can thrive. Treat techies as

bona fide members of the journalism team – not as IT robots who just do what you tell them to do. Let them be creative. Give them interesting problems to solve. Trust them. Even if j-schools start producing genius computer programmers, or if it becomes trendy for computer-science majors to seek employment at newspaper web sites, newspapers will need to change their attitudes, culture and resource allocation if they want these people to stick around. Otherwise, they'll pack their bags after a couple of months and go work for Google (Niles 2006).

## Journalism goes hyperlocal

A few months after that was published, Holovaty packed his own bags to develop and launch Everyblock.com – a hyperlocal journalism project – with a $1m grant from the Knight Foundation. Holovaty is exceptional – not many journalists would be capable of creating their own programming framework (in his case, Django, now widely used in many web projects) because existing languages were not up to the job – but both he and Weiss strike me as precisely the kind of individuals whom the newspaper industry would have done well to retain.

Still, four years later, and with Everyblock now snapped up by MSNBC.com, there are some signs that mainstream journalism is beginning to recognise the value of the journalist-programmers who have followed them. Certainly some highly respected voices are helping to make the case. Here's Tim Berners-Lee, one of the web's founding fathers, speaking at an event in November 2010 to launch the release of massive blocks of UK government data through an initiative he helped to devise:

> The responsibility [to analyse this data] needs to be with the press. Journalists need to be data-savvy. These are the people whose jobs are to interpret what government is doing to the people. So it used to be that you would get stories by chatting to people in bars, and it still might be that you'll do it that way sometimes. But now it's also going to be about poring over data and equipping yourself with the tools to analyse it and picking out what's interesting. And keeping it in perspective, helping people out by really seeing where it all fits together, and what's going on in the country (Arthur 2010).

Those news organisations which are already on the case are producing work that proves the point. *The New York Times*'s Interactive News Technology Group was set up in 2009 under the leadership of Aron Pilhofer. Profiled in *New York Magazine*, Pilhofer explained:

> The proposal was to create a newsroom: a group of developers-slash-journalists, or journalists-slash-developers, who would work on long-term, medium-term, short-term journalism – everything from elections to NFL penalties (Nussbaum 2009).

His team continues to produce truly innovative journalism, using new digital techniques both in the gathering of news and in the way they present it to, and engage with, their audience. A couple of examples: their "Health Care Conversations" feature was a creative way of encouraging reader debate and reaction to key issues on health reform, using what the team describe as a "bento box" visual structure; "Living With Less", a crowd-sourced feature in which readers shared their survival strategies for coping with the economic downturn; and "Casualties of War" used a mass of data collated from the Iraq War to mark the 3,000[th] US military fatality there in a graphically stunning way.

There are many others and, although not all of the team's experiments have proved successful, their numerous hits demonstrate what can be achieved when journalists are encouraged to think as programmers and vice versa.

Another organisation with a team of programmer journalists is ProPublica, the American non-profit investigative journalism organisation funded by philanthropists. At ProPublica the PJs develop "news applications" – which they describe as "interactive web pages that tell stories using software instead of words and pictures".

Using its Dollars For Docs tool, to give one example, readers can type in their own doctor's name to discover whether they have received money from drugs companies' marketing budgets. It was made possible by collection and aggregation of data made public following several legal cases, using "techniques [mostly] within the ability of the moderately experienced programmer", according to Dan Ngugen, who previously worked on the *Sacramento Bee* newspaper as a reporter, web programmer and multimedia producer.

## How ProPublica helps other programmer-journalists

The ProPublica team is also committed to sharing its techniques, so it publishes tutorials and tip sheets to help other programmer-journalists.

Bill Alpert, senior editor at the weekly stock market magazine, *Barrons*, has been using Dow Jones data in investigative journalism for a decade or so. When we spoke he was in the process of hiring a PJ intern. The advertisement for this post is the first I have seen that requires candidates to send examples of both computer code and journalism that they have written, along with their CV. Alpert has no doubt that this combination of skills will become commonplace:

> It will take a generation for programming to become as common as, say, the ability to read financial statements – a modestly-widespread capability...which was just starting to be taught in journalism schools when I was a student in 1980. Does that mean there will be a zillion programmer-journalist/journalist-programmer jobs available? I doubt it, but I hope I'm proven wrong...we're inventing this as we go along and no one ever knows how big or little their projects will prove to be.

It is harder to find teams of people who would describe themselves as programmer-journalists in the UK. At the *Guardian*, which has pinned its colours to a digital future more firmly than most newspaper groups, Simon Rogers runs a team which has been set up to find, tell and sell stories from data sets. He doesn't explicitly look for journalists with programming skills, although he is starting to see people joining at researcher level with specifically-useful data mining coding skills; instead the team works closely with the *Guardian's* specialist developers. He explains that he has encouraged his team to use relatively straightforward techniques with existing tools such as Microsoft Excel, which means they can focus on the real journalism – making sure the right questions are asked: "I do worry about getting dragged into a slightly esoteric world where the programming becomes more important than the answer."

## When the *Guardian* "crowdsourced" its reporting

But he also points out that he is in the fortunate position of having access to a well-resourced technology team that features developers such as Simon Willison, who built the MPs' expenses tool which the *Guardian* used to encourage readers to help "crowdsource" their reporting of the information. "I'm spoiled in that regard, but if I was working in a more isolated environment then absolutely I can see you will need people with both sets of skills."

Martin Belam, information architect at the same organisation, agrees that it's a "programming mindset" rather than a set of specific coding skills that the nascent digital journalist needs to develop. But there is still work to do. He counsels that there are risks in trying to be too prescriptive in setting trained journalists on the programming path: "It's hard to do it often enough to make it useful. If you're going to learn a programming language, it becomes difficult if you're only going to be using it once every three or four months. If you're learning to drive a car you need to practise more often than that and the same thing applies."

Nigel Vincent, head of online editorial development at regional newspaper group Newsquest, is one of a number of executives to take the pragmatic view. "There is a slight danger that if [journalists] get too obsessed or bogged down with writing code they lose sight of the basics of what they're here for – which is to find stories, to investigate stories and to get them out there as fast as they can." Like others in his position, he sees collaboration between journalists and developers as the more efficient approach – though he does expect greater opportunities for editorial staff who can bridge the divide through a deeper understanding of the technology. Another senior executive puts it more bluntly:

> We deliberately limit what journalists can do on our site in terms of HTML because in the past we've had people building things because they think they know how to – and I'm not trying to knock them, good on them for trying – but they're producing these things which are not tested across all browsers, they haven't considered usability at all, or accessibility. They're broken, they don't work, they look horrible. And they've spent a long time doing them. What's the point?

### (Mainly) young, digitally-engaged journalists

Nonetheless, there is an emerging group of (mainly) young, digitally-engaged journalists who clearly do want to add more coding and programming elements to their toolkits and are doing something about it – often in their own time. One such is Alison Gow, one of Trinity Mirror's rising stars of the digital era, who has just been made editor of

*Wales on Sunday* and Walesonline. Having started her career as a print reporter, she moved into digital journalism at the *Liverpool Echo*. Her technical epiphany came when she was watching multimedia guru Eric Ulken demonstrate a murder map he had put together for a US newspaper: "I realised that I didn't know how much I didn't know. I was looking at him thinking, I've no idea how to that, even though he's standing in front of me explaining it. That was when the knowledge gap really made me anxious. There weren't that many people that I could even ask."

One of her solutions was to begin teaching herself data "scraping" techniques which led to her working with an organisation called ScraperWiki, a start-up company in the north west of England. Now she sees the addition of programming skills as part of a natural progression of journalism's relationship with the web: "There seems to have been this shift: we went from conversation, to curation, then from that to how we write programs that help us to do that curation."

For others, an enthusiasm for programming, data and journalism has not proved so compatible with the harsh economics of newspaper publishing. Mary Hamilton was a reporter at Archant's *Eastern Daily Press* whose interest in data stories had given her newspaper some innovative hits both in print and online – using FoI-obtained parking ticket data, for example, to show readers which streets were being aggressively targeted by council officials. But she became increasingly frustrated at how much time she was able to spend on developing this sort of project. She had started to work with a local group of web developers on projects for the paper, but found that scarce resources meant that her line managers could no longer find time to let that happen.

> It got a lot more difficult in terms of having time to do that. They couldn't spare me even for a few hours a fortnight to work on these things. And I found it more and more difficult, on top of a ten hour day, to create the space you need. I had the overriding sense that online ideas had to take a back seat, always, to getting enough stories in the paper.

Hamilton is now a digital media executive at Citywire, the financial information specialist, where she describes part of her job as being a "geek to journalist translator, and vice versa".

## Support network: hackshackers.com

Striking from my conversations with industry practitioners is that the vast majority of those who can realistically claim the title programmer-journalist say that they have taught themselves the techie stuff. Hamilton, like other journalists trying to develop their programming skills, is part of a support network, hackshackers.com, formed in 2009 with the intention of bringing journalists and coders closer together and encouraging the sharing of ideas and skillsets. Established in the US, it has a growing branch of eager participants in the UK too, many of them journalists with a specific interest in learning particular coding languages. Its first four (not quite monthly) meetings, have seen numbers grow from 50 to more than 100.

All of which points to the fact that the industry – and I include journalism departments under that label – must ensure it is providing training and continuous professional development support to those who want it. Many university departments, including the one I work at, are already including significant strands of data journalism and digital storytelling into their programmes. We will surely see the emergence of more specialist programmes too, which allow some students to immerse themselves more thoroughly in the art of coding.

Rich Beckman, a professor of visual journalism at the University of Miami and a guru of new media education, told *The New York Times*: "There were deans all over the country saying, 'We're never going to teach computer programming in J-school.' Well, now they are" (Selter 2009).

Columbia Journalism School has just launched a new Master's programme in conjunction with the university's computer science department. Students will split their time 50/50 between studying traditional journalism skills and computer science. It expands on the logic of Northwestern University's scholarships aimed at recruiting computer programmers to study on its journalism programme. Former *Guardian* executive Emily Bell, now director of Columbia's Tow Center for Digital Journalism, where the new course will run, outlined the thinking when she opened the centre last October:

> No one from mainstream media thought to look at the computer science graduate programs of schools like Stanford, MIT and Columbia in the 1990s to help navigate the future. And what a huge

mistake that was...Our journalists will need to serve a far more complex world with the highest standards, and it is our job to provide the educational foundation for that. This sounds lofty and idealistic, but has immediate practical applications: they will be the journalists who know how to glean and interpret data and marry it to compelling narrative. They will understand the capacity and limitations of software, and how to optimize its use for journalism. They will understand the importance of finding, measuring and retaining an audience and what methods to use. They will be the first generation which eradicates the divide between technology and journalism (Bell 2010).

## Graduates going deeper into the technology behind production

Bill Grueskin, the school's academic dean, says he hopes that the programme will produce students capable of going much deeper than existing journalism students into the technology behind news creation and production: "Almost all of those skills rely on using existing software or programs to do digital journalism," he told *Wired* magazine. "We hope and expect that graduates of this program will be more able to innovate and create the solutions the news business so sorely needs" (Van Buskirk 2010).

It's not just a question of teaching journalists a few coding languages and giving them a deeper understanding of how databases are built. *Wired* asked Columbia computing professors how they thought the programmer journalist could shape the future of journalism. They came up with ideas including; developing more sophisticated automated journalism tools; "digital trust" systems – enabling users to sort the wheat from the chaff of online news; identification of underreported events from secretive states; and 3D visualisations.

More prosaically, a crucial question for today's would-be programmer journalists, and for those who want to teach them, is which languages or code frameworks to start with. When editors from the *Las Vegas Sun* showed the Online News Association how they had achieved their much-admired web site overhaul in 2008, the list of technologies read like a particularly unpalatable alphabet soup: XHTML, CSS, RSS, Javascript, Google Docs, Linux, Django, Python, Ajax. *The New York Times* and the *Guardian* use a coding framework called Ruby on Rails for much of their data work. Many social media sites – Facebook included – are based on

MySQL databases. And then there's PHP, Perl and jQuery. To say nothing of what you might need to master to get your work onto the new wave of mobile and tablet devices (I speak as someone who spent last summer learning Objective C to build the Centre for Journalism iPad app).

## Little consensus amongst practitioners on the core set

It's a terrifying list. And there's little consensus among the practitioners I have spoken to as to whether a core set exists – their answers tend to depend on what is used within their own organisations. My own suggested technical core for the nascent PJ would be this: a familiarity with HTML and CSS, the basic building blocks of web pages; a familiarity with url structures and the organisation of web pages; and an ability to set up and manipulate a simple MySQL relational database. From there, you could pick a framework like Ruby on Rails, Python or Django – Ruby on Rails is the friendliest for the newcomer – and dive right in. The good news is that there is a huge amount of help available online in the shape of tutorials, networks and forums.

This is the new environment in which we find ourselves. The data about us, the details of decisions that affect us, the workings of states and corporations, the messages we exchange, the transactions we make and the media we consume – so much of them are now contained within those ones and zeros stored on web servers around the planet. (If you still have any doubt about that, type your own name into 123people.co.uk and discover what the web thinks it knows about you.)

The journalists who can really understand and manipulate the fabric of that world give themselves a far better chance of fulfilling the vital functions necessary to keep their profession relevant. Many greats of journalism and communication have achieved their star status – and occasionally vast wealth – through a mastery of an emerging technology. Wynkin de Worde used his knowledge of soft metals, learned as Caxton's apprentice, to develop movable type printing and establish Fleet Street as a centre for mass market communication; Paul Reuter's grasp of the new cable and telegraph transmission technologies helped him found an enduring media empire; Ed Murrow's groundbreaking multi-point broadcast technique covering the 1938 Anschluss helped revolutionise news radio; Matt Drudge's understanding of the blogosphere and news aggregation techniques made him rich and famous.

The world stage awaits the programmer-journalist enterprising enough to follow in their footsteps.

## Technical index

**Ajax:** Asynchronous javascript and XML. A combination of techniques that allow web pages to perform operations in the background without reloading the entire page.

**BitTorrent:** Method of sharing large digital files (such as video) between large groups of users by breaking them down into chunks and sharing the distribution between the group.

**CSS**: Cascading Style Sheets. Used in conjunction with HTML to format content on web pages.

**Dipity:** Free online tool to organise and present information along an interactive timeline.

**Django:** Framework that allows design of web pages and applications. Established by journalist-programmer Adrian Holovaty, and used in newsrooms including the *Washington Post*.

**Google Docs:** Shareable web-based storage system for spreadsheets and other data.

**HTML**: Hypertext Markup Language. The code that tells browser software how to display web pages.

**Javascript:** Scripting language that allows web pages to provide better user interfaces and more dynamic content.

**jQuery:** An extensive library for use by javascript programmers, useful for simplifying complicated javascript tasks

**MySQL:** Database management system used by some of the biggest sites on the web, including Facebook and Wikipedia.

**Objective C:** Programming language used for creating applications for Apple devices, including the iPhone and iPad.

**PHP:** Web-scripting language (originally it stood for Personal Home Page) that allows pages to be created dynamically or "on the fly". Often used in web sites built around databases – such as Facebook.

**Python:** Programming language (named from the television series *Monty Python's Flying Circus*), used widely in newspaper web teams. Its code is designed to be particularly readable, and a growing number of journalists are learning it.

**RSS:** Rich Site Summary – but often referred to as Really Simple Syndication. Allows frequently-updated web content to be set up as "feeds" for use in other sites or by individual users.

**Ruby on Rails:** Web framework that simplifies the creation of complicated web sites. Used by *The New York Times* and the *Guardian*, among others.

**Scraperwiki:** A collaborative web site that helps its users to collect data from web sites and present it in more usable ways.

**Vuvox:** Free online tool used to present multimedia content and create interactive "collages".

**Wordpress:** Free content management software for publishing blogs and web sites.

**Yahoo Pipes:** Composition tool that allows content from various web sources to be customised

## References

Anderson, K. (2010) Journalists: Belittling digital staff is not acceptable, Strange Attractor blog. Available online at http://charman-anderson.com/2010/01/18/journalists-belittling-digital-staff-is-not-acceptable/, accessed on 2 February 2011

Arthur, C. (2010) Analysing data is the future for journalists, says Tim Berners-Lee, *Guardian*, 22 November. Available online at http://www.guardian.co.uk/media/2010/nov/22/data-analysis-tim-berners-lee, accessed on 2 February 2011

Bell, E. (2010) Opening of Tow Center For Digital Journalism [video]. Available online at http://www.journalism.columbia.edu/page/628-tow-center-for-digital-journalism/426, accessed on 20 December 2010

Niles, R. (2006) The programmer as journalist. A Q&A with Adrian Holovaty, Online Journalism Review. Available online at http://www.ojr.org/ojr/stories/060605niles/, accessed 2 February 2011

Nussbaum, E (2009) The New Journalism: Goosing the Gray Lady, *New York Magazine*, 11 January. Available online at http://nymag.com/news/features/all-new/53344/, accessed 20 January 2011

Selter, B. (2009) J-schools play catch-up, *New York Times*, 14 April. Available online at http://www.nytimes.com/2009/04/19/education/edlife/journ-t.html, accessed 2 February 2011

Van Buskirk, E. (2010) Will Columbia-trained, code-savvy journalists bridge the media/tech divide? *Wired*, 7 April. Available online at from http://www.wired.com/epicenter/2010/04/will-columbia-trained-code-savvy-journalists-bridge-the-mediatech-divide/#ixzz0kS9CXLwS, accessed 20 December 2010

## Note on the author

Ian Reeves is director of learning and teaching at the University of Kent's Centre for Journalism, a department he founded with Tim Luckhurst. He built the centre's web site at www.centreforjournalism.co.uk, and its new iPad app which is available from Apple's app store. He works on web and app development projects in the media and public sectors. He was previously editor of journalism's weekly news magazine, *Press Gazette*, and winner of the PPA's weekly business writer of the year award in 2005. He is also a former editor of features agency Central Press Features. The interviews for this chapter were conducted by telephone in December 2010 and January 2011.

# Out of the academe and into the living and bed room: Facing the future in higher education – the Coventry way

**John Mair and Peter Woodbridge**

## Breaking down institutional walls

The internet is the Great Disruptor of our time – of journalism, of media and of education. The rules are being rewritten literally minute by minute. The world wide web is just twenty years old yet it has generated change that previously took decades or even centuries to happen.

One of the most significant aspects of the impact of digital media technologies is that they have enabled old institutional walls to be broken down. "Journalism" is no longer just for professional journalists, "publication" is no longer just for professional authors, "documentary production" is no longer just for professional broadcasters. Although many of the old hierarchies and barriers still exist, they are seemingly dissolving day by day.

The challenge for universities is to understand, interpret and be part of this "open media" *zeitgeist*. Academia has yet to embrace properly much of this open ethic beyond the mere creation and dissemination of content. This is particularly true of letting the information flow the other way from the subjects/readers to the content generators.

Let us take, as an example, the arguments over media studies a subject that, for many years has undoubtedly lost touch with the organisational structures of the contemporary media industry. Hence its low esteem in those areas and the constant derision of "meeja studies" in the press. Media studies academics are perfectly entitled to develop their own paradigms for use within their own contexts, even if they are very myopic – but this has led to a somewhat difficult relationship understanding its value as a discipline. How many media studies PhDs land jobs working for broadcasters and actually effecting change? Michael Jackson, the former Chief Executive of Channel Four (and a Westminster University media graduate) is a true exception to this Iron Law of Media Studies Unemployment.

## Engage, disengage?

Part of our project at Coventry University has been about letting this interaction back in and engaging with the communities of practice that we have endlessly derided in our disciplines. Over the last five years the Coventry Conversations (Coventry.ac.uk/coventryconversations) have brought literally hundreds of professionals to our campus to discuss contemporary issues in a variety of contexts related to the media. They have ranged from the Director General of the BBC to the founders of Channel 4 to BAFTA/Emmy and RTS award winners and to famous on-screen faces – Jon Snow, Jeremy Paxman, Kirsty Wark, Jeremy Vine to name but four. All talking about themselves, their career, their craft, all engaging in active debate. The Conversations have turned Coventry into a cutting edge centre for media discussion. The Conversations have become part of the institutional fabric – the DNA – of the university and of the city too. They are the best known brand in CU and affectionately known by students as the "CovCons".

More importantly, however, has been the truly open approach that these have taken. All the Conversations are free and open to the public (some even partly filling up Coventry Cathedral) and all are published, in their entirety, online. Sometimes they are also "broadcast" live via Twitter and blogging. The result of this open approach has been wide-ranging, with more than 5,000 bums on seats each year, much attention in the local, national and press and a swathe of professional opportunities opening for our students. They have been recorded and podcast almost from the start. The university podcast site has had 65,000 downloads to date (March 2011); the most popular a *Panorama* reporter on how she uncovered the truth about Ritalin and ADHD which has been downloaded 2,000 times. Since 2009 we have also included these as part Apple's global education project *i*Tunes U. The impact of that platform has been stellar and global. The academe has literally gone out to the world via the world wide web. To date, 2.5 million people have hit the *i*tunesU button to the Coventry Conversations. One – on modern games – has had 70,000 hits. Others on what might think of as arcane niche subjects such as the media coverage of the Afghan war 40,000 hits. The average for each and every of the 200 "CovCon" podcasts out there is 12,000 hits. So, the 20 to 200 person live audience in Coventry is always multiplied hundred, even thousand fold, worldwide thanks to the digital connected universe. It is hard to conceive of such massive audiences but they are plainly there for intelligent talk about media matters. Lord Reith and his dictum that the BBC should "inform, educate and entertain" would recognise the Conversations as doing just that globally.

The Coventry Conversations often generate news stories and news angles in themselves. All are totally on the record and Coventry journalism students are firmly encouraged to report them in student publications, blogs, the local and the national press. This can lead to uncomfortable results well beyond Coventry. At least one senior BBC executive ruled himself out of the job of Controller BBC I twice in a Conversation, then being reported on that, then regretting it and trying (too late) to recall it. The students and the internet were too quick for these machinations. It was/is in the public domain. That individual did not get that job and now no longer works for the BBC. Another Conversationalist, a former tabloid editor, David Yelland, firmly put the boot into his erstwhile colleague Andy Coulson over his much proclaimed "ignorance" of phone hacking at the *News of the World*. The Twitterati, led by *Guardian* editor in chief Alan Rusbridger, went to town on that once it was "out there". Coulson resigned as Downing Street Director of Communications in January 2011 following sustained media pressure. Week in, week out the Conversations make the news.

On a pedagogic level they act as a very good teaching aid. Students faced with assignments on a wide variety of media subjects – privacy, news values, pay walls, reality television, production – find their way to the Conversations and to their podcasts. Hearsay evidence says that students from other universities in the UK also use the Conversation podcasts as their audio books. There is a "CovCon" encyclopedia out there on the net of British media movers and shakers all discussing live media issues. Those media chattering classes are reached via putting it all out there but also through thorough careful tagging and meta data implants. The search engine is the modern professor guiding students to suitable content.

Coventry University students are also encouraged to report – live or in more constructed pieces – the Conversations in their own blog/newspaper, cutoday.wordpress.com. That also has proved popular in cyberspace with at the time of writing 110,000 hits in less than two years. The winners on that particular open platform are the student reports on Debbie Isitt's *Nativity* film, Steve Cropley, of *Autocar*, talking *Top Gear*, and Jeremy Paxman, of the BBC, talking about stuffing (interviewees). One suspects, though, that the latter is a Christmas phenomenon and a result of over diligent search engine optimisation.

## Today Coventry...tomorrow the world?

Coventry has not just acquired 'possibly the best speaker programme in any British University'(Professor Richard Lance Keeble, of the University of Lincoln, 2008) live each week but also through the internet and *i*TunesU a method of engaging literally millions worldwide in media debate and in sampling the Coventry University brand. One recent estimate put the AVE (Advertising Value Equivalent) to the University in excess of £1 million per annum. Coventry has gained prestige, profile and potential recruits from the world wide web. This will be reflected in the recruitment pattern of Coventry students globally.

Luckily, however, Coventry University, although among the first in the UK to start taking such faltering steps to the future, is not the only HE institution to start thinking about how to use open routes to publishing to engage in wider debates and how to make more education available for free. There are now some 350,000 lectures available, completely free, on *i*Tunes. When you add up all of the higher education content available online it would take literally hundreds of years worth of time to consume it. Institutions such as the Open University, MIT and many others are starting to make resources, networks and knowledge available to anyone who wants it. The UK Open University announced in 2009 that their efforts in engaging the wider public in education online had resulted in more than 6,000 additional applications to their courses. The public demand for education in all forms and on all platforms has never been higher.

By joining a few communities of practice modern man or woman, either through participation in universities or through joining local groups on the internet or a combination, can achieve a nice mix potentially as good as any university could offer. The Coventry Conversations podcasts have found on line niches in games freaks, online news buffs, train spotters, Afghan coverage afficionados, celebrity followers and more. These knowledge niches are out there and hungry to learn. Recently, a colleague at Coventry, Jonathan Worth, ran an open photography course on "Phonar: Photography and narrative" (photography.covmedia.co.uk) which had an average of 700 participants engaging with it from outside the course.

The Coventry Conversations and "Phonar" projects are not just free online lectures or courses, they are networks of practice and debate that encourage our students to place their development in the context of the wider landscape of their disciplines. They also help to address one of the gaps in our current education system in that it is not always what, but who, you know that will help you get on in your media career. Giving our students the tools to negotiate these networks is much more crucial in vocational terms than any traditional chalk and talk course. Obviously we must negotiate the balance between education as vocation and education for education's sake but these are the core questions in the academe that we will have to start asking if our degrees are to be judged on their ability to create graduate level careers.

If access for all is genuinely a goal for us, we need to start enabling it through open pedagogies such as those we have been pioneering at Coventry. As academics perhaps we could even make the ethical decision of refusing our free labour to publish in closed, expensive, inaccessible journals and adopting our own means of peer-reviewed dissemination. This is what the *i*Tunes U, YouTube Edu and various other projects in Coventry University and elsewhere are about.

## Out of the academe... into everywhere

Interestingly, though, it's not just the universities that are starting to take responsibility for this opening up of and to the media. Many of the great cultural institutions such as our libraries, museums, galleries, the BBC, film and other archives and even many private organisations and companies are also using their access to resources and knowledge to open up themselves in freely accessible ways. If we also include the many dedicated individuals who help train the world via video/the net (from advice on how to fix your car, learn guitar scales right through to learning about political philosophy, history and programming) we are today looking at truly interesting times. Times in which even the most specialist, niche interests and activities and forms of learning can potentially be met by the long long tail of the world wide web

It could be that modern students feel they are not able to learn without universities. Without them whilst they will be able to learn, they just will not be able to get a degree for that learning. Do we need to open up our models of accreditation and certification to enable these people to gain formal credentials for this type of activity? Perhaps we face the future by allowing people only to pay for parts of the university experience (for example, the examinations, the feedback etc) rather than committing themselves to a lifetime of debt for a knowledge base they will have forgotten, and may even be out of date, just a few years down the line. Are we going far enough when it comes to opening access routes into and out of our ivory towers?

It is clear that in the UK, a country that is moving more and more to a knowledge-based economy, three years learning at the start of adult life are unable to provide this in many industries. Should we in universities be teaching people how to become independent learners so that they can continue to learn? Should we provide the opportunities for dipping in and out, as and when they need it, to update knowledge and skill reservoirs throughout life? That is a latent aim of the Coventry Conversations, the 5,000 annual bums on seats and millions of web hits. Is that a pointer that universities can become much more than crèches for 18 to 21-year-olds?

In a true meritocracy, could we weigh up the difference between the skills and capabilities of someone who went to university and someone who has not? This is especially true in creative and media careers where your worth and value is usually determined by your actual work and more importantly the networks that you have developed to nurture yourself. In journalism, film, photography and design it is rarely your degree or its classification that lands you the job. It is your portfolio of publications, your show reel of films, your website of designs and your contacts that make the major difference.

## The academe: Can it cope with the future?
There were some 204,000 students in the UK in 2010 who failed to get a university place. The demand for places shows no sign of abating with applications up again – by 2.5 per cent – for entry in September 2011. Many – some figures as high as 250,000 – will face disappointment again this autumn. Which higher education institution will be the first to wake up to the enormous potential of these "lost" people in terms of their desire for education and also for those who would like to retrain by taking a second degree? They could quite easily be achieved using these internet spaces to gain access to content, support networks and the basic infrastructure of a supported learning environment. Open media leads to open universities.

There are already a number of free radical projects that are going to undermine the university system. The P2P university (p2pu.org/) offers free higher education online courses to anyone who wants to participate, the School of Everything is a website (schoolofeverything.com/) which enables learners to connect directly with teachers, built on the proviso that everyone has something to learn and everyone has something to teach. In the discipline of media, sites such as Film Studies for Free (filmstudiesforfree.blogspot.com) offer links and analysis to the best resources on the web for film scholars; the Vimeo Video School (vimeo.com/videoschool) offers tutorials and a community of filmmakers helping to nurture each other through their craft.

Then there is the BBC Academy and the BBC College of Journalism (bbc.co.uk/journalism) which, if undergraduate journalism students discovered it, most would stop paying their university tuition fees! "BBC Cojo", as it is already known, has in just a year of existence put out there in cyberspace enough instructional videos to at least kick off a broadcasting career. "Cojo" is replete with masters of their craft giving of their knowledge to journeymen and hack/ettes manqué. In addition, "Cojo" encourages febrile open discussion of contemporary media issues and has, for example, co-sponsored four real/virtual conferences with the

Coventry Conversations on "The crisis in journalism", "Reporting Afghanistan", the "Internet and journalism" and "Investigative journalism". Three have led to volumes such as this. A simple case of two open platforms meeting and making up more than the sum of their parts.

In addition to all of these constructed, virtual learning, environments, there are solo professionals who are offering tutorials, mentoring and giving advice (if only through Twittering) as part of this gift economy. If more people, organisations and businesses made it part of their mantra to share their knowledge resources in such a way, would this not be a better way of spreading the cost of having an educated population? We could even reward the people in some way who make this a part of their agenda. If this were to happen, universities may have an important role here since they are, in principle, potentially neutral and places of trust.

More importantly than this, the academe needs to adopt wider strategies for engagement, not only so our disciplines can benefit from the untapped potential of inclusiveness, but so that we can continue to remain relevant in a rapidly changing media landscape. If our students are out there in the real world, and the real world comes literally into our lecture halls, then the work of our students can surely help to nurture and sustain some important areas such as the humanities which are under threat of funding starvation. This is the "gift-economy" that is so crucial to our work in universities.

## Is the academe now an outdated model?

In a connected digital world, higher education needs to be seen in its much wider sense and not just the preserve of academics and fee-paying students. Just as music doesn't necessarily need the record industry, just as journalists don't necessarily need newspapers, just as film makers don't need broadcasters, does education always need universities? Sometimes, but not always. The only difference is that in journalism and music, both of these modes of production seem to be able to co-exist – so why don't we allow both of them exist side by side in higher education?

It is in the university's short term interest to keep their processes opaque, complex and expensive, to keep their monopoly on the degree awarding and their piece of the pie. On one level education is really quite a simple task of connecting the learned with the learner. There is the question of access to resources – but in the arts and humanities these are relatively inexpensive. How long will it be before a few rogue-traders or entrepreneurs or pirates (they're all the same thing essentially) decide to break away from the present, and at times antiquated, system and set up the university version of the renegades who started the Huffington Post, Google, Facebook or the Virgin Megastore. Piggybacking on the world of resources that we have out there in cyberspace and using them for their own end.

Companies are already starting to make advances here too (McDonalds, for example, are offering "McDegrees" to their employees) but these are largely business school-based models. Should we try to set up a version of these for the Creative Arts and Humanities? Instead of trying to keep modeling our institutions around their needs (or the needs of the elite few) should we centre them on the needs of the academics and the students whom they are supposed to serve?

So, in essence then, if the web has given us anything over the last two decades, it has been the ability to re-imagine completely how our institutional-based structures can be conceived. Already, within education, we are seeing some examples that enable us to imagine how this restructuring might look like but are we going far enough? Is it time to come out of the academe and head via the bedroom computer and living room computer/television to connect with the real world more? That is the real challenge. Are the Coventry Conversations and Phonar important pointers as we turn in the acadame to face the future?

### Note on the authors
John Mair is a senior lecturer in broadcasting at Coventry University. He invented and runs the Coventry Conversations. He is a former BBC, ITV and Channel Four producer and director with 200 films to his credit. He has edited three books before this one with Professor Richard Lance Keeble.

Peter Woodbridge is a lecturer in Open Media at Coventry University. He is the former Creative Multi-media Manager for the university and set up the *i*tunesU, CUTV and Covtelly platforms for the university.

# Section 10. What does it all mean?

## Richard Lance Keeble

For the concluding section, three eminent thinkers ponder the deeper implications of the web revolution for journalism in the UK and globally. At the heart of this text is the simple belief that our focus on the rapidly changing technology of journalism should never serve to marginalise the profoundly important ethical and political dimensions of the job.

Kevin Marsh, former editor of Radio Four's *Today* programme and Executive Editor at the BBC College of Journalism, highlights this point by returning to a speech given by Beatrice Warde, the celebrated commentator on newspaper typography, to the men of the British Typographers Guild in 1930. The tools of any trade, she said, were best when they were invisible.

Whatever pride you have in the tools you make and build, never forget that they are *only* tools, she said. Containers (or what today we call "platforms") should never obscure nor detract attention from the ideas themselves, whether fiction, history, philosophy. Or journalism.

Following Warde's lead, Marsh here argues that British journalists tended to respond too submissively and hesitantly to the arrival of Web 2.0. They forgot how easily the tools could become our tyrants. They forgot that the best tools and platforms were those that did not obscure the content. "Like Beatrice Warde, we need to look beyond the mechanics – even the aesthetics – of our platforms. They will come and go." But, according to Marsh, they should not change the essential values "that distinguish journalism from everything else".

Next Professor Tim Luckhurst, Head of Journalism at Kent University and former Editor of the *Scotsman*, celebrates the "liberal faith that professional journalism exists to serve social and moral purposes". And he looks forward to "an age of partnership between representative journalism and participatory journalism, a future in which privately-owned, independent media will continue to play the role of an estate, not just an industry".

Leftist critics of the media, Professor Luckhurst argues, are too reluctant to admit its successes in exposing wrongdoings: for instance, Granada Television's *World in Action* series was first to investigate the convictions in 1975 of the Birmingham Six. The *Guardian's* exposure in 1995 of the lies told by Conservative cabinet minister Jonathan Aitken ended the career of a powerful politician while the *Daily Telegraph's* exposure of the details of MPs' expenses claims in 2009 revealed abuses by MPs from all parties and seriously damaged public faith in politicians. "Few stories have demonstrated more emphatically the willingness of liberal media to scrutinise in the public interest institutions they support and admire."

Finally Professor John Tulloch, Head of the School of Journalism at the University of Lincoln, mixes both seriousness and wit in his brilliantly coruscating application of the predictions of the celebrated sci-fi novelist, Philip K. Dick, to the emergence of the robotic reporter. Are we all Dickheads now? Tulloch wonders. Researchers at the Intelligent Systems Informatics Lab (ISI) of Tokyo University have, certainly, developed a journalist robot that can autonomously explore its environment and report what it finds. "The robot detects changes in its surroundings, decides if they are relevant and then takes pictures with its on-board camera. It can query nearby people for information and it uses internet searches to further round out its understanding."

Prof Tulloch delights in delving into Dick's predictions, arguing that quite a few of journalists' routine functions could be taken over by robots. For instance, its role in surveilling the environment could "easily be replicated by fixed CCTV cameras in car parks and parliament, drones, security cameras".

Various other species of robots could materialise – "opinionbots surveying and vox popping, sportsbots surveilling routine events, dronebots checking out demonstrations, even portly Simpsonbots wandering through the crowds in the Liberation Squares of the Third World patronising the locals while their princely progenitor sips gin and saves on insurance and security".

But then, could a robot emerge to take over the role of the eminent *Independent* war correspondent, Robert Fisk? Hardly. "One can't see a Fisk style of journalism dying out, even if newspapers do. And his long form mix of analytical journalism and street level reporting would in some way find a home online more easily than in an ailing broadsheet. Could one see a Fiskbot? Leaping on a US tank, or nimbly escaping enraged Afghans? In your dreams." In the end, there are reasons for optimism.

# Future tools: The crystal goblet

**Kevin Marsh**

In October 1930, in a building just off Fleet Street, a young American woman got to her feet to address an audience of dour, serious-minded men. Many had spent a lifetime in their trade and oozed knowledge and experience. She was the only woman in the room and barely into her thirties

Just around the corner, up and down the Street of Ink/Adventure/Shame, weasel-faced men with dirty fingernails scuttled purposefully, "PRESS" cards folded into their fedora hatbands, stained raincoat collars turned against the autumn wind. (Add your own favourite Fleet Street's golden age cliché here.)

The young woman was Beatrice Warde, already a celebrated commentator on newspaper typography, and the men she was about to speak to were not journalists – though they were the lords of their region of the print universe. They were the British Typographers Guild: the men who designed, engineered, maintained and set the type in the mighty presses that nightly kissed ink on to paper in the unlovely bowels of Fleet Street.

In that autumn of 1930, print was at its zenith. If you wanted news or the latest prices. Or to hear the rolls of thunder for or against the gold standard or read the witness of reporters in far away places of which you knew little, then you turned to a newspaper. You might have called it the platform of choice for journalism, for any form of mass communication. Except that there wasn't much choice. Not yet, anyway.

BBC Radio had broadcast its first news bulletin in 1922 – but those bulletins were thin, almost perfunctory and deliberately written not to compete with the written press. British Movietone news had only just appeared in cinemas, in 1929. Television wasn't to flicker into life for another six years, though the first TV news bulletin would not go out for an entire generation – in 1954.

So the men gathered in the St Bride's Institute in the autumn of 1930 were those who, for the time being at least, fashioned the very things – print and presses – that carried journalism. The tool that journalists had to understand to get their work out there. What, today, we would call their platform.

### Beatrice Warde: Wunderkind of an introverted trade

Beatrice Warde was already something of a wunderkind in this narrow, sometimes introverted trade. She had shown herself to be a woman of extraordinary vision and a gifted communicator who inspired and intimidated in roughly equal measure. She evidently had no fear of her audience nor saw any reason that day to trim what she had to say to overcome their possible prejudices. And the speech she delivered resonated far beyond the institute and the world of printing right down to the present day.

She called her address "The crystal goblet or printing should be invisible" – a title which seemed calculated to alienate and provoke an audience of typographers. Her thesis was a simple one, though she apologised for what she called the "long-winded and fragrant metaphor" with which she clothed it. "Imagine," she said, "that you have before you a flagon of wine" and two goblets – one very ornate, the other crystal clear:

According to your choice of goblet, I shall know whether or not you are a connoisseur of wine. For if you have no feelings about wine one way or the other, you will want the sensation of drinking the stuff out of a vessel that may have cost thousands of pounds; but if you are a member of that vanishing tribe, the amateurs of fine vintages, you will choose the crystal, because everything about it is calculated to reveal rather than to hide the beautiful thing which it was meant to contain...No cloud must come between your eyes and the fiery heart of the liquid...the glass is colourless or at the most only faintly tinged in the bowl, because the connoisseur judges wine partly by its colour and is impatient of anything that alters it. [i]

Metaphor it might have been. But her meaning was clear enough. Whatever pride you have in the tools you make and build, never forget that they are *only* tools. They are not the thing itself, the value of which exists wholly separate from the container that holds them. Containers, platforms, should never obscure nor detract attention from the ideas themselves, whether fiction, history, philosophy. Or journalism. She went on to explain how the tools of the trade were best when they went unnoticed. And that the thought and communication should not adapt themselves to the tools, the platforms:

It is sheer magic that I should be able to hold a one-sided conversation by means of black marks on paper with an unknown person halfway across the world. Talking, broadcasting, writing, and printing are all quite literally forms of thought transference, and it is this ability and eagerness to transfer and receive the contents of the mind that is almost alone responsible for human civilisation.

Far from being alienated, her audience in the hall and their counterparts across the English speaking world were inspired. Throughout America and England, printers displayed a copy of her famous poster that continued her theme: "This is a Printing Office" — its words resounding, urging these toolmakers of communication to invest every piece of type with "fearless truth against whispering rumour", creating words which "fly ...verified by proof". [ii]

It would be reassuring to think there were voices articulating a vision as clear and compelling as Beatrice Warde's as we contemplate journalism's current crises and uncertain future. Particularly when we consider how often we are told, explicitly or implicitly, that journalism is being changed fundamentally by the tools of social networking or, more latterly, the tools on which we read or experience journalism.

The fact is, journalism, over a decade or more, has been so weakened by an existential neurosis, coupled with financial catastrophe, brought on by the earliest tools of the internet that we now seem able to do little more than cower in the shadow of every new web tool, believing that we have to adapt journalism to the tools, not the tools to journalism.

## The multidimensional crisis

The roots and routes of journalism's existential neurosis are well explored. The effect of that neurosis on our ability to see beyond the mechanics of tools and platforms, as Beatrice Warde did eighty years ago, is less well understood. Here and now in 2011, thinking about journalism's future and the tools we will need feels like playing a multidimensional strategy game when the main rule is that we always have to play at least one move behind everyone else. All the time hearing real and imagined voices assuring us we have no right to be in the game in the first place. Because that's where Web 1.0 left us: doubting that journalism as a distinct form of human discourse with a public and civic purpose existed any more – certainly, not in the form we recognised it. We were in no shape to deal with the crowd-liberating tools of Web 2.0 when they rolled over us in the second half of the 2000s. *Oryctolagi cuniculi* transfixed in halogen crossbeams, we believed every new-web guru who told us that every new tool was a "gamechanger".

Thinking back to the tools of Web 1.0 – the web itself, search engines, news aggregators, free read/write software as well as digital broadcast distribution – we now see how they undermined everything we thought we were. They added a second trajectory to our communication, the "return path", turning what we wrote and said from one-to-many-lectures to many-to-many-conversations. They unbundled our carefully crafted daily bundles of "news". They fragmented the old-style mass audiences we were so attached to and which underpinned both classified and display advertising.

## "Journalism as we know it is over"

You didn't have to look very far for news executives ready to throw in their hand. "The long-building plaint is now undeniable: Journalism as we know it is over" (Overholser 2005). That happened to be Geneva Overholser in 2005. As director of the School of Journalism at the University of Southern California's Annenberg School for Communication, she is the doyen of journalism educators. She is also a former Pulitzer prize winner and US National Press Foundation Editor of the Year. Her language was as arresting as it was angst-ridden:

> A critical element of our democracy is threatened, for no self-governing people can long continue without a press that is not only free but also meets the basic needs of the citizenry (ibid).

Even those with less hangdog expressions, those who saw opportunities in the effects the old/new technologies were having on journalism – mostly, it has to be said, either engaged in publicly-funded journalism or outside the trade altogether – declared the game fundamentally changed.

The BBC's Richard Sambrook, for example, who as Director of Global News was at the forefront of educating the biggest news organisation in the world about journalism's changing times. Journalism, BBC journalism in particular, he argued:

> ...can only be strengthened by being open to more perspectives and the knowledge and understanding of the audience or users...by encouraging participation and being open to the views and the input of a wide range of users (Sambrook 2005).

And it certainly seemed true that if journalism embraced the possibilities of Web 1.0, grasped its tools firmly, there were clear positives:

> ...the big disasters of 2005, from the Tsunami, to the London bombings, to Hurricane Katrina, the Asian earthquake and the Buncefield oil explosion in the UK provided platforms for the public to contribute to newsgathering on an unprecedented scale (Sambrook 2006).

## The "news as conversation" thing

Some of us even persuaded ourselves we had got this "news as conversation" thing cracked – at least, those of us whose business model was not being macerated by advertisers' flight away from paper. We set up big name blogs and started to detect a difference between the kind of news you could break in an online conversation and the kind that was proper to a formal news bulletin or newspaper.

We talked about "evolving truth" to reassure ourselves it was OK to share our verification processes with the audience. OK to be "never wrong for long". And we set up User Generated Content (UGC) hubs and put in place protocols to check the authenticity of material our audiences sent us.

But it was a flawed understanding which did not quite recognise that nothing ever stood still nor the sheer weight of material generated by the tools of Web 2.0 that would be heading our way. Richard Sambrook's successor as BBC Director of Global News, Peter Horrocks, wrote on the BBC Editors' blog: "There is little doubt of the enormous value of audience-provided information and media in enhancing the coverage of news events" (Horrocks 2008).

The problem was this: he was writing not in 2005 nor 2006. It was 2008 and the tools the world was using to talk to itself appeared to some to be cutting us journalists out of the picture. Though not everyone had noticed. As I argued in response to Peter Horrocks, the newer, crowd-corralling tools of Web 2.0 meant that if we were to adapt to them, his "journocentric approach" was no longer viable. This view that all the new peer-to-peer activity on the web was just another source was, I wrote, a "vision of journalism (that) yields very little of the trade's role as the principal agent in the information business" (Marsh 2008).

## Journo-gurus' whiff of something invigorating

How to yield some or all of that role in the *information* business while still retaining its proper role in the *journalism* business (not the same thing) was a complex calculation we were ill placed to understand let alone achieve. In the United States, journo-gurus – (disillusioned) former journalists, academics and geeks – caught the whiff of something invigorating. They applauded and celebrated the way the old/new technologies of Web 1.0 had stripped the arrogant, swaggering trade of journalism of its sovereignty and, as they saw it, handed back to citizens the means to share their own (news and) information, invite attention to their own civic needs in their own way and with their own voices.

And when they called that "peer-to-peer" communication "journalism" (though, in reality, it was no different from the penny post and telephone calls…except the conversations had, potentially, the entire planet listening on speakerphone) we journalists – untrusted and unloved – were so uncertain of our place in the order of things that we felt unable to push back. And point out this wasn't journalism. We read writers such as Dan Gillmor with something like resignation. He wrote: "… the 'former audience'…has…turned its endless ideas into such unexpected, and in some cases superb, forms of journalism" (Gillmor 2004: 238). Journalism had failed, long live the net: "The net should be the ally of thought and nuance, not a booster shot for knee-jerk reaction. An informed citizenry cannot sit still for more of the same" (Rosen 2006).

## "The overthrow of everything" predicted

New York University's Jay Rosen took to calling those people who were now reading fewer papers and watching less television news "the people formerly known as the audience" and warned us journalists: "You don't own the eyeballs. You don't own the press, which is now divided into pro and amateur zones. You don't control production on the new platform, which isn't one-way. There's a new balance of power between you and us" (ibid).

A new balance we found hard to work out, while the new media/new politics guru Joe Trippi – the man who persuaded US Democrat presidential contender Howard Dean to put his trust in the web in the 2004 – predicted "the overthrow of everything" (2004). We read and listened and became depressed. There seemed no simple way ahead for journalism. Jay Rosen's images were typical, striking and uncompromising. Migrate or die. "Like reluctant migrants everywhere, the people in the news tribe have to decide what to take with them. When to leave. Where to land. They have to figure out what is essential to their way of life. They have to ask if what they know is portable" (Rosen 2008).

## The tyranny of tools

As if this wasn't enough of a crisis for journalism, just as we were beginning to work out what to take with us in the handcarts, the mechanical revolution of Web 2.0 hit us. Web 2.0 took all the tergiversative tendencies of the old/new web, multiplied and accelerated them. Tool after tool emerged from college frat houses or the minds of the new masters of the universe in Mountain View or Cupertino – all calculated to make the inter-personal communications of "the people formerly known as the audience" media rich or global or instant or more or less anything and anyhow that by-passed terminally neurotic journalism. These new tools became the new tyranny.

How did journalism respond? Submissively. Uncertainly. Unsure which tools mattered, which didn't. Which actually contributed to journalism, could support and enhance it. And which were just another way of idly connecting people who wanted a chat...but more so. But because of our neurosis after half a decade of hearing we were no longer necessary or important, we questioned our own right even to be part of the calculation. And there were plenty of journophobes out there only too ready to tell us that we had no such right and this or that new tool replaced us.

But we forgot something. Or perhaps we didn't have the confidence in ourselves to articulate it any more. We forgot that it was the tools that were the tyrants – not us. We forgot Beatrice Warde's stricture that the best tools, the best platforms, were those that didn't obscure the content. There was a pattern in journalism's responses to the social networking tools that emerged in the second half of the decade. At first we looked away – not ignoring them exactly, more unaware of any potential they might have until it was too late and they'd become ubiquitous on the world's desktops, their more journophobicly zealous fans lecturing us on how they did all the things that we did but better.

## When Facebook and YouTube seemed geeky toys

So it was that Facebook (February 2004) and YouTube (February 2005) seemed geeky teenage toys at first. Then, as a result often of grim news stories involving young people such as the Virginia Tech shootings (of April 2007), we recognised their marginal worth as potential sources. Trouble was, we failed to argue convincingly that they were no more than what they actually were – simple tools of communication and sharing. Instead, we allowed ourselves to be persuaded that they were tools of journalism...and we would have to change to be embraced by them.

The sheer weight of content on YouTube pitted ubiquity – someone, somewhere, has a camera pointed at even the most trivial event – against salience, undermining the notion, fundamental to journalism, of bearing witness. And that ubiquity, combined with falling attention and concentration spans and the impatience of the hand in control of the mouse, persuaded us that "seeing the thing" was what mattered – not the carefully constructed context and explanation journalism offered.

Innovative journalists such as BBC *Panorama*'s Derren Lawford [iii] tried to capitalise on the You Tube and Facebook way by adapting long-form, current affairs journalism to Web 2.0's demands. He took the material and content that went into a traditional television documentary on teenage girls' self-harm and pregnancy and turned it into bite-sized gobbets, posting them on YouTube and creating debate and discussion around them on Facebook.

The upside of adapting his work to sharing and networking was that he reached an audience he would never have reached on BBC1 or even BBC3. The downside was that the venture succeeded only because it fragmented journalism's fundamentals: the idea of the story; narrative sequence; the balance between testimony, context and analysis; even the schedule.

## News organisations desperately trying to understand Twitter

But it's Twitter (March-July 2006) that attracts the most outrageous claims about its right to be thought of as journalism, its ability to supplant it. And which most news organisations are still desperately trying to understand. Twitter poses problems for many of journalism's fundamentals – not the least being verification. And yet, there are many within and without journalism who seem to want to strain journalism into the Twitter mould.

Alf Hermida is an Assistant Professor at the School of Journalism, University of British Columbia and formerly a BBC News website editor. He's a vociferous Twitter-as-journalism advocate who believes social networking is more than just a communication tool. It's changed the way we acquire news and information. He calls this info-universe "ambient journalism" (2010):

Today, the process of journalism is taking place in public on media platforms such as Twitter. Information is published, disseminated, checked, confirmed or denied in public through a collaboration facilitated by social networks. The process of journalism in this media system turns on its head the traditional approach of filter, then publish. Instead, breaking news becomes a process of publish, then filter. The journalistic functions of verification and authentication take place in public, done by both professional journalists and citizens.

What he's describing here is not journalism – not even with qualification. It's ambient allright – the background noise that has always been there. The only difference now is that the volume is turned up and, via Twitter and other social networking tools, ignorant whispers resonate globally. Our mistake, as journalists, is to believe those who tell us that it has changed our trade in some fundamental way. A mistake that arises directly from that existential neurosis.

And it's not just the mechanics. The tools of Web 2.0: collaborative tools which enable crowdsourcing [iv] seem calculated either to bypass journalism (Paul Bradshaw's Help Me Investigate, [v] for example) or undermine it – one apparent purpose of Julian Assange's Wikileaks (Brock 2010). Though, of course, both need the mediation of traditional journalism to have any real impact and make any meaningful contribution to public discourse.

## Conclusion

Journalism now has no Beatrice Warde to raise its vision. Few have sufficient confidence in our trade to look, as she did in her day, through the tools we use to communicate to each other to see the message within. Ours is an unloved and untrusted trade and anyone rising to their feet to describe journalism today as wielding an "armoury of fearless truth against whispering rumour" would be laughed off the stage – unless their audience were one of self-deluding, disingenuous tabloid editors inhabiting a world of their own.

Some are trying. Charlie Beckett (2008), who runs the politics/media thinktank POLIS at the London School of Economics, argues that the Web 2.0 entails a new emerging shape for journalism, but one that's rooted in its enduring skills and tools – the tools that differentiate it from mere information retailing:

> The whole point of the networked model is that you do not surrender the journalistic judgement, the journalistic values and the journalistic nous that enables you to filter out information, to edit and prioritise stories and to package information in a way that can be consumed.[vi]

Martin Moore, who is Director of the Media Standards Trust, a charity whose aim is to improve standards in British journalism, also argues that journalists are agents of a specific role in the information universe.

> Their role should be as much about collecting information, verifying that information and then providing the tools for the public to assess that information, to investigate it, to compare it. And I think only by empowering them to do that will journalism reinvent itself. [vii]

Whether journalism needs reinvention or simply the perspicacity to see that each new communication tool has not changed its fundamental place in our media ecologies is the key question. The tools we need for the future, for the future of journalism are little to do with the mechanics of the Web 2.0, 3.0, X.0 or digital technologies – we have to take those as read, givens in the age of the new literacies.

The tools we really need are everything to do with the mindsets and mental tools that have always distinguished journalism from civilisation's ambient hum. And they have always differentiated journalism from mere information:

- the curiosity and inquisitiveness to investigate and bear witness on behalf of others and in the public interest;
- the sense of what's salient, timely, worthy of attention in the mass of data and information;
- an ear for narrative and an eye for the telling or poignant detail;
- a sense of the tragedy of human experience;
- but more than anything else, the sense that what we do matters: that it's important, that it's different from gossip, chatter, rumour, prejudice; the sense that mere information – no matter how well

disseminated – that mere data – no matter how well mined and scraped – are not enough.

Like Beatrice Warde, we need to look beyond the mechanics – even the aesthetics – of our platforms. They will come and go – but they do not and should not change those things that distinguish journalism from everything else.

In January 2010, I put it like this to a conference of journalism students in London. Skills and tools are a means to an end:

> And no matter how exciting multimedia and social media are – the way in which new, easier ways of doing things come on stream – they're not an end in themselves. Don't become a Twitterhead – like the petrolhead who knows everything about cars but forgets the point of them is to go from one place to another. Make sure you stay outside the bubble.[viii]

Not Beatrice Warde, I'll admit. And perhaps not the vision and inspiration we need right now. But certainly intended as a warning that unless we can rediscover the confidence to articulate and advocate journalism's unchanged and unchanging purpose, we will feel pressed by any and every new web or digital tool to dilute our values and relegate ourselves in importance to the public sphere.

In short, we will deserve to lose our role in what Beatrice Warde called the "magic" of that "ability and eagerness to transfer and receive the contents of the mind that is almost alone responsible for human civilisation".

# Notes

---

[i] "The crystal goblet or printing should be invisible" went through many versions between its original delivery in 1930 and final publication in 1956 in *The crystal goblet: Sixteen essays in typography*. The text of the 1930 speech is available online at http://www.upload.likeyougiveadamn.com/PG_03_TEXT.pdf, accessed on 12 January 2011

[ii] The full text of "This is a Printing Office" reads: "This is a Printing Office, Crossroads of civilisation, Refuge of all the arts Against the ravages of time, Armoury of fearless truth Against whispering rumour, Incessant trumpet of trade. From this place words may fly abroad, Not to perish on waves of sound, not to vary with the writer's hand, But fixed in time having been verified in proof. Friend you stand on sacred ground. This is a Printing Office." Available online at http://infoshare1.princeton.edu/rbsc2/ga/unseenhands/labels/wardePrintOffice.html, accessed on 13 January 2011

[iii] The details of Derren Lawford's "multisodes" experiment can be found online at http://www.bbc.co.uk/journalism/skills/production/developing-audiences/minisodes.shtml, accessed on 17 January 2011

[iv] For a critique of insufficiently-curated crowdsourcing, see Marsh, K. (2011) The attention deficit of crowds, BBC College of Journalism. Available online at http://www.bbc.co.uk/journalism/blog/2010/11/the-attention-deficit-of-crowd.shtml, accessed on 20 January 2011

[v] See Help Me Investigate. Available online at http://www.helpmeinvestigate.com/, accessed on 20 January 2011

[vi] Interview with author for *Analysis* on BBC Radio 4, 3 July 2008. Transcript available online at http://news.bbc.co.uk/1/hi/programmes/analysis/7487525.stm, accessed on 17 January 2011

[vii] Interview with author for *Analysis* on BBC Radio 4, 3 July 2008: Transcript available online at http://news.bbc.co.uk/1/hi/programmes/analysis/7487525.stm, accessed on 17 January 2011

[viii] Marsh, K. (2010) Keynote speech to Newsrewired conference, January. Available online at http://storycurve.blogspot.com/2010/01/challenges-of-learning-new-multimedia.html, accessed 16 January 2011

# References

Beckett, C. (2008) *Supermedia: Saving journalism so that it can save the world,* Oxford, Wiley-Blackwell

Brock G. (2010) Julian Assange and the Wikileaks agenda, 12 July. Available online at http://georgebrock.net/julian-assange-and-the-wikileaks-agenda/, accessed on 17 January 2011

Gillmor, D. (2004) *We the media: Grassroots journalism for the people by the people,* New York, O'Reilly

Hermida, A. (2010) From TV to Twitter: How ambient news became ambient journalism, *M/C Journal,* Vol. 13, No. 2, May. Available online at http://journal.media-culture.org.au/index.php/mcjournal/article/viewArticle/220/0

Hermida, A. (2011) Giffords' shooting shows process of journalism on Twitter, reportr.net, 10 January. Available online at http://www.reportr.net/2011/01/10/giffords_shooting_twitter/, accessed on 19 January 2011

Horrocks, P. (2008) Value of citizen journalism, BBC News online, 7 January. Available online at http://www.bbc.co.uk/blogs/theeditors/2006/11/the_future_of_news.html, accessed on 16 January

Marsh, K. (2008) Future(ish) news(ish), Storycurve, 11 January. Available online at http://storycurve.blogspot.com/2008/01/recently-my-good-friend-and-head-of-bbc.html, accessed on 16 January 2011

Overholser, G. (2005) *On behalf of journalism: A manifesto for change,* the Annenberg Foundations Trust, University of Southern California

Rosen, J. (2006) The people formerly known as the audience, 27 June. Available online at Pressthink http://archive.pressthink.org/2006/06/27/ppl_frmr.html, accessed on 17 January 2011

Rosen, J. (2008) Migration point for the press tribe, 26 June. Available online at http://journalism.nyu.edu/pubzone/weblogs/pressthink/2008/06/26/pdf.html, accessed on 17 January 2011

Sambrook, R. (2005) Email interview with Hypergene Media Blog, 11 April. Available online at http://www.hypergene.net/blog/weblog.php?id=P266, accessed on 17 January 2011

Sambrook, R. (2006) Guest blog at cybersoc.com, 20 March. Available online at http://www.cybersoc.com/2006/03/guest_blogger_r.html 17/1, accessed on 17 January 2011

Trippi, J. (2004) *The revolution will not be televised: Democracy, the internet and the overthrow of everything*, New York, Regan Books

**Note on the author**

Kevin Marsh is Executive Editor at the BBC College of Journalism. He is a former Editor of the *Today* programme and also edited *The World at One*, *PM* and *Broadcasting House* on BBC Radio 4. He writes a regular column in *Press Gazette* and blogs at http://storycurve.blogspot.com/.

# Dr Hack, I presume? Liberal journalism in the multimedia age

**Tim Luckhurst**

Amid the familiar misery of ailing newspapers, impoverished broadcasters and a worldwide web that prefers not to remunerate professional journalists, one thing at least is clear. The future of journalism lies on a different planet. They will do things differently there.

Several thinkers believe they know what conditions will be like. Seth Lewis imagines a hospitable environment in which there will exist "vast new opportunities for the formerly atomised audience to participate on their terms, connect and coordinate horizontally with each other, and do so in a way that creates value through collective intelligence and contributions"(Lewis 2010).

Stephen Moss and Joris Luyendijk are optimistic for similar reasons. They envisage a journalism of multiple online "agoras" (an agora was a place for assembly and debate in ancient Greece), where web users will congregate to produce organic, non-linear story-telling informed by the wisdom of crowds (Moss and Luyendijk 2010). Jay Rosen argues a similar case and, in common with others who share his perspective, appears pleased that the internet may weaken the authority of large-scale professional media organisations (Rosen 2009).

Such enthusiasm for citizen journalism – an oxymoron so hoary it should be abandoned – often starts from the assertion that professional journalism in representative democracies restricts debate to perspectives that are acceptable to governing and financial elites. It is rooted in a belief that top-down journalism privileges the views of the powerful and that it excludes popular opinion. Such arguments assume that millions of free citizens are routinely duped or seduced by big media reporting. They encompass a version of Friedrich Engels' thesis of false consciousness (Engels [1893] 1968). They predict the death of big media because it serves the interests of liberal, capitalist democracy. Many of their proponents would like that to die too.

This chapter challenges theories of change that foresee the relocation of media power in the hands of consumers. It foresees, instead, an age of partnership between representative journalism and participatory journalism, a future in which privately-owned, independent media will continue to play the role of an estate, not just an industry.

## "Greater need for traditional journalistic skills"

Newman suggests that, as the pace of the news cycle accelerates, "it can be argued that there is an even greater need for traditional journalistic skills of sorting fact from fiction; selecting the key facts for a mass audience". He cites as evidence of partnership the uploading of user-generated pictures and videos to Persian TV and CNN by Iranian citizens during the protests that followed that country's election in 2009 (Newman 2009: 50-51).

These protesters understood that only professionally edited, mass media outlets have the power and authority to influence opinion widely and fast. Newman notes that most of the information and links shared via social networks during the Iranian protests following the disputed election of President Ahmadinejad in 2009 "came from, or pushed people to, the work of the mainstream media itself" (ibid).

Charlie Beckett notes that mainstream journalists are beginning to regain some of their lost confidence: "They look at big stories like Iran and they see the value of what they do magnified, amplified and not contradicted by new media" (cited in ibid). Alan Rusbridger, editor of the *Guardian*, glimpsed the same possibility in his January 2010 Hugh Cudlipp Lecture: "Journalists may remain one source of authority, but people may also be less interested to receive journalism in an inert context – i.e. which can't be responded to, challenged, or knitted in with other sources" (Busfield 2010).

Belief that large-scale, mass-audience media may remain healthy and influential does not rely on panglossianism. Freedman notes that the BBC news website remains Britain's most popular source of news online (Freedman 2010). Other news sites produced by mainstream, private media companies also attract huge audiences. Leading examples include Mail Online, Guardian Unlimited and Sky.Com.

## Growing partnerships between professional journalists and their audiences

Small wonder, then, that journalists in big media institutions including the BBC, Sky News, *The New York Times* and the *Guardian* are learning to think in terms of active partnerships in which professional journalists and their audiences report events together, the former responding to the latter's requests, suggestions and demands and filtering information to privilege fact over rumour and objectivity over ideology.

A consensus is beginning to emerge among professional journalists that Dutton's fifth estate of networked individuals and groups really can live and work alongside traditional media instead of replacing it (Dutton 2007). The fifth estate will help the fourth estate to curate news in the multimedia environment. It will help the professionals to do a better job of keeping the powerful honest and accountable to the people they serve.

This consensus raises a question that is absent from much ideologically predisposed debate about the future of journalism: what intellectual skills will the professional journalist of the future require to fulfil their duties to their fellow citizen and to representative democracy? How will these watchdogs be equipped to offer, in Eric Hobsbawm's words, the engaged citizens of the 21st century democracies "an explanatory narrative adequate to its complexities"? (see Holden 2002).

To attempt an answer it is necessary first to contest an orthodoxy that, while useful to the study of journalism, does not merit the level of acceptance it has achieved in the decades since the academy encouraged such study to drift apart from the established disciplines in which it was born.

## Fourth estate "myth" – an impoverished, ideological stance

Thirty-two years have passed since the fourth estate theory was described as "a political myth" (Boyce, Curran and Wingate 1978). Since then, this view has come to be treated as fact by some academic analysts of professional journalism and, through their agency, by their students. But to accord it such status is to embrace an impoverished ideological stance not conducive to understanding journalism's social purpose.

When Mark Thompson, Director General of the BBC, signed a letter to the Secretary of State for Business warning that a buyout of BSkyB by News Corporation "could have serious consequences for media plurality" (BBC News 2010a), his objection relied on the classic fourth estate argument that plurality of media ownership and diversity of media content are crucial to the health of liberal democracy.

According to liberal theory, plurality and diversity promote competition, which allows good to drive out bad in the market for ideas. In this Darwinian struggle towards light, the truth – or its near equivalent – emerges triumphant and allows informed citizens to hold power to account within the rules and systems of representative democracy. It encourages reform, not revolutionary change.

Julian Assange, editor of Wikileaks, appears committed to these ideals. He says: "The truth must come first. First the truth, because without the truth no public policy is coherent" (Assange 2010). It is hard to imagine a more emphatic statement of the fourth estate doctrine that journalism functions as a watchdog on the activities of government.

Assange's version of journalism's social purpose is not very different from the one described in 1852 by Henry Reeve, leader writer for *The Times*, who wrote that it exists "to find out the true state of facts, to report them with fidelity, to apply to them strict and fixed principles of justice, humanity and law, to inform as far as possible, the very conscience of nations and to call down the judgement of the world on what is false, or base, or tyrannical" (*The Times* 1939: 149).

Despite a revolution in media technology, that argument has barely changed since. The 1947-1949 Royal Commission observed: "The number and variety of newspapers should be such that the press as a whole gives an opportunity for all important points of view to be effectively presented in terms of the varying standards of taste, political opinion, and education among the principal groups of the population" (Royal Commission on the Press 1949: 1).

## Liberal faith in the social and moral purpose of the media

Furthermore, the liberal faith that professional journalism exists to serve social and moral purposes unites editors with wildly different editorial policies. It is present in the speech by Paul Dacre, editor of the *Daily Mail*, to the Society of Editors in which he promoted journalism's duty to expose "the crooks, the liars, the cheats, the rich and the corrupt [who shelter] behind a law of privacy being created by an unaccountable judge" (Dacre 2008).

It explains better than profit-motive alone the pride expressed by Bob Bird, Scottish editor of the *News of the World*, when Tommy Sheridan, the Scottish Socialist Party politician, was found guilty at the High Court in Glasgow on 23 December 2010, of perjury during his successful defamation case against the *News of the World* in 2006 (BBC 2010).

It underpins Alan Rusbridger's account of what C. P. Scott, the *Guardian*'s creator, might have thought of its online reach: "Scott would, I think, have been intensely intrigued to know that the paper he edited for so long…was so openly available and read around the world…that its reporting could change the minds of governments, inspire thinking, defy censorship, give a voice to the powerless and previously voice-less" (Rusbridger 2010).

James Murdoch professed similar confidence in journalism's capacity to serve liberal purposes in his 2009 MacTaggart Lecture to the Edinburgh International Television Festival. He said "the provision of independent news" and "investment in professional journalism" were "important spheres of human enterprise and endeavour" that might be harmed by excessive state regulation of the media industries (Murdoch 2009).

Of course, the endurance of a myth does not mean that it is not a myth, nor does continuing support for it by professional journalists. To paraphrase Mandy Rice-Davis, they would support it, wouldn't they? But this myth is not just resilient. In 21st century Britain, liberal fourth estate theory has the support of vast audiences who, despite decades of trenchant criticism, consume the journalism it inspires online, in print and via broadcast transmission in unprecedented volume.

Myths are not lies. One of their foremost functions is to promote models for social behaviour. Within professions or social groups they may validate certain values and practices. There is, however, a chasm separating the plain truth that myths may be used to promote virtuous professional conduct and the contention that they are merely sentimental devices by which groups promote unjustified self-regard.

Liberal press theory does not endure because it makes journalists feel good about themselves by depicting their profession as more than a commercial activity designed to make profits by selling news. It endures because it describes more accurately than the profession's most entrenched critics are happy to acknowledge what public service journalism does and what its consumers want it to do.

## Journalism's ability to expose wrongdoing

Since the emergence of representative democracy in economically liberal nation states, liberal press theory has promoted journalism as a servant of the public sphere, the realm in which citizens engage in critical debate about the practices of government and state. It has promoted journalism's ability to expose wrongdoing, to keep power honest and to advance the cause of reform. It has pledged to defend democracy and civil rights by deploying the sword of truth and the shield of fairness.

Liberal fourth estate theory was invented to describe journalism's role within representative democracy. Liberals who believed in that system's virtue and in its ability to evolve and reform in the public interest devised it. People who share their faith support it now. That it is opposed by thinkers who would prefer journalism to advocate the replacement of representative democracy in its present form is unremarkable. But it is important to recognise that their analyses are intended to promote change in the media and in society, not simply to describe it.

Among influential thinkers about journalism, the best acknowledge this candidly. Richard Keeble does so with admirable clarity: "It is clearly important to work for radical, progressive change to the corporate media from within. The closeness of the mainstream to dominant economic, cultural and ideological forces means that the mainstream largely functions to promote the interests of the military/industrial/political complex" (Keeble 2010).

Liberal theory has become a more accurate guide to journalism's social purpose as time has passed. The intense scepticism of 1978 looks jaded today. Boyce was right to pour scorn on editors who, like H. A. Gwynne of the *Morning Post,* derived influence "not from any aloof, distinct posture, but from his contacts and friendships with people at the very centre of power" (Boyce 1978: 31). But liberal journalists have learned not to be friends with politicians. Today, the evidence suggests that those who exercise media power have embraced H. L. Mencken's advice that "the proper relationship between a journalist and a politician should be akin to that between a dog and a lamp-post" (see BBC 1999).

That politicians also understand this is illustrated by the frequency with which they piss back. For much of her time in office Mrs. Thatcher enjoyed a mutually supportive relationship with important national newspapers. Her gripe was with broadcast journalists, particularly those working for the BBC. Following a series of *Panorama* documentaries on topics including Northern Ireland, the 1982 Falklands War the 1984 Brighton bombing, and the miners' strike (1984-1985), Mrs Thatcher demanded that the BBC "put its house in order" (McQueen 2008).

Members of the Iron Lady's cabinet were caustic about BBC Radio 4's *Today* programme. Nigel Lawson accused its presenter, Brian Redhead, of voting Labour and Dennis Thatcher decorated a wall at 10 Downing Street with a picture of Broadcasting House leaning to the left.

John Major enjoyed only a very brief honeymoon in his relationship with journalists before the British media turned its critical eye on him. Seymour-Ure notes that Major found the experience dispiriting and complained about "negligible response time, reductive soundbites, ritualistic rhetoric (often misleading), skeleton reporting (even in the broadsheets), [and] pressure to produce sensational stories" (Seymour-Ure 2003: 8).

Tony Blair basked in the glow of largely favourable coverage until the invasion of Iraq harmed his reputation. Afterwards he compared the media to a "feral beast", determined to destroy politicians for selfish gain (Blair 2007). The former Prime Minister also noted that his efforts to circumnavigate mainstream media by using the internet had failed utterly.

## Journalists as independent critics of government

Supporters of liberal theory see these examples of criticism from both wings of British politics as evidence that journalists are independent critics of government. Work originally inspired by the Glasgow Media Group in the 1970s has, nevertheless, continued to dismiss the liberal position, arguing that excessive reliance on official sources and mainstream representatives of politics and business erodes journalism's autonomy and makes it power's lackey (McQueen op cit).

British journalism's achievements in the years since James Callaghan surrendered office to Margaret Thatcher in 1979 are too numerous to list, but a few examples may serve to illustrate the profession's potency as a watchdog. Granada Television's *World in Action* series was first to investigate the convictions in 1975 of the Birmingham Six. The company's journalism was instrumental in correcting a grave miscarriage of justice.

*The Scotsman's* dedication to the cause of constitutional change helped to keep the case for devolution of power to a Scottish Parliament on the UK political agenda despite Conservative opposition. After 1997, it helped to maintain the pressure on Tony Blair's New Labour administration when the Prime Minister's doubts about devolution resurfaced (Peterkin 2010).

The *Guardian's* exposure in 1995 of the lies told by Conservative cabinet minister Jonathan Aitken ended the career of a powerful politician who had betrayed the confidence shown in him by the electorate. Independent Television News held to account a regime responsible for brutal abuses of power when it broadcast, on 6 August 1992, evidence of the barbaric mistreatment of Bosnian Muslim prisoners in the Serb-run detention camp at Trnopolje, in northern Bosnia. These examples date from before the dawn of the multimedia age.

## MPs' expenses scandal – and the liberal theory of the media

It is noteworthy that although the internet has damaged journalism's profitability, it has done less to dampen the profession's pursuit of liberal ideals. The *Daily Telegraph's* exposure of the details of MPs' expenses claims in 2009 revealed abuses by MPs from all parties and seriously damaged public faith in politicians. Few stories have demonstrated more emphatically the willingness of liberal media to scrutinise in the public interest institutions they support and admire.

In December 2010, the *Daily Telegraph* returned to the fray by deploying subterfuge and misrepresentation to record Liberal Democrat ministers in Britain's coalition government expressing fierce disapproval of coalition policy and of their conservative ministerial colleagues (Prince 2010). The *Telegraph's* claim that it acted in the public interest – the only justification under Section 10 of the Editor's Code of Conduct – was only partially undermined by its failure to publish immediately comments by Vince Cable, the Business Secretary, revealing his personal hostility to a complete takeover of BSkyB by News Corporation (BBC News 2010c).

The expenses files also demonstrated the potential of partnerships between the fourth and fifth estates as newspapers including the *Daily Telegraph* and the *Guardian* invited readers to mine online data about expenses claims for details about their MP.

Another example of partnership emerged following the death in April 2009 of Ian Tomlinson, a newspaper seller who collapsed and died in the City of London during mass protests against the G20 summit then taking place in the city. Initial post-mortem findings indicated that Tomlinson had died of natural causes. That version was challenged when the *Guardian* obtained film taken by an American fund manager which showed him being hit and pushed by a police officer wielding a baton (*Guardian* 2009).

## The importance of user-generated content

Such use by mainstream media of user-generated content is not a new phenomenon, but it has become more common in the digital era and media companies now encourage it actively. Thus Sky News uses its home page to appeal for "your videos" and "your photos" (Sky News, 2010). BBC News makes a comparable appeal via the "have your say" section of its website which is also advertised on its home page (BBC News 2010d).

Rusbridger detects tension between the authority enjoyed by professional journalists and the desire of some news consumers to create their own content and make their own judgements (Rusbridger op cit). But will citizens with busy lives really make time to hold power to account via Facebook and Twitter or will they rely at least as heavily as their pre-internet ancestors on the power, independence and professionalism of big media to do the job with them?

Crowdsourcing has taken journalists beyond appeals for individual stories, photographs and videos to a new understanding that a newsroom which works in symbiosis with its audience may produce more richly informed news. Richard Sambrook believes that this curatorial approach to news gathering and production may spawn a new breed of foreign reporting in which traditional foreign correspondents will be replaced by teams consisting of foreign news desk staff and local journalists working collaboratively with their audiences (Sambrook 2010). One Reuters editor told him: "We used to need hunter-gatherers; in future we'll need farmers."

What skills will these farmers of news require to nurture, fertilise and reap collaborative journalism? The vocational toolkit is reasonably easy to describe. Convergence has reduced the market value of single-medium skills. Today's multimedia reporter needs the ability to gather, organise and deploy information, images and data from primary and secondary sources and to create and deploy text and images for publication in print, for broadcast and online. They need to be able to use cameras and audio recording equipment and the relevant editing software. They also need advanced ability to build, edit and update web pages.

To these practical competencies must be added advanced awareness of and familiarity with social networking technologies and sites and editorial ability to exploit them fully. Creating content for and interacting with online audiences and, in particular, with mobile online audiences is an essential editorial skill. Learning to deploy journalism via mobile operating systems such as Google's Android and Apple's iPad is already important and will become more so.

### Basic skills for the multimedia environment
For journalists, team-building has been a core skill since the professionalisation of the news industry in the second half of the

nineteenth century. Now, the modern journalist needs the flexibility to work in and organise teams creating output in single, bi- and multimedia formats.

This basic skill is useful at every level of the free media's social hierarchy. It applies when a journalist toils to produce the novelist Jay McInerney's recipe for tabloid success: "Killer Bees, Hero Cops, Sex Fiends, Lottery Winners, Teenage Terrorists, Liz Taylor [Cheryl Cole?], Tough Tots, Sicko Creeps, Living Nightmares, Life on Other Planets, Spontaneous Human Combustion, Miracle Diets and Coma Babies" (McInerney 1985: 11).

It is as useful to BBC journalists who are enjoined to "apply due impartiality to all of our subject matter" and to "reflect a breadth and diversity of opinion across our output as a whole, over an appropriate period, so that no significant strand of thought is knowingly unreflected or under-represented" (BBC 2010: 9 section 1.2.3.).

But technical virtuosity alone does not a great liberal journalist make. To serve the purposes defined in fourth estate theory the profession demands intellectual acuity too. Leonard Downie and Michael Schudson note: "Although much basic news reporting is routine, enterprise and accountability journalism, which by definition bring new information to light, can grow into society-changing work not that dissimilar to academic research that makes original contributions to knowledge in history and the social sciences" (Downie and Schudson 2009: 89).

For decades aspiring British journalists have questioned how best to realise their ambitions. Well-intentioned advice from veteran liberal journalists has tended to recommend a degree in history, politics or English literature and a graduate traineeship at a newspaper or broadcaster. Universities offering degrees in journalism have made the case for learning core skills as an undergraduate in order to enter the market place with a competitive advantage.

Even in today's restricted job market either route can work, provided the aspirant has drawn to their attention the unavoidable truths that journalism jobs are exceptionally hard to get, that competition is ferocious and that few professions are as intensely meritocratic. Too few universities which offer journalism degrees identify students who are plainly not bright enough to work in journalism and warn them of their shortcomings. Many that offer candour are accredited by the National Council for the Training of Journalists.

## Basic knowledge for today's journalists

Absent from the debate is much sincere effort to define the academic learning journalists will require. In fact, the answer is implicit in the typical veteran liberal's answer. To perform their job effectively journalists need to understand the history of liberal, capitalist, representative democracy and how it works. They also need the ability to express themselves clearly. In other words, they need to add to their multimedia skill set thorough grounding in history, politics, law and literature.

A very basic reading list should include Milton, Jean-Jacques Rousseau, Voltaire, and Adam Smith, Tom Paine, Jeremy Bentham, Karl Marx and J. S. Mill. It should offer an introduction to the development of representative democracy through works including Boyd Hilton's *A mad, bad and dangerous people – England 1783-1846* (2006), Hugh Cunningham's *The challenge of democracy – Britain 1832-1918* (2001) and David Marquand's *Britain since 1918 – The strange career of British democracy* (2008). It should offer understanding of the Second World War through Angus Calder's *The people's war* (1969) and Robert Kee's *1945: The world we fought for* (1985) and of its aftermath via Peter Hennessy's *Never again – Britain 1945-1951* (1992) and *Having it so good – Britain in the Fifties* (2006).

It should introduce readers to a basic understanding of contemporary politics through works including Vernon Bogdanor's *The new British constitution* (2009), Bill Jones, Dennis Kavanagh, Michael Moran and Phillip Norton's *Politics UK* (fourth edition, 2006) and David Judge's *Political institutions in the United Kingdom* (2005). Journalism's relationship with the law should be approached through *McNae's essential law for journalists* (20th edition, 2010) and Frances Quinn's *Law for journalists* (2009).

With such foundations built, the education of aspiring journalists should begin to incorporate study of the role of the press. Andrew Marr's *My trade* (2004) offers an invaluable introduction. Students should also read *Power without responsibility* (sixth edition, 2001) by James Curran and Jean Seaton, *Newspaper history from the 17th century to the present day*, edited by

George Boyce, James Curran and Pauline Wingate (1978) (including Boyce's essay The Fourth Estate: The reappraisal of a concept*)*, and *Why democracies need an unlovable press* (2008), by Michael Schudson. Their education will be incomplete if they do not also read *Obscure scribblers – A history of parliamentary journalism* (2003) by Andrew Sparrow, *Flat earth news* (2008), by Nick Davies and *The universal journalist* (2000), by David Randall.

## The essential media diet

None of this will be of any value unless the student also consumes journalism daily. A basic diet of *Today* on BBC Radio Four and/or *Breakfast* on Five Live, one quality daily newspaper, one tabloid (in print or online) and the *Daily Mail* should be reinforced by evening consumption of television news and current affairs, ideally Channel 4 News and Newsnight on BBC2. Students should check authoritative news websites including BBC News, Guardian Unlimited and Mail Online constantly.

Journalism students at Kent often blanch when I remind them that such daily consumption is the essential starting point for a career in public service journalism. But I tell them because I know hardly any successful journalists who do not consume news avidly. And the same discipline is essential in niche journalism. Motorcycle journalists read *Motorcycle News* and magazines including *Bike* and *Ride* as closely as political correspondents read websites including *Conservative Home*, and Guido Fawkes' blog (www.Order-Order.com).

Such dedicated attention is essential to success in journalism and the profession's demands will only become more gruelling as the number of outlets and the opportunities to respond to audience demands expand in parallel with the creative opportunities for multimedia story-telling.

Critics of the mainstream media may deride these recommendations as a recipe for creating new servants of the liberal capitalist media. They are designed for that purpose. Mainstream media is not hostile to dissident opinion. Indeed, as Richard Keeble notes, "progressive" writers have often written for professional, liberal media outlets as well as contributing to campaigning outlets (Keeble op cit).

Such partnership will be more common in the multimedia era. The alliance between *Wikileaks* and the *Guardian, New York Times, Le Monde* etc. which placed the US embassy cables in the public domain, is a compelling example. It illustrates the efficiency with which mainstream liberal media outlets can now work in partnership with consumers to serve core fourth estate purposes, and the enthusiasm with which they pursue that virtuous ideal.

Journalists with advanced multimedia skills, intense academic training and Stakhanovite work ethics are better placed than ever before to hold power to account on behalf of, and in partnership with, their audiences.

## References

Assange, Julian (2010) Video interview with Kirsty Wark. Available online at http://www.bbc.co.uk/news/world-11047811, accessed on 8 December 2010.

BBC (1999) Scotland tabloid bites back at Steel, 6 September. Available online at http://news.bbc.co.uk/1/hi/scotland/439580.stm, accessed on 20 December 2010

BBC News (2010a) Mark Thompson expresses "regret" over Sky letter, 8 November. Available online at http://www.bbc.co.uk/news/entertainment-arts-11713108, accessed on 2 December 2010

BBC News (2010b) Tommy Sheridan found guilty of perjury. Available online at http://www.bbc.co.uk/news/uk-scotland-glasgow-west-12059037, accessed on 24/ December 2010

BBC News (2010c) Peston on Cable's BsKyB comments. Available online at http://www.bbc.co.uk/news/business-12053179, accessed on 24 December 2010

BBC News (2010d) Home page available online at http://www.bbc.co.uk/news/, accessed on 13 December 2010

BBC (2010e) Editorial guidelines. Available online at http://www.bbc.co.uk/bbctrust/assets/files/pdf/our_work/editorial_gu idelines/2010/trust_commentary.pdf, accessed on 13 December 2010

Blair, Tony (2010) On public life: Speech to Reuters, 12 June 2007. Available online at http://news.bbc.co.uk/1/hi/uk_politics/6744581.stm, accessed on 17 December 10

Boyce, George (1978) The Fourth Estate: The reappraisal of a concept, Curran, James and Wingate, Pauline, *Newspaper history: From the 17th century to the present day*, London, Constable pp 19-41

Busfield, Steve (2010) Guardian editor hits back at paywalls, *Guardian*, 25 January. Available online at http://www.guardian.co.uk/media/2010/jan/25/guardian-editor-paywalls, accessed on 27 January 2010

Dacre, Paul (2008) Speech to the annual conference of the Society of Editors 2008. Available online at http://www.societyofeditors.co.uk/page-view.php?pagename=TheSOELecture2008, accessed on 9 December 2010

Downie, Leonard and Schudson, Michael (2009) The reconstruction of American journalism, 20 October. Columbia University Graduate School of Journalism. Available online at http://www.journalism.columbia.edu/system/documents/1/original/Reconstruction_of_Journalism.pdf, accessed on 13 December 2010

Dutton, William H. (2007) *Through the network of networks*, Oxford, Oxford Internet Institute

Engels, Friedrich (1893 [1968]) Letter to Franz Mehring, *Marx and Engels correspondence*, London, International Publishers

Freedman, Des, (2010) The political economy of the "new" news environment, Fenton, Natalie (ed.) *New media old news*, London, Sage pp 35-50

*Guardian* (2009) Video of officer hitting Ian Tomlinson. Available online at http://www.guardian.co.uk/uk/g20-police-assault-ian-tomlinson, accessed on 13 December 2010

Holden, Anthony (2002) Reporting the reporters: Review of *People's witness* by Fred Inglis, *Observer*, 5 May. Available online at http://www.guardian.co.uk/education/2002/may/05/highereducation.news, accessed on 20 December 2010

Keeble, Richard (2010) How alternative media provide the crucial critique of the mainstream. Available online at http://medialens.org/alerts/10/100120_the_future_of.php, accessed on 20 December 2010

Lewis, Seth (2010) The future of journalism, A class blog for J349T Writing for Online Publication, in the School of Journalism at UT-Austin. Available online at http://writingforonline.wordpress.com/2010/03/19/citizen-journalism-2/, accessed on 2 December 2010

McInerney, Jay (1985) *Bright lights big city*, London, Jonathan Cape

McQueen, David (2008) BBC's *Panorama*, war coverage and the "Westminster consensus", Westminster Papers in Communication and Culture, 2008. Available online at http://www.westminster.ac.uk/__data/assets/pdf_file/0009/20007/WPCC-Vol5-No3-David_McQueen.pdf, accessed on 17 December 2010

Moss, Stephen and Joris Luyendijk (2010) The old model of journalism is broken, *Guardian*, 30 November. Available online at www.guardian.co.uk/media/2010/nov/30/future-of-journalism-joris-luyendijk, accessed on 2 December 2010

Murdoch, James (2009) The McTaggart lecture. Available online at http://www.guardian.co.uk/media/video/2009/aug/29/james-murdoch-edinburgh-festival-mactaggart, accessed on 2 December 2010

Newman, Nick (2009) The rise of social media and its impact on mainstream journalism, London, Reuters Institute for the Study of Journalism. Available online at http://reutersinstitute.politics.ox.ac.uk/about/news/item/article/the-use-of-citizen-journalism-by-tr.html, accessed on 12 December 2010

Peterkin, Tom (2010) Tony Blair memoirs: I was never convinced on devolution – it was dangerous, 2 September. Available online at http://thescotsman.scotsman.com/scotland/Tony-Blair-memoirs-39I-was.6508131.jp, accessed on 17 December 2010

Prince, Rosa (2010) Liberal Democrat ministers backed after expressing concerns, *Daily Telegraph*, 23 December. Available online at http://www.telegraph.co.uk/news/newstopics/politics/liberaldemocrats/8221220/Liberal-Democrat-ministers-backed-after-expressing-concern-over-Coalition.html, accessed on 2 December 2010

Rosen, Jay (2010) Audience atomization overcome: Why the internet weakens the authority of the press. Available online at http://archive.pressthink.org/2009/01/12/atomization.html, accessed on 2 December 2010

Royal Commission on the Press 1947-1949 (1949). Report available online at http://openlibrary.org/books/OL21768421M/Royal_Commission_on_the_Press_1947-1949_Report, accessed on 2 December 2010

Rusbridger, Alan (2010) The Hugh Cudlipp Lecture 2010. Available online at http://www.guardian.co.uk/media/2010/jan/25/cudlipp-lecture-alan-rusbridger, accessed on 9 December 2010

Sambrook, Richard (2010) Are foreign correspondents redundant? The changing face of international news, Oxford, Reuters Institute for the Study of Journalism. Available online at http://reutersinstitute.politics.ox.ac.uk/publications/risj-challenges/are-foreign-correspondents-redundant.html, accessed on 2 December 2010

Seymour-Ure, Colin (2003) *Prime Ministers and the media*, Oxford,:Blackwell

*The Times* (1939) *The history of The Times 1841-1884*, London, *The Times*

Sky News (2010) Home page available online at http://news.sky.com/skynews/, accessed on 13 December 2010

## Note on the author

Tim Luckhurst is Professor of Journalism at the University of Kent and the founding head of the university's Centre for Journalism. He is best known as a former editor of the *Scotsman*, Scotland's national newspaper. He began his career in journalism on BBC Radio 4's *Today* programme for which he produced, edited and reported from the UK and abroad. For BBC Radio he covered the Romanian Revolution of 1989, reported from Iraq, Israel, Jordan and Kuwait during the first Gulf War and reported the Waco Siege. He reported conflict in Former Yugoslavia from Kosovo, Macedonia and Serbia for the *Scotsman*. He was co-editor of Today's coverage of the 1992 General Election and worked as the BBC's Washington Producer during the first year of the Clinton presidency. He returned to the UK to become a senior member of the team that designed, launched and edited BBC Radio Five Live. From 1995 to 1997 he was Editor of News Programmes at BBC Scotland. He joined the *Scotsman* in 1997 as Assistant Editor and was appointed Deputy Editor in 2008 and editor in January 2000. He has won two Sony Radio Academy Gold Awards for news broadcasting (*The Romanian revolution 1989* for Radio 4's *Today* programme and the *IRA ceasefire of 1995* for Radio Five Live). His publications include *This is Today: A biography of the Today programme* and contributions to *What a State: Is Devolution for Scotland the End of Britain?* He writes for publications including the *Guardian* and the *Independent* and is a frequent contributor to programmes on BBC Radio and Television, Sky News, LBC and Talksport. He is a member of the jury for the annual UACES/Reuters Reporting Europe Competition.

# We are all Dickheads now: Reflections on the future of journalism

**John Tulloch**

Researchers at the Intelligent Systems Informatics Lab (ISI) at Tokyo University have developed a journalist robot that can autonomously explore its environment and report what it finds. The robot detects changes in its surroundings, decides if they are relevant and then takes pictures with its on-board camera. It can query nearby people for information and it uses internet searches to further round out its understanding. If something appears newsworthy, the robot will even write a short article and publish it to the web (Saenz 2010).

Fans of the late science fiction writer Philip K. Dick (1928-82), once a tight little body of believers banded together as Dickheads, are now vastly increased by the nine movies based on his science fiction novels, which have allegedly amassed revenues of more than $1 billion.[i]

Dickheads can also rejoice that the master's lost android head – the subject of a BBC Radio 3 play *Bring me the head of Philip K Dick* – has been rebuilt by a robotics company and a Dutch public broadcaster.[ii] Soon the BBC is to embark on a four-hour mini-series based on his finest novel, *The man in the high castle*, produced by Ridley Scott, director of *Blade runner*.[iii]

The temper of these times tends towards the dystopian vision and Hollywood's Dick-mining has mainly served the purpose of presenting variously miserable alternate futures, whether it is LA shrouded by climatic ruin (*Blade runner*) or a Washington where police can detect murders before they are committed – a development of Orwell's "thought crime" (*Minority report*). Even grimmer, *The man in the high castle* presents a future in which Nazi Germany and Imperial Japan have won World War Two.

Dickheads now have a further source of pride in the master's foresight, up there with H. G. Wells, with the naturalisation of the concept of the robot reporter. Dick, of course, was there first, loosely predicting it in 1969 in his novel *Ubik*:

> In a corner of the large room a chime sounded and a tinkling mechanical voice called: "I'm your free homeopape machine, a service supplied exclusively by all the fine Rootes hotels throughout Earth and the colonies. Simply dial the classification of news that you wish, and in a matter of seconds I'll speedily provide you with a fresh, up-to-the-minute homeopape tailored to your individual requirements; and, let me repeat, at no cost to you!" (Dick 1969: 79).

One of the many handy Dickhead websites defines it thus: "HOMEOPAPE: A newspaper that filters the news so it only shows what you are interested in…The homeopape asks you what you want to read about and then prints it on paper".[iv]

## Dick's jape at mass-produced Cold War newspapers

The problem with future predictions in fiction, of course, is that they are principally concerned with satirising the present. Just as "thoughtcrime" is Orwell's crack at contemporary propagandists at the British Ministry of Information and the Kremlin, the homeopape is a jape at mass-produced Cold War newspapers – whose deadening weight of free-market ideology and news agency style could justly be described as "robotic". The inverted pyramid might as easily be plucked from a dangerous SF vision (Hackgate?) as from a training manual for reporters.

The origins of robot journalism, like so much technicist utopianism in the dark abysm of time, lies in the 19th century and the triumph of factory journalism in the UK and the US. This came a generation after the advent of the industrial factory system and was congruent with the rise of the professional classes, in which "the journalist" booked a disreputable third class ticket, just above steerage. This system took hold in the London mass circulation Sundays and larger dailies of the mid 19th century, developing to a high point in the 1910-60s with the second, electrical-based revolution and the full flowering of daily journalism. In retrospect, the 1960s glorydays of *The Sunday Times* heralded a slow decline, to end perhaps a generation after the factory system and British industry was dealt fatal blows by the Thatcher administrations – which is where we are now. The rise and decline is nearly circumscribed in the lives of Murdoch *pere* et *fils* (Sir Keith Murdoch 1885-1952, Rupert Murdoch 1931- ?).

The sentient robot reporter was the outgrowth of these journalism factories and their attendant, state-sponsored bureaucracies. The advent of the real thing is, therefore, no surprise and reporters who covered the story adopted three jokey lines: either (1) "Robots are after my job" (Saenz 2010) but gee, now you think about it; (2) "Robot reporters could help alleviate workload in some newsrooms" (Grimm 2010) and that (3) people might actually prefer being accosted by a machine rather than a human hack – perhaps with superior trust potential and the added bonus that they don't whine or skive off – "finally a likeable reporter" (ibid).

## How a robot would make sense of central Cairo
One wonders what Tokyo's robot would have made of central Cairo, as January edged into February 2011. It would have no problem detecting anomalies in the environment of the order of an extra few hundred thousand people. If it was identifiably Japanese rather than American it might attract less hostility as the Obamabot quailed over supporting or dumping his most dependable ally, the Mubarakbot. It would be more impervious to police truncheons than the average reporter's skull. And it could take lots of pictures and do all sorts of on the spot surveys of public opinion devised by a flummoxed newsroom. Are you an Islamist?

How do you feel about Israel? Should he stay a bit or should he go now? Should he be hung from a handy palm tree? How high?

Could it do more? For example, could it jump on a tank and talk to the crew? Could we make one like Robert Fisk? What would a Fiskbot need? I suppose the instruction book re Cairo might say: learn Arabic, live for 30 years in the Middle East, passionately immerse yourself in the history and politics, learn painful lessons about the limits of courage, go to the scene, and report what you see in Maidan al-Tahrir – Cairo's so-called Liberation Square. Here's Fisk himself reporting:

> The Egyptian tanks, the delirious protesters sitting atop them, the flags, the 40,000 protesters weeping and crying and cheering in Freedom Square and praying around them, the Muslim Brotherhood official sitting amid the tank passengers. Should this be compared to the liberation of Bucharest? Climbing on to an American-made battle tank myself, I could only remember those wonderful films of the liberation of Paris. A few hundred metres away, Hosni Mubarak's black-uniformed security police were still firing at demonstrators near the interior ministry. It was a wild, historical victory celebration, Mubarak's own tanks freeing his capital from his own dictatorship....
>
> Their crews, in battledress and smiling and in some cases clapping their hands, made no attempt to wipe off the graffiti that the crowds had spray-painted on their tanks. "Mubarak Out – Get Out" and "Your regime is over, Mubarak" have now been plastered on almost every Egyptian tank on the streets of Cairo. On one of the tanks circling Freedom Square was a senior member of the Muslim Brotherhood, Mohamed Beltagi. Earlier, I had walked beside a convoy of tanks near the suburb of Garden City as crowds scrambled on to the machines to hand oranges to the crews, applauding them as Egyptian patriots. However crazed Mubarak's choice of vice-president and his gradual appointment of a powerless new government of cronies, the streets of Cairo proved what the United States and EU leaders have simply failed to grasp. It is over (Fisk 2011).

A basic low order function of journalism might be described as surveillance of the environment and most of it, indeed, can be replicated by fixed CCTV cameras in car parks and parliament, drones, security cameras. This stuff is important to our safety and general sense of connection to human society. A second function is the summarising and translating of relatively complicated and/or boring information in a readable, entertaining form that we can understand and make use of. The third function is to explain to us what the hell is going on in as honest and as well-informed a way as possible. The explanation does not need to be objective, but it does need to be honest enough to show us where the author is coming from, the quality of the sources and where we might profitably graze on alternative accounts.

## What chances of a Fiskbot emerging?

One can't see a Fisk style of journalism dying out, even if newspapers do. And his long form mix of analytical journalism and street level reporting would in some way find a home online more easily than in an ailing broadsheet. Could one see a Fiskbot? Leaping on a US tank, or nimbly escaping enraged Afghans? In your dreams. This is a man who doesn't do emails and even had his cat sleeping on the fax machine (Fisk 2009: 235). But while he would not wear it with his anti-technicist prejudices, one can conceive of a kind of Fiskimator 2 able to sit in his Beirut flat and drive his metal simulacrum interesting places.

Confirmed anti-technicists such as Fisk will be hard to persuade. But he has written eloquently about the phenomenon of "mouse journalism": "popping up at the scene of an event and staying just long enough to get the story, before the men with guns arrive" (Lewin 2005). Like the robot mine detectors and killer drones, Robohack may be the future of a journalism which has become too dangerous and expensive to practise, in an age of disintegrating hegemonies.

## Conclusion: There's more to life than Robohack

There must be more to life than Robohack. Here are five thoughts about the future of journalism – only one about a robot:

1. All production is footloose and will be outsourced to the cheapest available English language competent destination. Hello Sri Lanka.

2. Ultimately the UK press will be forced to accept a statutory system of regulation – the Press Complaints Commission is

heading out of the last chance saloon to the Tombstone undertaker – it's hard to see what could replace this most busted of flushes. The longer the hapless Baroness Peta Buscombe stays in control the sooner it may be.

3. Vast swathes of "journalism" clearly are for the chop. All the in-house celebrity material could be simply outsourced to PR agencies. Surveillance-based (inc telephone-hacking) and negative celebrity coverage will be increasingly outsourced to mercenaries, with cut-offs to avoid more Coulsongate scandals. Serious long-form journalism migrates to the web.

4. Much routine reporting can, indeed, be done by various species of robots – opinionbots surveying and vox popping, sportsbots surveilling routine events, dronebots checking out demonstrations, even portly Simpsonbots wandering through the crowds in the Liberation Squares of the Third World patronising the locals while their princely progenitor sips gin and saves on insurance and security.

5. The role of the generalist journalist/reporter will inevitably diminish. Malcolm Gladwell, of the *New Yorker*, says that "journalism has to get smarter" and argues that aspiring journalists should avoid journalism school and develop their specialist knowledge: "If I was studying today, I would go get a Masters in statistics" (Pasternack 2009). In response, many J-schools may adopt joint postgraduate degrees, such as Columbia's model of a joint programme in journalism and computer science, currently being heavily hyped, if they can bear the thought of producing, in a phrase that should be treasured in the annals of technicist-drivel, "a whole new breed of cross-disciplinary techno/journalist ninjas" (Fenwick 2010).

## Notes

[i] See http://www.philipkdick.com/films_intro.html, accessed on 31 January 2011
[ii] See http://io9.com/5731075/the-lost-robotic-head-of-philip-k-dick-has-been-rebuilt, accessed on 31 January 2011
[iii] See http://www.deadline.com/2010/10/ridley-scott-returns-to-philip-

k-dick-25-years-after-directing-'blade-runner'/, accessed on 31 January 2011

[iv] See http://downlode.org/Etext/pkdicktionary.html#h, accessed on 1 January 2011

## References

Dick, P. K. (1969) *Ubik*, New York, Daw Books

Fenwick, A. (2010) Robot journalism and the future of digital media, *Columbia Journalism Review*, 19 April. Available online at http://www.cjr.org/the_news_frontier/robot_journalism_and_the_futur.php, accessed on 5 January 2011

Fisk, R. (2009) *The age of the warrior: Selected writings*, London, Fourth Estate

Fisk, R. (2011) Egypt: Death throes of a dictatorship, *Independent*, 30 January. Available online at http://www.independent.co.uk/opinion/commentators/fisk/robert-fisk-egypt-death-throes-of-a-dictatorship-2198444.html, accessed on 31 January 2011

Gopnik, A. (2007) Blows against the empire: The return of Philip K. Dick, *New Yorker*, 20 August. Available online at http://www.newyorker.com/arts/critics/books/2007/08/20/070820crbo_books_gopnik?printable=true, accessed on 5 January 2011

Grimm, J. (2010) Robot reporters could alleviate workload in some newsroom, Poynter.org, 8 April. Available online at http://www.poynter.org/how-tos/career-development/ask-the-recruiter/101915/robot-reporters-could-help-alleviate-workload-in-some-newsrooms/, accessed on 5 January 2011

Lewin, M. (2005) "Mouse journalism" is the only way we can report on Iraq — Fisk, *Press Gazette*, 14 October. Available online at http://www.pressgazette.co.uk/story.asp?storyCode=32198&sectioncode=1, accessed on 31 January 2011

Pasternack, A. (2009) Columbia axes environmental journalism and Malcolm Gladwell is OK with that, The Huffington Post, 21 October. Available online at http://www.huffingtonpost.com/alex-pasternack/columbia-axes-environment_b_328167.html, accessed on 5 January 2011

Saenz, A. (2010) Robot journalist takes pictures, asks questions, publishes online, Singularity Hub, 18 March. Available online at http://singularityhub.com/2010/03/18/robot-journalist-takes-pictures-ask-questions-publishes-online/, accessed on 5 January 2011

**Note on the author**

John Tulloch is Professor of Journalism and Head of the School of Journalism, Lincoln University. He is co-director of the Centre for Journalism Research (CRJ). Previously (1995-2003) he was Head of the Department of Journalism and Mass Communication, University of Westminster. Edited books include *Tabloid tales* (2000) (edited with Colin Sparks) *Peace journalism, war and conflict resolution* (2010) (edited with Richard Lance Keeble and Florian Zollmann), and *Global literary journalism* (edited with Richard Lance Keeble), forthcoming 2011. He has also written recently on extraordinary rendition and on the journalism of Charles Dickens.